EMPOWERED LIVING

A Twelve-Week Plan for Improving Your Most Significant Relationships

Jim Hohnberger

with Tim & Julie Canuteson

Pacific Press® Publishing Association
Nampa, Idaho
Oshawa, Ontario, Canada
www.pacificpress.com

Edited by Tim Lale
Inside design by Tim Larson
Cover design and art by Linda Griffith

Copyright 2002 by
Pacific Press® Publishing Association
Printed in United States of America
All Rights Reserved

Additional copies of this book may be purchased at
http://www.adventistbookcenter.com

ISBN: 0-8163-1917-0

05 06 • 5 4

Dedication

To those who, like me, would rejoice to hear the words of our Savior saying,

Is your life strained? Come to Me.
If your marriage is troubled, come nearer to Me.
Has your family fractured? Come.
No matter how impossible your situation,
My strength is made perfect in your weakness.
Come to Me, and I will empower thee.

Acknowledgments

The authors wish to acknowledge the contribution made by each of the individuals named below and in many cases their families as well. This book could not have been as complete or as useful to the reader without your willingness to allow others to see you as you really were, and we thank you. All other names used in the book are pseudonyms.

Heike Clark
James and Donna Ehrlich
Janell Garey
Denny and Brenda Kaneshiro
Mark and Maria Lodenkamp
Edwin and Maria Nebblett
Paul and Carolyn Rayne
Sarah Swearingen
Barry and Pam Van Petten
Tom and Alane Waters
Ron and Karen Wood

Contents

Preface 6

Introduction 10

Part 1   **Empowered Life**

Chapter 1   Batteries Not Included 15

Chapter 2   Crossing Over 29

Chapter 3   Attached and Receiving 61

Chapter 4   Less Attempted , More Achieved 93

Part 2   **Empowered Marriage**

Chapter 5   Lost and Found 114

Chapter 6   Kindling the Flame 149

Chapter 7   Swing Time 168

Chapter 8   Removing the Thorns 191

Part 3   **Empowered Family**

Chapter 9   Independent Atoms 212

Chapter 10 Time to Be a Family 234

Chapter 11 The Family Firm 251

Chapter 12 Family Councils 266

Chapter 13 Failure Is Not an Option 282

Appendix 1 Recommended Book List 292

Appendix 2 Time Management and Schedules 294

Preface

"Coldwater, Michigan? Where on earth is Coldwater, Michigan?" you might ask. Well, it's not quite as much at the end of the earth as Polebridge, Montana, but it is a small unassuming town just north of, and nearly equal to, the Ohio-Indiana state line. Yet in its own way, Coldwater is responsible for the book you hold in your hands.

When the Lord called me to ministry, I often wondered where the calls to speak would come from. The Lord knew what He was doing, and I have always turned down far more invitations than I have accepted. I have learned from personal experience that just because you are engaged in good activities, even ministry-related activities, doesn't mean you can allow yourself to become over-committed without reaping the same bad rewards other workaholics do. Still, the more I see the needs of people, the more I have longed to reach them with the good news that life can be different for them—starting today! Every trip I take, I wonder whom God has in mind for me to reach. But even if I preached every weekend to a gathering of a thousand people, I could only reach fifty-two thousand people a year, and that is not even a fraction of the birth rate, let alone all those who are already living.

It is thoughts like these that burden me as we fly across the continent. My wife, Sally, sitting beside me, looks tired. It's no wonder. We have given ourselves to the work of God and poured ourselves out for others until we are spent. And something has to change. My health has suffered, my sleep patterns are destroyed, and age is making slow inroads into what used to be a ceaseless supply of energy and enthusiasm. I'm not complaining. If God desired I continue this way, I would gladly do so, but it is God who has impressed me with the need to change direction, to preserve my energy, and use the strength He provides to advantage. The problem is that I just don't know what to do. I pray earnestly that He will give me some guidance.

Coldwater, Michigan in February is, well, cold! I live in what many people perceive as a frigid location next to Canada and Glacier National Park, but the cold there is dry, the snow powder. This moist cold from the Great Lakes goes right through you. Whoever named this place knew what they were talking about. Thankfully the people there almost make you forget the cold with their warmth and friendliness.

We had a wonderful weekend of meetings and enjoyed staying with our old friends Dwight and Deb, who, before we flew out Tuesday, invited us to tour their business. They run a health club with state-of-the-art equipment. Everything about the club was cheerful and bright. It was the wall, however, that caught my attention. There was a huge display of "before and after" pictures of clients, who had transformed their bodies from flab to fitness. I mean, these people had gone from couch potatoes to Mr. and Mrs. Universe. "How long did it take these people to get these results?" I queried.

"Just twelve weeks," they replied.

"Just twelve weeks!" I exclaimed. "I was sure it had been years!"

"It's our special lifestyle routine, which includes not only exercise, but also a healthy diet," they explained, sensing my disbelief. "It is one of our greatest selling points when prospective clients visit. There's a contest every six months to reward those who show the most improvement."

The pictures were hard to discount, and their effect lingered in my mind long after we left. I was still thinking about them on the long flight home. I tried to turn my mind back to my problem of outreach, but I couldn't seem to focus. That twelve-week plan to transform your life with all its success stories kept floating before my eyes. Somehow I sensed amid my jumbled thoughts there was something important here, even though I couldn't express it as a coherent idea yet. I knew there had to be something that could help me with my dilemma. Turning to Sally, I asked, "Do you still want to be flying to Coldwater, Michigan ten years from now?"

"No, Jim, I don't," she replied without hesitation.

It was an accurate reflection of my own feelings. I love the work God has called me to, but increasingly I had been coming to see the limitations of my own human frame, and I could appreciate the need to consider new methods of presenting the message God has laid on my heart.

My first book was an object lesson to me. In less than a year, it was going to reach more people than our ministry has contacted in a decade. Yes, I could write another book, but what did that have to do with the events of this weekend in Coldwater? What was the essence of my ministry? What did we do in the personal counseling sessions that so benefited others? Could we somehow do that for you, the reader, in a book format? Suddenly it all made sense! The concept fell into place. Excitement and animation coursed through my veins as Sally and I discussed my ideas, which now seemed crystal clear.

Just like the clients at the health club, the people I deal with know they need help, but they are reluctant to trust in something that they have not seen working for others. Can you blame them? Average Christians differ little from those about them who make no profession. The world has become skeptical, and with good cause, about the claims of Christianity. What I needed to convince them was a wall just like the one at the health club. I needed before and after "pictures" of real-life people who had, through the grace of God, transformed their lives, marriages, and families.

The next problem was "Who?" Who should I profile, Lord, and who in the world would be willing to open themselves up for that type of scrutiny? It seemed an almost impossible task, but I started compiling a list of individuals and families that I could ask. They are all people I have known for years. I have been in their homes, watched how they live Christianity in their families, and while I know they aren't perfect, I know they have an experience with God that is living and vibrant. These same dear people are also very humble and private, and they would all have very good reasons not to want this type of public exposure. What if they all turned me down?

I took my idea to my co-authors and managed to convey my vision for the book. They understood what I wanted but also grasped the complexity of writing the many different stories, styles, and personalities involved in such a venture. They were a little doubtful as to whether or not we could pull it off. Then I asked them to write their story first so we could send it to all the others as an example of what we wanted to do.

I sensed their reluctance. To share on an intimate level is hard. To be the first to do so is even harder. Still, as I look back I see God's hand moving as He provided them, through this hard experience, the knowledge necessary to help the others through the same process.

My request put some families in turmoil as they relived certain events. In many homes there were tears as old wounds were reopened and dealt with, but they all re-emerged healed and more strongly bonded to each other than they were at the beginning. Almost everyone I asked agreed to share, and while not every story was used, this book is as much a product of those whose experiences were not included as those whose stories were used extensively. Each of you is an encouragement to my heart. Thank you!

It is up to you, dear reader, to decide how effective I have been in my presentation of their stories and experiences. If you choose to live an empowered life, form an empowered marriage, and experience an empowered family, my efforts will be more than repaid. May God's richest blessing attend your reading and may it be He, and not this poor servant, who leads your feet into the way of an empowered life.

Jim Hohnberger
Polebridge, Montana
October 2001

Introduction

Have you ever been discouraged with your own behavior? Have you ever listened to a sermon from a minister or read a book written by someone who you just knew could never understand your particular problems? Do you ever look at your coworkers, neighbors, the apparently spiritual people at church, or even the minister and wonder what they are really like behind closed doors? If you have, you're probably not alone, because most of us look about us and see lots of people who seem to have their act together. Then we wonder if we're the only ones who are struggling.

Often during the war in Vietnam, our troops in the field would read the favorably slanted news reports filled with inflated body counts and would draw the conclusion that everyone else was winning, that it was only their unit or their part of the country that was struggling. Yet, if you had brought soldiers from every unit together, they would have told the same depressing stories of taking the same ground again and again with ever-increasing losses, while the enemy continued to gain strength and support.

Today's Christian army is in no better shape. I know. I have spoken with thousands of Christians casually and counseled extensively with many, many hundreds more over the last two decades. Based on this firsthand knowledge, I think that if some doctor trained to evaluate ecclesiastical health examined today's churches, every Christian church would have to be issued a certificate of at least partial or full disability! Shocking!

But it is not so shocking when you get a chance to see behind the scenes, beyond the company manners, and look inside the private lives of the very people who stand behind you in the grocery store or share the pew with you at church. Let me introduce you to a few people, real people, just like you and me. You'll have the opportunity to become even better acquainted with them in subsequent chapters. But before I go on, let me explain a little about the design of this book.

Each chapter is based on the premise that you are motivated and that your schedule is typically American—meaning that you are rushed and hurried and working Monday through Friday. Therefore, Sunday, the first day of the week, is committed to reading the chapter, and subsequent days have shorter activities planned for them. If you don't fit this stereotype, feel free to alter the study guide to suit your lifestyle and personality. Don't force yourself to go through it faster than you can easily assimilate the information you are gaining.

You will notice that no activity is planned for Saturday. This is not an error but rather the acknowledgment of the authors that after an intense week of study and application of new ideas and principles you will need a day to "come ye yourselves apart … and rest a while"(Mark 6:31, KJV). Use this time, if possible, to rest from life's burdens and trials, or, if needed, use it as a catch-up day if you had to skip an exercise.

To get you started, we have placed the instructions for Sunday's activities in this introduction. Through the remainder of the book they will come at the end of the chapter with the other days' instructions.

Sunday

Prayer time: No matter what your religious background or lack thereof, approach God as if He were friendly, for He is. Ask Him to guide you as you read and to free your mind from all other cares and concerns. Ask Him to draw near to you for He has promised, "I will instruct thee and teach thee in the way which thou shalt go: I will guide thee with mine eye" (Psalm 32:8). Above all else, draw near to God and ask Him to draw near to you just as He promises in James 4:8: "Draw nigh to God, and he will draw nigh to you."

Activity: Read chapter 1, "Batteries Not Included." Highlight or underline as you desire. Allow yourself to enter into the experiences portrayed. Enjoy getting to know the families. I know I speak for every family whose story appears when I say we hope you will benefit as much as we have in the sharing. Now, let's continue on with "Batteries Not Included."

Part 1

Empowered Life

Batteries Not Included

"I can of mine own self do nothing" (John 5:30).

CHAPTER GOAL

Come to understand that we are powerless to move beyond our own weakness in order to experience empowered living.

Julie was a beautiful young woman. Her face faded in the ethereal moonlight as she pulled momentarily back from the steamy embrace. She looked at Tim, the man she loved, and her only wish was to get closer.

The thought flitted briefly through Tim's mind that they shouldn't be doing this. Oh, they hadn't gone too far, but they were becoming far too familiar. She was after all a denominational employee—if someone found out, it could really cause a scandal. More to the point, they were both Christians who seriously wanted God's blessing on their relationship, but the feelings were too good, and who was going to know anyway? They continued to cuddle as the eastern sky started to show the first rosy hints of dawn.

With the dawn, a flood of anger washed over the guilty pair. Somehow the knowledge of what they hadn't done was little comfort to them now. Tim tried to soothe their anguish. "Why can't we be married?" he queried. "We can be 'good' until then." It seemed a whole lot better than the alternative of breaking off their relationship.

So they tried, honestly tried, but sooner or later one of them would push for indulgence, and the other would give in. It seemed that the more they indulged the more they wanted. "We grew to hate ourselves, both for what we were, and for what we weren't." They were powerless Christians. Am I picking on an isolated example? I think not.

In England I found a young couple that were very energetic Christians. They were lay workers and gave numerous Bible studies each week and had a great reputation in the church for their missionary service. Paul and Carolyn were up-and-coming leaders, but behind closed doors the façade was hard to maintain.

"If you could have visited us then, you would have found two days' worth of dishes carefully tucked away under the sink. When you have thirteen Bible studies going, there is just no time to get to them. We had only a little time for personal time with God or private study, and despite our efforts our lives remained inconsistent with the Bible truths we tried to share. One evening on the way to a study we had one of the biggest arguments of our married life.

"We had been offered a chance to travel to Eastern Europe to train people to give studies. Paul was all in favor, but I held back, overwhelmed by our current commitments.

" 'You told him, yes. Didn't you?'

" 'Well, I said we'd probably be interested.'

" 'You're eager to go, aren't you?'

" 'I said I'd have to ask you, but I was keen to go.'

" 'Just like you to jump in with both feet. Haven't we enough on our plate? What about the people we are already studying with?'

" 'They'll be fine for a couple of weeks.' "

There was more, but I'll cut it short by saying that about this time they arrived at the home of the person they were studying with. Carolyn told me, "We had been arguing. I hadn't been treating him as a Christian," and Paul added, "I was treating her with much disrespect." They got out of the car, walked up to the door, and were transformed into animated, happy Christians.

"Hi. Are you ready for your study tonight on the second coming of Jesus? Do you want to be ready when Jesus comes?"

They had a wonderful study and then got back in the car and picked up their arguing and bickering right where they had left off. Surely people who do such good works are Christians. Or could it be that they, too, were powerless?

And then there's Maria. Educated, professional, happily married to an up-and-coming physician, living in a 3,000-square-foot house, Maria had everything she needed in life to make her happy, or so she thought. She loved children and had given birth to four in the preceding six years, but life was beginning to fray around the edges.

"I struggled to keep my cool and not lose my temper with the little ones. I tried to patiently bear the noise and disorder in the home that seems inevitable with four children under the age of six. But I would finally blow up and speak harshly to them. It became a regular pattern. I'll never forget the evening when I got a good hard look at myself.

"It was late, and Edwin had gone to deliver a baby. The children seemed especially active and mischievous just before bedtime. I had put up with it until I couldn't stand it any longer and finally yelled at them to get their attention, to force some kind of obedience. Feeling miserable that I had blown it again, I continued ranting at them, justifying my loss of self-control, blaming their childish misbehavior for my actions. 'Don't you care about me?' I blurted out.

"With big tears in her eyes my five-year-old daughter answered, 'I do care. I try to please you, but no matter how hard I try, I can't. I'll never be able to please you!'

"I was shocked to hear the words. They broke my heart. My anger turned to despair as I realized how I was hurting the very children that were so precious to me. I lay in my bed crying after I had tucked them in for the night. I had been a Christian for years, yet it didn't seem to make any difference. I cried out to God for deliverance, but I felt as though I was hopeless."

Maria's husband, Edwin, was a success. As a family practice physician, he had risen at a young age to become the director of the residency program, but it had come at a terrible price. "With greater responsibilities had come greater challenges and greater demands on my time. I had to face a number of character weaknesses in my new position, and I could feel myself slowly separating from my wife and family. Even when I was home I was always on the phone. I had been religious my whole life. I was the son of a missionary, but by age thirty-nine I was just going through the motions. I had the best of everything, a beautiful wife, great children, and a fantastic job. Almost everyone was affirming me for the great job I was doing, but I was nearly dead inside, and no one—not even my wife—knew how miserable I really was."

Miserable Christians? You had better believe it! For the last seventeen years, I have traveled the world, and these kinds of Christians are not exceptions but the rule. They are people who look great on the outside. Sometimes even their own families don't know it, but they know it; they're miserable inside!

And yet, it doesn't have to be that way—no matter what your past is like. No matter what situation you find yourself in, things can be different for you starting today! But before we can look at the solution, we need to take a good long look at ourselves. We have to understand the problems we are trying to resolve. So, come with me back through my life, for we are not that different, you and I, and every one of us has experienced the disappointment of finding out that the batteries are not included.

I can still recall the thrill of discovery as I examined a gaily wrapped Christmas gift, wondering what was inside. Was it the new baseball mitt I wanted? A canteen? The pair of PF Flyer tennis shoes, the ones I just knew would make me the fastest kid on the block?

My fingers shredded the paper and quickly revealed a replica jeep. I wish you could've seen me with that jeep. I had it out of the package in an instant, wasted no time on the label or instructions, and before you knew it, I was pushing it along. *Vrooom! Vroom! Beep! Beep! Splash!* I made all the proper noises for the motor, the brakes, and of course all the imaginary obstacles I was climbing over or splashing through in four-wheel drive. What joy it brought to my little heart and to my brothers and sister as they watched and sometimes joined in my play. I probably would have stayed content with this self-directed level of play had it not been for someone wiser and more experienced than myself. He said, "Son, bring your new vehicle over here."

I was busy pushing my jeep through a thick carpet jungle, but at the sound of his voice I gladly placed my jeep on my father's lap with all the pride of ownership I would feel when I owned a real car. I could see he had picked up the remains of the packaging, and he showed me two items he had rescued from the wrapping, a small control box and a label that read, "Batteries not included." I wasn't sure of the meaning of those words in relation to my prized jeep, but my father drew me close to explain. He said that the jeep wasn't like my other toys I played "truckie" with. This toy was designed to run on a separate source of power. He showed me the instructions and explained the working of the control box. What a flutter of joy rose up in me as my budding intellect grasped hold of this concept, and I blurted out, "Why, I won't have to push it around anymore!"

"That's right son. You won't have to push it around."

Somehow as I grew up into manhood I never equated my battery-less toy experience with the life I was leading. But if we honestly stop and think about it, most of us are just like little Jimmy Hohnberger—pushing ourselves around through life like batteryless toys. I'm not putting anybody down; I'm talking about me person-ally, and the life I've led.

I was raised to be a hard worker. I come from a stoic German family—good people, achievers, and a stubborn people. When we were told to do something, it was expected that we would jump to it, and if we didn't, we would soon wish we had. I approached religion in the same manner. If this is what I am supposed to do, then I will do it. So I did do it, and I had a reputation as a good kid, but there was only one problem. I could go to church, attend classes, be accepted by my church, and yet be powerless to control the areas of my life that most often got me in trouble. I had an honest desire to serve God, and yet it was frustrating to fall on my face time and time again over the same obstacles. I had a powerless religion. At last I gave up trying because it just didn't seem to work for me.

Years later a client of mine opened the Bible to me, and out of what I had considered a book of fables and old stories came logic, order, and answers to the questions I had always had about how we should conduct our lives. All my life I had wanted someone to show me how to be a Christian, how to have peace with God. Now through an understanding of the doctrines, I felt I was going to achieve that goal. I had that same old strong will that had been trained into me, and I set off wholeheartedly to do what the Bible taught. What I didn't understand was that doctrine, however correct it may be, along with strong human will power to implement lifestyle changes, is not Christianity. No, the Bible speaks of this experience as "having a form of godliness, but denying the power thereof" (2 Timothy 3:5).

Playing church is offensive to God and to man, and that's exactly what I was doing. I was playing church. I had a pretense of religion, a pulpit religion, as it is sometimes called. I looked pretty good on the outside, but the acid test of one's character is in private. It is how I treat my child, my wife, or my dog. It is in the thoughts I think and the emotions I cherish that determine if my religious practices are doing me any "saving" good. If I am pushing myself around with no real power, then the religion I practice isn't worthy of the name.

The disciples had power. They were just a handful of men, and yet they turned the world upside-down in less than a generation. Today there are millions upon millions of professed Christians and yet we seem powerless. Is it possible that we are not really what we claim to be? Please be honest with yourself. Is your temper consistently controlled? How about your feelings and emotions? Do you keep them surrendered to God? Do you ever get irritated at your spouse, your boss, or your children? Are your appetites and passions under the control of your intellect, or do they control you? What about your words? Do you filter every word through God before you utter it? Would you go to church if you knew that they would be showing a video of how you acted in your own home during the last week?

A minister came to speak to me during a lunch break in a daylong seminar. He sat there at the table and said, "Jim, I'm a front and a fraud."

I turned to my wife, Sally, and said, in astonished disbelief, "What did he just say?"

"He said, he was a front and a fraud!" she responded much too loudly.

"Shh! I know what he said; I just don't believe he said it." I looked at this man who sat beside me. He was a leader in his denomination, not just the head of a local congregation. "What do you mean, you're a 'front and a fraud'?"

"Well, when I'm in a church, you know—up front, the denominational representative—everyone thinks I'm some kind of spiritual giant. I play the game, I put on a front, but at home with my wife, I'm a fraud." He was honest, friends. Are we? What would the video of our lives look like?

The alarm clock jarred my senses, as I dragged my tired body out of bed. It was 6:00 A.M. I knelt by my bed and prayed a short, shopping-list type of prayer. You know the kind that informs God of what you want Him to do for you? And then I showered and dressed in one of the several beautiful suits in my closet and came downstairs. My wife had some toast and a glass of juice waiting. After eating I kissed Sally and my boys goodbye and headed out the door. I stopped at the post office as it opened and was at my desk a little after eight. As the owner of an insurance firm, I worked all day to meet the needs of my clients, and if you had done business with me, you would have found an orderly office where I treated you, the customer, and my employees with Christian courtesy. By 5:00 P.M. when I left work, I knew it had been a long day. Most days at work seemed that way more and more, but I didn't mind. I was making it in the world, with all the toys and trappings of success. I arrived home dead tired and ready to just vegetate in my recliner. As I walked in my wife, Sally, who I must confess is one of the least confrontational people I have ever met, was waiting for me with a message.

"Mr. Vandenburg called for you."

"What did he want?" He was one of my clients. Calls at home from a client can mean many things, but few of them are good.

"He didn't say."

"Didn't you ask him?"

"No. I didn't think of it at the time."

"Well, why didn't you think of it?" I said, my voice rising in anger. Sally's shoulders slumped. She had looked forward to seeing me, and now she knew that her hopes of a pleasant evening were gone and she was "in for it" again.

"I don't know . . . I just don't think like you do ..."

"Isn't it about time you learn to think!" I bellowed and stormed off to call the client. Somehow I was able to treat him very nicely, while the girl I had promised to love and care for ached and suffered from my harshness.

Leave that scene now and view my family driving down the country road to church. We were leaders. I taught an adult class, and Sally taught the young people. Neither of us had much to offer.

"Jim, turn around. I forgot something."

"What do you mean, you forgot something?" I turned the car around but continued to stab at her for inconveniencing me a whole five minutes. "Can't you ever remember anything?"

"Jim, I just forgot something," she said reasonably, although I was clearly beyond reason.

"It's about time you started thinking," I lashed out angrily.

"I wish your Bible study class could see their teacher right now!" she stabbed back. It was an eloquent form of ridicule, because it allowed my own conscience to humiliate and mock me.

By the time we got to church, we were good and mad at each other. But we put smiles on our faces and went forth to our various duties and responsibilities, both of us playing the roles of Jimmy and Sally Christian. It was a ludicrous display of human effort that lasted throughout the day's whirl of activities. We presumed to show others the path to happiness and peace while so utterly devoid of these characteristics ourselves. We skipped opportunities to be intimate with each other, averted our eyes from each other, and refrained from any activities that might require us to be more than acceptably civil with each other. By the time we headed home after a long day, the fire of anger was out and in its place was a void, a cold reserve. Neither of us apologized. We never talked about the incident, and we did all we knew how to do, which was to stuff the hurts and the guilt down and pretend that everything was all right. But it wasn't all right and somewhere, deep down, almost against our wills, the coals of frustration smoldered, just waiting for release.

Things continued like this for years. Our frustrations increased daily, until it all came to a head the day we had the "Big Fight." It was the worst fight we ever had. It was a verbal knock-down, drag-out fight that terrified our children and ended with my wife locked out on the porch of our 3,000-square-foot log home, pleading to get back in while our boys, then three and five, wailed in terror at their father's temper.

Sally took a walk down the road. After a while I calmed down and unlocked the door. When she returned, we just looked at each other in shock. We had no idea that either of us could act this way. "What's happened to us?" I asked, bewildered. Sally could only shake her head. Right then and there we took ten days off and headed to an isolated lake with our camper so we could talk and assess the path we were traveling. The conclusion was that we were not Christians, not even converted, no matter what our profession.

I was a success by worldly standards. If I had any doubts, all I had to do was to look in my checkbook. After all, if I make a lot of money I must be successful, right? I looked the part on the outside and in public, but the acid test of our batteries is at home. Here, I was a dismal failure. I longed for something that would save me from myself. I wasn't even sure how to describe it, but I desired it all the same. There had to be more than I had found.

When Christ walked this earth, He came upon a well-leafed fig tree along the road he traveled. Hungry, he searched the branches for the fruits that form before the leaves, but the tree was barren. Christ cursed that tree: "No man eat fruit of thee forever." The tree had, by having foliage, made a pretentious claim of fruitfulness. Those looking upon the leaves might think it a fruitful tree, but a close examination reveals its lack. The leaves were actually deceitful.

Most churches, nay, most Christians are like the fig tree Christ cursed. They make an outward show—they play church. Their branches are covered with the foliage of pretense, tradition, forms, ceremonies, and rites, but they lack the fruit that would come from a connection with the living God.

What does it mean to be a Christian? We unite so closely with Christ that we are one. Just as in human marriage, when we take Christ's name we become one with Him. That's what it means to be a Christian.

"I am the vine, ye are the branches: He that abideth in me, and I in him, the same bringeth forth much fruit: for without me ye can do nothing" (John 15:5). The branch is one with the vine. It must stay connected if it is to bear any fruit, in fact to sustain life itself. The only test of our connection to the Vine, to Christ, is our fruitfulness. Christ said, "Wherefore by their fruits ye shall know them" (Matthew 7:20).

Our self-will is crossed most often at home, and it is when we are crossed—by our spouse, by our children, or even by some tricky home repair—that the religious experience made up of outward show fails its practitioner. You see, I thought Christ and I were one, but in my relationship to God, I was the one. It was I, not Christ, who had control of my life. Here I was, decades after that jeep, still pushing myself around—a batteryless toy. It was depressing.

Thankfully the Lord didn't let me rest at that stage, but for my friend Jeff, the problem of his powerlessness left him so distraught that life seemed worthless. Lest you think Jeff a failure, let me tell you he and his wife are college educated. They have a nice home, and their children look just like any other church member's children. There was nothing that showed on the outside how bad things were for him and his family, and yet they were falling apart. Jeff and his wife tried very hard to make Christianity work in their home, but nothing seemed to change except the credit card balances. Debts were mounting faster than their income until they had amassed more than $160,000 in consumer debt. The extra shifts he worked to help pay the ever-increasing debts hurt family cohesiveness. They started having arguments over the situation that deteriorated over a period of weeks into hurtful screaming matches. At last Jeff felt estranged from his wife, his children, and God. They had all the trappings of Christianity—church offices, Bible storybooks, and religious music tapes for their children, and they were still painfully dissatisfied. *If this is all there is to life and all there is to religion, then I'm going to kill myself,* Jeff thought. *I don't want to go on hurting.*

So, carefully loading his 9mm handgun with hollow-point bullets, the most destructive shells he owned, he placed the gun in his pocket and prepared to go and find a secluded spot on their country estate to end it all. He ignored his wife's pleas not to do anything rash and asked her to keep the children inside for a while. He didn't want them to hear the sound or come and investigate.

He walked out the door and met his four-year-old son riding his pint-sized bike and singing. Children, especially young children, unaware of the nature of the problems and conflicts in the home, are content to live happily in the moment. So it was with this little lad. He was singing, "Jesus loves me, this I know." Jeff walked past his son and out into the surrounding countryside to a little knoll. He pulled out the gun, and in his final moments, he thought of his son and what it would do to his child if he killed himself. The tears flowed freely as at last he lowered the gun, put it back in his pocket, and returned it to the house.

"I was depressed," he said. "I was never a depressed person before this, but I was depressed now. I couldn't make Christianity work, and I knew that it should work. I was a failure as a Christian, a failure as a husband, a failure as a dad, a financial failure, and now I couldn't even succeed in killing myself."

Soon after, Jeff came to one of my meetings. I spoke with him and shared the concepts that appear in the following chapters. I encouraged him to put them into practice, not just allow them to be an intellectual reality, and I hoped and prayed he'd turn his life around.

Six months later I was again speaking within driving distance of Jeff and he came to the meetings. He was a different person! His religion had become practical, and it was affecting his wife and his children, but most of all it had changed Jeff. In just half a year they had repaid more than half their debt. In half a year, they had a new attitude toward life and each other. Jeff and his family still have a long way to go, but if you were to ask them, they would tell you how much better things are today and how much they look forward to making things even better.

Activities for Week 1

Sunday

Reflection: Which characters did you relate to and why? Was it because you've been there and done that? How have you tried in the past to overcome this powerless condition? How well have these methods worked? Are you ready to try something different?

Monday

Prayer time: Seek God in a practical sense today. Ask Him to make you sensitive to your powerlessness in every situation of life.

Activity: Mentally keep track of your reactions to the day's events. Pay special attention to areas in which you failed or ones you wish you had handled better.

Reflection: Where did you find it hardest to be a Christian? Was it with friends, at work, or in the home?

Tuesday

Prayer time: Ask God to help you subdue self and have honest reflection upon your true condition.

Activity: Take a look at that problem area you identified. The majority will have found home to be the hardest area. Is there an activity or time of day that consistently derails you? Do your children, your spouse, or your in-laws drive you to the edge of insanity?

Reflection: When watching yourself throughout the day, were there things you wish you hadn't done, or words and attitudes you would like to take back? Likely there were, and this on a day when you were consciously scrutinizing your actions. What does this teach us about our own powerlessness?

Wednesday

Prayer time: Ask God for divine insight into the areas you identified yesterday.

Activity: Listen carefully for God's quiet voice speaking in your thoughts today. You will be surprised at how often God may call upon you to exercise self-denial in your home. Now imagine what your home would be like if you possessed the power to actually do what God is asking of you. I'm not suggesting you imagine a home where everyone else was Christian in their actions, but just how much of an impact you would have if all your actions were truly Christian. You may be as surprised as I was when I discovered that the real problem in my children's spiritual life was none other than their own father—me!

Reflection: Did you find as I did that while I perceived others to be at fault, the real problems in the home lay at my own door?

Thursday

Prayer time: While it can be hard to have true introspection in the home setting, it can be equally challenging with those outside the home. Ask God for objectivity to evaluate your role in today's activity.

Activity: A huge proportion of our day is spent at work or at school. One would think that in such a structured setting, it would be easy to be a Christian, but often the distractions and problems of the day can prevent us from dependence upon God. Examine your day. See if you even remember in the hustle of the day's activities that God is supposed to be leading.

Reflection: Did you find the workplace distracting to your concentration on the spiritual life? How could you alter things to make it easier?

Friday

Prayer time: For some, today's topic may be the hardest of all. Ask God for new insights into your relationships with those special people we call friends.

Activity: I love my friends and yet it is easy to be drawn into behaviors I regret because of their influence. Peer pressure is not just something children have to worry about, but something that affects adults too. Watch today for little things that influence you to do wrong.

Reflection: Were there settings in which you found it hard to be a Christian? Did some friends lift you up toward the heavenly kingdom, while others hindered your growth in grace? Are you weaker with some friends than others?

Saturday

Reflection: Consider what you have learned about yourself this week. If you see problems without a lot of solutions, rejoice because God has a solution for you. All of us are batteryless toys ... but we can become empowered. We can live an empowered life, acquire empowered marriages, and enjoy empowered families. It has worked for others and it will work for you as well. The choice is yours. You too can enjoy empowered living by a prayerful daily application of the principles and tools in the following chapters.

CHAPTER 2

Crossing Over

"For as many as are led by the Spirit of God, they are the sons of God" (Romans 8:14).

CHAPTER GOAL

Reach out across the gulf between a self-directed life and start experiencing the Spirit-directed life.

Back in the days when I was growing up, television was just be-coming popular. And those of you who happen to be as old as me will remember those early TV sets as big, heavy, filled with a variety of vacuum tubes, and by today's standards, notoriously unreliable. The maintenance needs of these new home appliances kept a small army of TV repairmen hopping.

One of my friends had a father who loved to watch television, but one day his set wouldn't work. He promptly called a repairman, who, upon arrival, walked up to the set and plugged it into the wall. And before he left charged him a handsome sum for the privilege.

In a very real sense you and I need to do the same thing with our lives. Running our own lives isn't working! Intellectually, we may know the solution is as simple as plugging into the power Source—God. But while we may assent to the idea of needing God to run our lives, the concept is essentially foreign to most human beings. Even among those who claim to be Christians, few understand on a practical level how to communicate with God and have His presence direct their thoughts and actions throughout the day. For far too many, Christianity has become like a shiny new chain saw. They brought it home because they heard it could make their job easier. They enjoyed the feelings it generated. Holding it in their hands made them feel like a real lumberjack! However, back at home it just didn't work out that way. They took it out to the wood lot, but no matter how much they shoved it back and forth, they made little progress. Their new saw was heavy; it became a burden to lug around and took more work to cut something than the old bucksaw did. Eventually they fell back into the old ways of cutting wood because it was just easier. Friends, they never learned to start the motor. They never experienced the chain saw as a *powered* instrument. A preposterous parable? Unfortunately, it's not. The overwhelming majority tries to use Christianity to cut through life without the power to make it happen.

Paul and Carolyn, the devoted young couple in the previous chapter, finally gained this revelation through an idea that came to Paul during a period of prayerful reflection. It seemed to Paul that he and a whole group of gospel workers were cultivating a field. And what a field it was, stretching almost farther than the eye could see. He and his fellow workers were diligently cultivating the soil with—teaspoons! That's right, teaspoons! In his mind's eye he could see the whole scenario, and it seemed as if he could hear the Lord calling him away from this useless endeavor of "teaspoon cultivation" with these words: "Come on, Paul. I'll show you how to drive the tractor."

Friends, this is what the Lord is calling each of us to in this chapter. It is time we learned to drive the tractor, to start our motors and plug in our sets.

So, *how* do we do it? Where do we begin?

Everyone hopes, desires, indeed suspects that the life we have led thus far is but a dim shadow of what could, or in fact should be our birthright as children of God. The Bible holds forth the promise of victory and inner peace to the Christian, and yet how very few ever seem to find it. The reason is that self-will dominates our lives, our decisions, and even our emotions. We may claim to have Christ as Lord of our lives, but the truth is that while we may frequently ask Him for help, we tie His hands by refusing to give up our control.

Contemporary Christians frequently reveal their true attitudes in such culturally expressive venues as bumper stickers. A popular one states, "God is my copilot." And this indeed is how we *want* to treat Him. The copilot helps the captain, acts on the orders of the captain, but is never truly in charge. He can exercise authority only as the commander grants it to him. You and I are running our own shows, and until we give up the right to operate our own controls, failure will continue to haunt us. So let's look at how we can start crossing over to something different in a practical way.

Every morning as I rise, the first and foremost piece of business I must attend to is the surrendering of myself to the present will of God for my life. This means that I choose of my own volition to give to another—that is God—control of every aspect of my life. What do I mean by that? I mean surrender of every choice, every thought, and every emotion to the control of God. Then this surrender must be maintained through the influence of God's Spirit upon my mind throughout the day.

It is so easy for us to assent to this intellectually, but in the real world, there are unlimited problems to distract us. Satan loves to stir up controversy and conflicts to stimulate our interest and entice our minds. Sometimes it seems that we are absolute fools because we fall into the same traps again and again. The crossing-over experience is where we begin allowing God to rescue us from these pitfalls.

For example, I once had a really good friend. I had done an awful lot for him, as he had for me. We really clicked, but later he turned on me, started telling lies about me. Soon rumors spurred by his un-truths traveled far and wide. I was hurt, really hurt, and in my heart there was a tendency to feel angry and bitter over being betrayed. God, through His Spirit, spoke to my mind and asked me to give these feelings to Him and let Him carry them. It is hard to really put down these hurts and let God have them, but it is the only way to happiness. All of us have cherished such feelings before, and as we mull them over in our minds, they become larger and larger, just like a little snowball rolled around in the snow becomes larger and larger until its weight is overwhelming. How much better it is to cleanse our minds of these feelings right away before they become a burden that crushes the soul and spirit, leaving us gloomy and bitter.

The consistent surrender of all such thoughts, feelings, and, yes, our actions comprises freedom in the Christian life. When we are fully surrendered to all God asks of us in the moment, then we are truly His. As we remain willing, God will reveal to us the areas of our lives that He wants us to surrender to Him. As long as we continue to grow in grace and remain surrendered, we maintain our sweet fellowship with God. When God asks for something and we choose to say No and not to surrender it, we move almost imperceptibly from being Spirit-controlled to being self-controlled.

A picture is worth a thousand words, so let me draw for you a scene of two days in the life of my friend and coauthor, Tim Canuteson.

It was November in the mountains of Pennsylvania—a changeable season of frigid winds alternating with periods of mild temperatures. Rain and snow mix as if the very elements themselves are confused. I've been there in November, and it is not the season I would choose to open a forty-square-foot hole in the side of my home for new doors, but sometimes such tasks are unavoidable. In Tim's words:

"The doors had arrived weeks before, but my schedule did not allow me to set a day aside until late in the month. It was Tuesday morning, and I knew I needed to be surrendered to God for the struggles of the day, but I didn't feel 'un-surrendered,' and the urgency of the task before me impelled me to hurry. That's how life is; it hurries us along, demands our attention and pressures us to act before we have had time to think. I yielded to its demands. Instead of spending the time needed to make sure I was submitted to God that morning, I rushed though my personal time with God and charged out the door to the hardware store for supplies.

"Certainly I was not openly rebellious to God, and yet I wasn't completely at peace. A quiet little voice nagged in my mind, questioning my course—acting without consulting God. First it spoke about cutting short my worship, but I knew better. 'Quick beginnings make for quick endings,' I told myself. Deep down I knew I was trying to coast through the day on my Christian experience of the day before. But I had things to do and taking some of my limited time and wasting it (so it seemed to me) on a time-consuming worship just didn't fit in my plans for the day. God was trying to help me; to guide me through the day, but I was not willing to listen."

Tim is like many of us. Unless we decisively place ourselves on God's side we are by inclination bound to yield to our self-will, and while his first choice of the day to reject God's guidance was seemingly minor, it prepared the way for its repetition.

"My next choice came after I had completed my measurements. I skipped breakfast to save time, so I could leave for the lumberyard sooner. As I drove, that same small voice kept speaking to me. The message was most unwelcome. 'You should have eaten a proper breakfast,' but again I reasoned it away. I don't like most breakfast foods anyway, especially cooked cereal, so I didn't find it hard to reason away this suggestion!

"After obtaining the supplies, I removed the old doors and found something I hadn't planned on. The old doors had been pre-hung, and I was going to have to reframe the opening for the new doors. Of course I didn't have the right lumber for this unplanned job, so back to the lumberyard I went, feeling pressured for time with this new problem.

"Back home again, I removed the old pre-hung framing and re-framed the door, discovering in the process that I had forgotten to get the right type of nails for this new project. Back to the store I went for the third time that morning. I had headed out to the store for the first time at 6:00 A.M. It was now 11:30 A.M. and I was only where I should have been when I removed the doors. I had lost most of the morning. The new glass sliders were not the easiest things I have ever assembled. It took a frustrating hour to assemble the frame, carefully sealing all joints. Now I had to level the door in the opening and shim the frames perfectly square and true.

"When I had the frame in place, I discovered a new problem. I owned two levels, one small and one large. The small one covered too little distance to accurately level the doors over the six-foot span, and the large one was too big to fit into the recesses in the doorframe. So as the clock ticked away the precious moments, I headed back to the hardware store for a medium-size level, all the while growing increasingly agitated. At the store I heard some really unwelcome news. Snow was coming and soon. Now I really had to hurry. The situation was becoming increasingly infuriating!

"The frame was at last level and square, and I moved on to install the doors. These too carried their share of frustrations involving many adjustments of weather stripping and other things. My wife had lunch ready, but I urged her and the children to eat without me because I had to get this project done. The voice in my thoughts spoke loud and clear, warning me that I was becoming driven and was off track, but at last I was getting something done. Self had been rising bit by bit. Irritation reigned, and I found myself resenting my family for eating lunch while I worked, in spite of the fact that it was my idea.

"I had just finished the basic installation and was tightening the handles when my wife asked a simple question. 'Honey, why didn't you remove the molding on the inside of the door?'

"I hadn't done it because the new doors were slightly smaller than the old, allowing me to work without their interfering in the job. They would, however, have to be replaced with new moldings when the job was complete. Julie had asked about this two or three times, and each time I had replied in a noncommittal way, 'Don't worry about it.' The problem was that she didn't know I planned to replace them with new molding and worried that they were being damaged. Now in response to her question, I lost my temper. 'All right. If you want those boards off so you can see the ugly wall behind I'll take them off!' And I ripped them off the wall. She tried to explain, and even though I realized it was a misunderstanding, I was still frustrated and tired.

"Because the new doors were ever so slightly smaller than the old ones, the exterior trim could not be done in the old molding. It was just too narrow. So off to the lumberyard I went to find the right molding. This was my fifth trip of the day, and it's a twenty-five mile round trip! Getting just what I needed was easy from their large selection, but the cashier was starting to look at me a little funny after all these trips. I resolved to use a different register if I had to come back yet again.

"At home I sealed all the cracks with caulking and mitered the trim. It was cold. The sun had set, and the wind blew down from Canada. The air had a moist bite to it and carried the scent of snow. Now I could relax. My problems were basically over. Two last cuts, a few nails, and I would be done. The door would be weather tight.

" 'Daddy, it's family fun time,' Ellen called down from an upstairs window.

"Every night we spend time together having fun, reading, playing, and just enjoying our family. Nothing is supposed to interfere. 'OK,' I replied as I drove in the last few finishing nails. I could take time for my family now, because the pressure was off. After all, I was almost done. I glanced up at her in the window, nodded, and turned back to the job, striking a final blow to the nail to drive it home. I had, however, let my attention waver, and I crushed my thumb with the hammer.

"Clutching the injured thumb, I danced about on the darkened deck, performing what must have looked like an Indian war dance. Moaning, I staggered into the house, and my daughter, Ellen, to whom I had just responded sweetly when she called me to family fun time, said, 'Are you OK, Daddy?'

"I was really hurting. This was not your typical crushed thumbnail—you know, the kind you get when you are holding a nail and miss. No, I had been holding the board, so when I hit the thumb there was nowhere for it to move, no way to mitigate the impact or roll with the punch. The whole of my thumb was turning purple and swelling rapidly. There wasn't even a question as to whether I had broken it. I could feel the bones move.

"It is in a crisis that we reveal our characters, and I had been cultivating my self-will all day. Now I had had it. 'Does it look like I'm OK?' I bellowed. 'What kind of a stupid daughter have I got who'd ask such a dumb question?'

"My wife then said, 'Did you crush your thumb?'

"She was trying to be solicitous, but I burst out caustically, 'Boy, I can see where she gets her stupid questions from.'

"I had wasted a day. I got my project done, but it would take days to recover from the damage, both to my thumb and my relationships. As I sat there feeling miserable, I couldn't help remembering another day that I had slated for a project when things had been so different.

"Like the day I had installed the door, I was enjoying a day off from my regular employment, at least until midnight when the hospital would need me again. Yard work that I had been putting off was on my agenda. The weather forecast was perfect for outdoor work. I awoke at a very early hour. Fighting off the urge to go back to sleep, I padded quietly out into the sleeping house. The soft sounds of breathing came from the children's rooms, and I wasn't sure what had awakened me when I heard a soft sound on the deck. I flipped on the light, and there were three late-night visitors, looking for all the world like kids caught with their hands in the cookie jar. Three masked faces stared at me as six paws poised over or stood in the bowl of food we leave out for the raccoons each night. Realizing they were not going to be disturbed, they resumed eating, each trying to hog it all for themselves amid the protests of their friends. I enjoyed their antics for a few moments, but it was not their squabbles that had awakened me.

"I can't explain how God can be a personal presence to me, while He can at the same time be personally present with you, but He is. It was He who had called for me and was waiting like a secret friend to visit with me. He knows me so well and understands my weaknesses. He wanted to pour His strength into me for the coming day, and all He needed from me was my cooperation. I picked up the book I had been reading each morning to guide my devotional thoughts, but communion with God was all I desired, and the book remained open but unread before me. I passed a magical time of introspection, the minutes slipping away, one by one, until I suddenly realized that those minutes had turned into hours. Three o'clock in the morning had silently glided into five, and now I must awaken my wife.

"Predawn light was bringing trees into sharp relief against the brightening sky as I moved down the hall to the bedroom. Slipping into the covers I cuddled her gently, easing her into wakefulness. There was so much I wanted to share, to visit about, and yet, I sensed the time was not right. Amid my personal desire to enjoy her company, there was a persistent thought that ran counter to my wishes. And in its still, small voice I heard the call of God upon my heart saying, 'She needs time, time to wake up, to spend with God, time to prepare herself for the day.' I didn't like what God was asking of me, and yet I saw the wisdom and chose to yield my way for His.

"There was no great feeling of victory as I made my way back into the living room. I was living by principle, not by feelings, and my feelings and emotions didn't like the self-denial that is part and parcel of truly following God.

"Just as I settled in with my book, I heard the sound of tiny foot falls and a sleep-tousled head made its way down the stairs to my lap. He was warm and so very soft in the fleece pajamas his mother had sewn for him, that I felt as if I was petting a warm, furry animal.

"My son has always been a challenge for me. He is stubborn, resentful under correction, and quick-tempered. Coupled with this, he is smart, too smart for his own good, and frustrates easily when his intellect wants to accomplish things his body is incapable of doing. In short, he is so much like me that it is frightening. When he chooses to yield to God and hence his parents, he is as sweet as any child could be. When he chooses not to yield his way to ours, he can literally drive you crazy!

"Holding him that morning, his little head resting contentedly on my shoulder, I felt a surge of resentment rising within me. With my wife just awakened and my worship completed, I knew it was my responsibility to help my son with his personal time with God. Since he still wasn't reading proficiently, it meant I would have to read to him, but this would be much more than just sharing a Bible story. I would have to take my child to Jesus and present the option of yielding and obeying in a way that appealed in a practical manner to him. I often share how Jesus is willing to take from us the feelings we don't want—fears, upsets, and anger. I must show religion as a practical part of the household, something he sees affecting mother and father each and every day. My wife, Julie, usually does his worships and takes our often-stubborn child to the Lord to be softened and refined. Surely one of the greatest privileges given parents is the opportunity to bring our children to God and teach them practical Christianity. The problem is that we can't teach them to be submitted if we ourselves are not.

"As I prayed for us at the beginning of his worship and asked God for a clean heart and a willing spirit, I was in dead earnest. I needed to be resubmitted to God, and God did just what He promised. He supplied the need, took my resentful feelings, and we both came out of those happy minutes together fortified for the day. We were submitted to God's will and willing to obey no matter what He asked. How very important it is for us to start out the day that way, because it is a choice we will have to reaffirm many times each and every day.

"As you can see, a lot happens in our house early in the morning, and already I had had to choose repeatedly to stay surrendered. By the time I finished with my son and he dressed and made his bed, it was nearing seven. My whole family likes what the kids call 'Daddy breakfasts.' My wife is certainly no slouch in the kitchen, but with so many responsibilities that draw on her time she tends to make simple, but hearty meals of cooked cereal, toast, and fruit. I enjoy more exotic fare of waffles, pancakes, hashbrowns, baked apples, and the like, which are great to eat but take more time. When I have the time to make breakfast, I will often serve the more complex foods. I see my wife head for the bathtub, and I know for sure that breakfast is mine. I like to cook, so I don't mind and as an added advantage I get to make whatever I'm hungry for.

"After breakfast, my thoughts are about getting to work, but while she says nothing I can just see my wife is burdened with home schooling and the housework. Promptly a thought pops into my head that I know didn't emanate from me, 'Tim, take over the breakfast cleanup for your wife.'

"I didn't want to do that. It wasn't in my plans, but I surrendered to it, and Julie quickly headed upstairs to prepare for her lessons before the children finished their morning chores. Both children had started their schoolwork before I headed upstairs to say I was going outside to work. One glance at the desk told me Julie had the checkbook out and was sorting the bills. Clearly she wanted to pay them that morning. We like to do it together, or I should say, Julie likes to do it and I would rather do it with her than do it myself or let her do it solo and then be in the dark as to what is going on with the money.

"I was all ready to head outside to do my jobs, my pet projects, but again I felt the impression to put my wishes aside and help balance the checkbook. By the time I finished balancing the checkbook, Julie was in a small fix. Both children need instruction for their next subject, and she can only teach one at a time. Yet another time, I found myself being asked by the still, small voice to set my tasks aside and put my family first. I found myself teaching phonics—my worst subject. You may laugh to hear a writer say it, but when I took phonics in school I was so lost I didn't even know that it had to do with sounds!

"At last I finished teaching and returned to the bills. After Julie and I sorted them out, paid them and prepared some packages to mail, it was late morning. Seeing all the work my wife still had to do, I again felt inspired to help out. I volunteered to make the afternoon meal. By the time I got it cooked and we had eaten, school was done for the day and the children were fully involved with their afternoon jobs. Several packages were ready to mail—the result of our morning's work, so I headed to the post office to mail them before it closed. Back at home I threw myself into family fun time, enjoying the special people I am privileged to live with.

"The strange thing is, I found that my whole attitude had shifted. In the morning it was hard to put others first and my ideas second, but now it was flowing smoothly. As the kids got their baths, Julie and I had a few quiet minutes to visit. Often she rubs my feet in the evening, but that night I took hers in my hands. After the children were in bed, I tucked Julie in. The hour of parting had arrived. She needed to sleep and I had to leave for my night shift at the hospital. I had gotten nothing done that I'd wanted to do. Yet I was at peace and the day had not seemed wasted at all. We kissed, and she turned serious. 'You know, when I see you surrendered like this it makes me want to go forward too.'

"I smoothed down her hair, tucked in a corner of a blanket, and turned off the light as I left the room. Heading down the hall, I thought about her words and the events of the day. I hadn't done anything I wanted to do all day long, and yet I can never remember a better day or a happier feeling.

"It's about choices, I thought as my thumb throbbed. God's guidance was the same both days. What differed was my reaction to that guidance. Why did I make such poor choices today as I installed the doors? Because I would not let my will be submitted to God's will, because I wouldn't allow self to die, and because I wouldn't put others first. That is why my day was wasted. May God from here forward grant me the wisdom to see self-will for what it truly is—the enemy of true happiness and peace in my life."

You see, the human mind is like an Internet site. You can put a Web page out there and anyone who desires can visit your site. Every visit to your site is referred to as a hit, and you can keep track of the popularity of your site by the number of hits it gets. What about you? How many hits do you get from God each day? Would you like to get a printout or would you find it too depressing to realize all the times God has tried to get your attention, tried to get you to "download" vital data, and you chose to ignore His message? I've talked with scores of people just like you. You're frustrated trying to live the Christian life. You're discouraged and want to give up. But there *is* hope. That hope is found in entering into the experience held forth in the text found in Ephesians 2:8: "For by grace are ye saved through faith; and that not of yourselves: it is the gift of God: not of works, lest any man should boast."

What is God's grace? I'm not going to give you a theological explanation. Instead, here is my practical, down-to-earth analysis. After almost two decades of study and experience I have come to only one definition for God's grace. Grace is God's continual presence with me throughout every minute of every day of my life. God's grace is always trying to woo me, trying to entreat me, trying to beckon to me because He wants to save me from myself. Right here and right now, God wants to guide, direct, and empower me, so that He might restore me and redeem me. God is with me, and He is going to show me how to get out of all my troubles.

Let's talk more about this "gift of God." If someone gives me a gift, have I done anything to earn it? No! It's free! It's mine. All I have to do is accept it and open it. Is there a part I play with a gift? Yes, there is. What if I take the beautiful gift, all wrapped up in shiny paper with the ribbon and the bow just right, and I never open it, never take it home with me, and never use it? Has it done me any good? No, of course not.

But there is another side to gifts. Have you ever opened a gift from some well-meaning friend or family member and had to ask in all honesty, "What is it?" Most of us have, and I think that it is here that perhaps we find a clue as to why God's gift of grace so often goes unopened and unappreciated. God freely bestows the gift of His grace—that is, His guidance to every man, woman, and child. But by choosing to let our self-will direct us rather than His will, we have been conditioned through years of repetition to ignore His gift because we simply do not sense its value.

The salvation of man is made up of two parts. The first part is grace, and in the practical application of these principles we'll see that grace always comes first, always precedes anything I can do, anything I can think, and anything I can say. Grace is God's part, and it always comes first.

Faith is our part, and it always comes second. The exercise of faith is always in the present, inseparably linked with an action verb. Paul, in Hebrews 11, tells of person after person who did something through faith. "By faith Noah. ... built an ark to save his family.... By faith Abraham ... went, even though he did not know where he was going.... By faith Moses ... left Egypt, not fearing the king's anger" (verses 7-23). Paul also speaks of the faith of "Gideon, Barak, Samson, Jephtha, David, Samuel, and the prophets, who through faith conquered kingdoms, administered justice, and gained what was promised; who shut the mouths of lions" (verses 32, 33, NIV). Faith is our response to God's grace in the moment, in the here and the now. Faith is the choice that I make to allow the present operation of grace in my life by cooperating with God through my actions.

Several winters ago I was driving up our North Fork Road and hit a patch of ice. I was going too fast and slid into the snowbank. Even with four-wheel drive I couldn't get out. Thankfully another truck came along and when it stopped, I asked the driver if he would mind pulling me out of the ditch. "I have this tow strap," I told him. "Would you mind pulling me out of here?" He consented, and I was out in moments. I was elated, but I didn't say "Wow! What a tow strap!" No, I told him, "Wow! What a vehicle!"

The tow strap is like faith. In and of itself it has no value unless it connects me to a source of power. The same is true in the Christian life. There are a lot of things that masquerade as faith, but true faith is simple, and it connects us to the power Source.

Maybe faith can be simplified by looking at its three elements. Most people think of faith as belief. This is not wrong, but it is incomplete. Faith is belief, but belief is only one part of faith. Many of us think we have faith because we believe. But belief doesn't make us Christians. Belief doesn't mean we're converted, doesn't mean that we're going to treat our spouses properly; belief doesn't even mean we're not evil. "The devils believe and tremble."

So you see, belief is not complete in and of itself. For belief to have any practical value in our lives, we must surrender to God's grace, to His will, and have a willingness to do whatever He asks us to do. Unfortunately, most of us do not operate on the basis of belief coupled with surrender, but rather, we are led by our feelings and emotions and find ourselves in trouble.

In summary, we see that belief provides the motivation for our actions, while surrender is an intellectual choice for God's will. Motivation and surrender are vital, but still missing is the key to making this experience consistent, and that key is *dependence.* It is only as we make a decisive choice to remain dependent upon God that He can continue to work in and for us.

It is here that I believe the vast majority of those who earnestly hope and desire to be Christians find their experience lacking. When we first come to God, we soon gain the realization that God wants to direct us through His grace. Who among us doesn't desire this intimate guidance from God? But despite our wishing, we remain powerless due to the simple fact that we have not developed the skill of remaining dependent and allowing God to work in us, "both to will and do His good pleasure."

When a person has been severely injured, they often require extensive therapy just to gain the ability to accomplish what are professionally referred to as "activities of daily living," such as washing, dressing, and eating. No patient masters these skills without an investment of hard work and time; likewise we cannot learn the activities of daily Christian living without undergoing some struggles against long-established habits.

Don't be discouraged because you find it difficult to cross over from your current, self-directed experience to what you desire. The activities in this book are your therapy exercises. It takes time to retrain your hearing to be sensitive to God's voice and longer still to learn dependence. Independence from God is the biggest curse of my life and yours, but we do come by it honestly. It is the flesh we are born with and often all we have known up to this point. However, we do not have to stay in bondage to its powerlessness any longer. Oh yes, you will doubtless have times where you fall flat on your face. Don't give up. God promises that He who has begun a good work in you will complete it. So, go forth in newness of life, trusting Him to do just that.

The problem is that in this world of sin we have been conditioned to view dependence in a most disparaging manner. Adult children who are still dependent upon their parents are viewed with disgust. Women have been conditioned over the past forty years to throw off the idea of being dependent. Teenagers can't wait to discard their dependence. Every one of us has been trained to obtain our own independence, and in the process we have become ill-prepared to experience what could and should be to us the most rewarding relationship a human being is capable of entering into. Dependence is not a dirty word when there is no ability to be successfully independent.

Newborn babies are the most dependent creatures on earth. Human beings spend many of their early years dependent upon others. Perhaps because we take so long to achieve it we humans are loath to give up what we view as independence. Dependence upon another at this advanced stage in our life is viewed as insulting, an affront to our pride, an insult to our abilities. In many ways we are like an old tomcat I once heard of. This cat, being independent, as most cats are, took it into his head to climb atop a shed. Just why he climbed there is a mystery known only to him, but he was there and didn't know how to get back down over the roof's overhang, so he was stuck. His owner spotted him and, seeing the problem, set up a ladder and climbed to rescue him. Now analyze the situation with me.

The cat saw the owner coming and believed the owner loved him and was going to help him—that's belief. He came right up to the owner and submitted to the idea of the owner rescuing him—here is surrender. But when his master grabbed him and started down the ladder he dug his claws into the roof and held on for all he was worth. You see he wanted to get out of his situation but not badly enough to let go of his control. He wasn't willing to be dependent, and all the efforts expended on his behalf were unable to save him from himself.

You and I are in trouble—stuck just like that cat—in a bad situation from which we are powerless to rescue ourselves. Without a cultivated dependence on God, our belief and surrender, no matter how vital a part of faith they are, cannot save us. Let me illustrate from my life.

It was March 7, 1999. We had finished a series of meetings in Hawaii and were enjoying a few days of rest and relaxation before boarding a flight to Australia. After counseling with people and preaching for days at a time I needed a chance to unwind. We made our way to a sparsely populated beach where we planned to do some body surfing. I love to relax in the water. When you're on top of a wave heading into the beach, you can't do a lot of thinking and your mind has a chance to relax.

I had just spent two weeks speaking about living a Spirit-led life, but you're going to see that preaching truth is not quite the same as living that truth in the moment. There I was on the beach, just watching the waves come in and soaking up the sunshine. If you have done any surfing, you know that not every wave that comes in is the same. There is a pattern, a rhythm, and as you watch the waves, you'll notice they come ashore in sets, so you can figure out the pattern. On this day, every third or fourth wave was the big one, and I don't like to ride the small waves when I can ride the big ones. As I stood there on the beach watching the pattern, I had it all figured out. So I shouted to Sally, "Come on, honey! Let's go!"

As I started toward the water, this little thought came into my mind. *Jim, take off your watch. You might lose it.*

Bah! I'm not going to lose it. It's held on tight by my twist-o-flex band. I have swum with it many times. There's no need to remove it. And with those famous last words, I headed out into the ocean.

In the water I tried to reorient myself to the timing of the big waves and again that impression came. *Jim, take off your watch. Even with its twist-o-flex band, you might lose it.*

No way! Not me, not Jim Hohnberger. I know better than God does, or so I thought. I ask God to speak to me every day, to guide me, direct me, and empower me, so I won't get into any trouble. And then I don't listen to Him! Are you that way? Have you done that? Remember this is after two full weekends of preaching about God and how to listen to His Spirit. Anyway, there I was. I had been preaching about it, teaching others about it, and I didn't listen. The thing that troubles Jim Hohnberger is that the problem always comes differently than the way I think it's going to come. If it happened the same way every time, we'd learn to listen, wouldn't we?

So far in this story we've been talking about grace—God's continual presence with me to guide, instruct, and empower me over myself, so I don't get myself in trouble. The Bible describes it this way: "And thine ears shall hear a voice behind thee, saying, This is the way, walk ye in it" (Isaiah 30:21). When I was out there in that ocean, God was trying to tell me something, to give me some insight. That's how God's grace works in the present moment.

What about you? Are you resisting the operation of grace in your life right now? God's grace is always there. He is always willing to help and always sufficient for the task at hand. But as powerful as grace is, it is powerless without faith and I mean faith, real faith, not belief, not even belief coupled with surrender. I mean a vibrant dependence that transforms belief and surrender into a powerful Spirit-led life.

God was trying to help me through the gift of His grace. Was I opening His gift? No, because the biggest flaw in Jim Hohnberger's life is that I want to be self-sufficient. I love to manage myself. I want to make my own decisions, think my own thoughts, and run my own day. I'm really good at it—or at least, I think I'm good at it. Even though I claim to be a Christian, I like to manage myself, and the language of my heart is that I know more than God does.

My watch forgotten, we played on a few waves and got used to the water. As I looked out to sea, I saw the pattern and I could pick out the big wave on its way. I said, "There it is, honey. Do you see it coming?" And when those waves come, they really come. To get on top of the wave you can't just stand there and expect it to pick you up. You have to get some momentum so that as the wave comes you're already moving and can ride it all the way to shore. I threw my arm out in front of me to start a powerful crawl stroke and my watch flew off my wrist, sailed in a short arch, and dropped out of sight into the ocean.

I caught the wave, and as I rode it to shore, I said, "Lord, will I ever *listen?*" I berated myself all the way in, and as I looked about I realized Sally had missed the big wave. She was still out where we started. I headed back out, and as I came up to her, she could tell something was wrong.

"What?" she asked.

"I caught the wave, but I lost my watch."

"Well, let's find it."

I just kind of looked at her—my dear, sweet, innocent wife. I knew there was no sense in looking for it. When those waves come in, they churn up the whole bottom. It looks like a washing machine. There's no way you can find anything!

My wife said to me, "Let's pray about it."

Now, you know that God could find that watch, and you know that if He wanted to He could send an angel to locate it for me. But I was logical. Men tend to be that way. And I knew there wasn't a chance of finding that watch. So I said, "All right, you pray." I had analyzed the situation, and I knew my watch was gone. As I looked at my wife, so hopeful and earnest, I thought to myself, *This woman is nuts!*

After she prayed she started feeling around on the bottom with her feet, and I thought, *You've got to be kidding me.* I actually looked around us to see if anyone else was noticing what this crazy woman was up to. She looked up at me as if to say, "Aren't you going to look too?" There was no way I was going to make a fool of myself, doing something like that. I said, "Go ahead, honey. You look for it." I was embarrassed. I didn't want anyone to see Sally searching the bottom, let alone do it myself.

After a little while, Sally reached down and then handed me my watch. What a rebuke to the preacher! Isn't that something? God did send an angel to find my watch, the angel I'm married to!

It doesn't matter what kind of problem you are in. God says, "I will never leave thee, nor forsake thee. So that we may boldly say, The Lord is my helper" (Hebrews 13:5, 6). God always has a solution no matter how impossible the situation is. His solution is grace, and if you will have faith like my wife, you will find the watch! I humbly told my wife, "Honey, you just showed me what I've been preaching about all weekend. Thank you!" You see, it was Sally who found the watch. Sally exercised faith.

Are we living a life of continual faith? No, we're not. That's why it's so hard! We have been trying to accomplish our religion in the power of the flesh, and we're ignoring grace. In our evangelism, we've only been providing people with belief in God and in doctrines. Knowledge of God and knowledge of biblical truth has not made a Christian out of the devil. He knows more about truth than we could ever hope to learn, and he believes in God, but he is not surrendered to God or dependent on Him. So I ask you, Whose religion are we really following? Whose children are we? Which experience do we possess?

Many of us are longing, hoping, desiring, and desperately trying to be Christians, yet lacking the key which will unlock the door to the experience we yearn for. Friends, it can be different. And it can be different beginning today! If you will incorporate the knowledge gained in just this chapter, it will transform your life. Yes, it will be awkward and maybe even a bit scary to give up control. Don't despair if you don't always listen properly or if things go wrong. We don't throw out our children when they don't listen well or are forgetful. Our heavenly Father loves us the same way. He knows this is new to us. He knows how difficult change is, and He is as delighted with our progress as earthly parents are with the first tottering baby steps taken by their little pride and joy.

I know there are those who would like to say, "You just don't understand. If you came from my background and had my kind of baggage you would know this will never work for me." Well, friend, no matter what our background or history, no matter how hurt we have been, no matter how bitter we may feel, God understands, and it is He, not Jim Hohnberger, who is calling you to experience His continual direction.

Karen understands as well as anyone what it's like when your background is rough, when your life circumstances are far less than ideal. She says,

"I was only a little girl when I was robbed of the purity, beauty, and joy that are a child's right by an older relative who exposed me to activities far beyond my age. He was always messing with me, trying to get me to do and see things that even my little-girl mind knew were wrong. I was told things like, 'Your parents won't care. They do this too.' It continued for years. I was so confused. This violation of the trust a child should be able to have in their elders left me emotionally distraught and fearful around almost everyone. The only person I was really comfortable with was my mother.

"I became very shy and withdrawn. When I went to school, my teachers noticed it right away, but never pried deeply enough to find the real cause. They just concluded that I needed a little help adjusting socially, and they singled me out for attention and prominence. They tried me in different classes, chose friends for me, and quizzed my mother for suggestions. Their efforts were useless. All I knew was that I didn't want all the attention. I had already attracted far too much of the wrong sort of attention from adults. As I looked around me at school, I saw that none of the other children were receiving so much adult attention, and I concluded that there must be something wrong with me. Because of all this, I never liked school and didn't do well.

"In junior high school I learned to speak out in self-defense. There were big, rough boys who tormented other kids, and I was a regular target for one of them. I'm not just talking about teasing and making fun of kids, although there was plenty of that, but pushing kids in shop who are operating saws or poking girls from behind while they were operating a sewing machine, their hands perilously close to the needles. It was truly dangerous, and I cried out to my mom and the teachers for help. But they didn't understand my cry. The teachers seemed afraid of the boys because they would ignore their behavior and walk away. It made me so angry. I was forced to learn how to defend myself. I ranted and cursed at my tormentors until they backed off, but inside I was crying at the injustice of those who would not defend the weak.

"By high school I started having fun. I was maturing into a 'normal' girl—getting in trouble for talking too much and so on. Guys didn't seem so bad anymore, and I went out with a few, just as friends, and felt pretty safe. During my senior year, I started dating some of the older guys who seemed gentle and nice. There was this one fellow who asked me out. My friends told me rumors that he was involved in some gang, but I discounted their warnings. After all, he went to school with us and everyone knew him. He seemed nice, and I trusted his kindness.

"I didn't know he was setting me up for his fellow gang members. That night was a taste of hell. I won't go into details for it would only serve to glorify their satanic deeds, but looking back I realize it was a miracle of God that I made it back home the next morning—alive!

"I never told my parents. I was afraid to hurt my mother and father, so I confided what had happened only to my best friend. We decided the only thing to do was for me to act as if nothing had happened. So I tried, but it wasn't easy. Word got around, and people started to talk. You know how it goes. Since I had remained silent about what had really happened, rumors soon spread about how easy I was. It was horrible. That night had devastated me, and I couldn't defend myself. Even the other employees at my after-school job found out and approached me about it. It didn't take long for the rumor mill to turn me into a girl with a reputation.

"While all this was going on, I started dating Ron. What a great guy! We had a wonderful four months before the word got to him about the past, and he lost all respect for me. We broke up several months after graduation. I couldn't defend myself against the rumor mill, and through it I was being violated—again and again. My heart was crushed, and I started using social drinking as a way to cope with life.

"I became very independent—rented a house with a friend, enjoyed a booming social life. I could take care of myself materially, but I felt dead inside—like a walking corpse.

"Ron came back into my life, but I was confused about his feelings for me. He said he cared for me, and I certainly had feelings for him, but he would openly flirt with other girls. I was confused at the mixed messages he was sending. Deep down I longed to be loved by the down-to-earth, gentle person he was.

"When Ron proposed, I accepted, in spite of our problems. Finally I felt someone loved and wanted me! My friends were happy for me even though some joked and kidded, saying things like, 'You won't make it. You'll be divorced in a year. You won't stay faithful.' Some of them were just sorry to lose the friend they partied with.

"I started getting threatening phone calls almost every night. All through my engagement the calls came, telling me in graphic detail that they would kill me. They seemed to enjoy sharing with me their plans to end my life. It seemed these terrifying calls would last forever, but the last call came the morning of my wedding.

"Marriage seemed great … at first. But as the months went by, Ron and I drifted apart. I had given up my old life and friends at Ronnie's request, along with my single life and independence, but he hadn't given up his. He couldn't understand why I objected to his going out with the guys. I needed him. He was my life now, but I was just a part of his life. Before our first anniversary, I found myself sitting in the office of a man who was supposedly one of the best psychiatrists in Dallas. I'll let Ron tell about this."

Ron says,

"Karen came home after her third session lividly angry, and told me she'd never go back! I was paying this counselor money, lots of money, to help my wife and my marriage, only to find out that he wanted to be a 'sugar daddy' to my wife. He hadn't helped; he'd made things even worse."

Karen continues,

"Ron was right. I went downhill from there. I felt I was starting to come unglued. I took out the one Bible we had and prayed over it, weeping and begging God to save me. I had heard of Jesus saving people, and I wanted to find out if it was for real. We started attending an evangelical church, stopped drinking, and thought we had become Christians. Ron quit going out with the guys, and my contentment at home and with Ron improved. The people at the church were nice, but I didn't fit in. I really had little interest in making new friends. I wanted my husband to be my friend.

"We started church hopping, hoping to find some church, somewhere, that taught the Bible. I was pregnant with our first child and desperately wanted a church home to raise my children in. We received a pamphlet in the mail about some meetings where they claimed they would teach everything from the Bible. It was just what we had been longing for. They showed us truth, not theory. I never knew the Bible was so easy to understand. We were delighted and soon joined that church, but the one thing they didn't teach us was how to have God lead in our daily life.

"Two years later, our second daughter was born. Those years were some of the happiest times in our married life. We started planning to move to a more rural environment on land my parents owned. Then Ron's job uprooted us and sent him to Maryland. Maryland! It sure wasn't where I had planned to live, but to Maryland we went. We found a conservative church and started to really think Christianity was working for us. We learned a lot of practical Bible-based actions in those days. For example, I learned to dress in a more feminine way with less revealing styles than I used to wear. We became active church members, and I even helped give Bible studies to others. I had a zeal for my marriage and my children. For the first time we really began to bond with God and each other. We were sincere and really trying, but while we could transform our outer lives, I longed for help in overcoming the power of emotions in my life! Oh, our lives were better, far better than they had been, but we still didn't truly possess what we were searching for.

"Yet through this dark time God was working, and for the first time in my life I came to understand what self is. Self, that part of me that got irritated, frustrated, and angry with my husband was the root of all my problems. Self was that part of me that was determined to do things my way, to run my life, and overrule every decision. I had served my self-will for my entire life. I didn't know anything else or even that there was an alternative, until I talked with and got some tapes from a man named Jim Hohnberger.

"The things he said baffled me, yet it excited me to think that maybe things could be different. He gave me hope that my husband could be the man I needed. Even more important, I got a new and different view of myself and where my problems lay. Feelings and emotions had controlled me my whole life, but hope was born in my heart that it didn't have to be that way. Self no longer had to rule me.

"This revelation that self was my own worst enemy opened a whole new field of inquiry up for me. I started listening to God's still, small voice to my conscience, and for the first time in my life I found I didn't have to respond the same old way. It is so exciting! Let me share a couple of instances with you.

"I was in town with my two teenage girls doing some final errands before we left for a trip out of state. We had completed our first stop, and all of us were excited about our coming trip—when the van wouldn't start. It was raining, in fact pouring, and I was parallel parked on a busy street with little expectation that someone was going to be willing to stop in the road beside me and risk an accident just so they could stand in the rain and jump-start my van.

"I called Ron at work, but he had just left. I tried another friend, but they were out. At last I found a towing company who said they'd come out for twenty-five dollars. I was so tempted to think evil of my husband. After all, he had just told me the van was working fine. But just as quickly the Lord spoke to my heart, reminding me that I had a lot to be thankful for. It was daylight, we were safe and dry in the van, and I had a cell phone with me. *Yes Lord, thank You for Your blessings,* I prayed. The man arrived and jumped the van to life. 'Everything should be fine,' he assured me. 'The battery is good.'

"With a thankful heart I set off to the bank. Unfortunately I reverted to my old habit of turning off the vehicle while the transaction is being completed, and after I received my cash and turned the key, I was greeted with silence. "Oh, why did I turn the engine off? Girls, I'm afraid the produce stand will be closed." As soon as I said these negative words, the Lord spoke to my heart again, prompting me to use encouraging words with my girls. I told the drive-thru clerk the problem, and she said they would ask people coming in if they could jump-start us. While waiting for someone to help, we hunted up our jumper cables—not the easiest task with the van packed for vacation!

"Meanwhile my thoughts were running like this: *Why isn't Ronnie home yet? I need to know what to do with this van. Should I take it to a mechanic? I sure don't trust it for the trip right now. Why doesn't Ronnie ever have a decent vehicle for me to drive?*

"God called for me to surrender those thoughts of self-pity and to think good of my husband. I remembered how years ago, he gave me his brand-new car and drove an old broken-down car to save money. That was self-sacrifice! I really was thankful that Ronnie is not the type to go into debt for expensive vehicles.

"Someone pulled around to help me, and soon the engine started. On the way home we found a produce stand and got what we needed, this time *without* turning off the engine. At last I reached Ron by phone, and he agreed to meet me at a gas station, where he energetically went looking for the problem and fixed it! When Ronnie and I met I had joy in my heart for him. I was truly glad to see him and greeted him with a hug and a kiss. Ronnie was so sweet. He expressed sorrow and sympathy for what I had been through. I was so thankful I had let the Lord redirect my thoughts. In the past, I would have greeted him with a cold, condemning spirit. Now thanks to surrendering to the Lord, we had cheerful hearts for each other.

"Another time Ronnie had to go to the doctor for removal of a tiny metal fragment from his eye. I didn't want to go. The last few days had been rough. We had had some trials. Our relationship was a little rocky, and my emotions had been stirred. I didn't want to forgive and forget. Still I prayed that the Lord would put forgiveness in my heart and zeal back into my life. You mothers know what it's like some weeks. There had been endless trips to the doctors that week. The older man I take care of had fallen and ended up with a cast. In addition, that very day I had taken my daughter to the orthodontist, so the last thing I wanted to do was wait in yet another doctor's office. Then came the familiar prompting from the Lord, *Karen, I want you to go with Ronnie to the doctor's office.*

"Driving down the road, I was still struggling. I didn't want to do this, but I rationalized that maybe there was something wrong with his eye. Maybe there was some type of damage, and that was why the Lord wanted me to go along.

"The office was packed. The girls found a place to sit, and Ronnie took a bunch of papers from the receptionist to fill out and sat in a folding chair—the only seat left in the room. I stood over him, watching as he filled out the papers. Just then a couple left, and there was a cute little love seat just right for us to sit on. 'Come on, there's a chair for us to sit on,' I told him.

"He just shook his head and kept his eyes on the paperwork. I went and sat down. *Surely he will come soon,* I thought. *He's not coming, Lord. He is my husband. He should be sitting with me.* I motioned for him to come and sit next to me, but he again shook his head. Rejection! *What's wrong with me? I am wearing one of his favorite outfits. Lord, You want me to love him and just look what he's doing!*

'Karen, quit anticipating your husband is going to sit next to you. I love your husband. You don't know what he is thinking, and I want you to not think of him as rejecting you.'

"I sat quietly with peace in my heart. I didn't even look up to see when or if Ronnie was going to sit beside me. Minutes later he came over and sat down. He wanted some help with a couple of questions. I gladly helped him fill in the answers. It felt so nice to have him next to me.

"In the exam room with Ronnie, my attention had been on the nurse when I glanced at the man I love and thought, *Wow! It's Ronnie. I feel young, Lord. May I have some fun?*

"Yes. Karen, I am taking you and Ronnie deeper in your Christian walk. I just need you to cooperate with Me.

"I caught a gleam in Ronnie's eye, and I teased him by mouthing a few silent words behind the nurse's back. She left. Now I could really have some fun. I got up and started playing doctor. We were quietly laughing together when the doctor came in. Was I ever embarrassed to be caught playing doctor! I felt a little awkward as I shook hands and she smiled at me.

"As I reflected on the providence of God and His plans for us that day, I am so glad I listened to Him. I had started the day feeling estranged from Ronnie, but when he headed to work after the doctor's appointment, I departed from him feeling so refreshed, it was like we had just spent a weekend at a resort. This is how my new life is going. Day by day, I'm learning to become more distrustful of self, more willing to surrender my feelings, and more in love with my husband, my children, and my life."

Karen's childhood experience is light-years removed from my "normal" upbringing and probably from yours, yet all of us can relate to her. Why? Because no matter what our background, whether it is better or, God forbid, worse, we share a commonality of suffering. No one has lived so pampered that they have never been misunderstood, hurt, or used. Disappointments and pain are the same for everyone, and we relate to each other's suffering through what we have experienced ourselves. Sin has to a greater or lesser extent damaged all of us, and, like victims of an epidemic, some may have more pronounced symptoms. But all must have a cure lest they die of the disease. The possibility that you or I have struggles that are more socially acceptable than someone else does not negate the seriousness of our condition.

Today's Christian often longs for true communion with God as was seen in Bible times. People often lament, "Things were easier back then when God spoke to people and told them what to do." Well, friend, that type of intimate involvement with God is available to all. He is just as willing to talk to you and to me as He was to David or Paul. The continuous interchange between God and man is the heart of saving grace and living faith. This is the gospel experience that saves us. It's not our doctrine or our beliefs but a continual *communion* between the soul and God. It is reaching out over the gulf that separates us and crossing over from a self-directed life to a new and better, Spirit-directed way of living. It is only in realizing our powerlessness and in stepping out in faith to cooperate in the strength of heaven that we wrest ourselves from the bonds of sin and selfishness that have so long held us captive.

I once heard a story about a man who had to cross a creek by means of a rope secured to an overhead branch. In this situation it was necessary for him to take a running start, grab the rope, and let the momentum carry him over to the other side, where he could let go of the rope and drop safely on dry ground.

The man in our story took a good running start and made a good swing on the rope, but he didn't let go. When the rope swung like a pendulum back to the place he started, he still didn't let go, and as the rope lost its momentum, he called out to his friends, "I don't think I can make it!" Indeed he couldn't, for now he hung on the rope over the creek, and there he would remain, straining to hang on until his strength gave way and he fell into the water.

Most Christians are just like this man. They leap out to leave the old life but are never willing to let go and drop into the new life; hence they find they are in a worse condition than they were at the start. They are "hanging in there," but every moment is a struggle, a battle, which they must inevitably lose. Don't let this happen to you. Cross over into newness of life. It is there on the other shore just waiting for you to experience. The only question that remains is "Are you willing to let go?"

Activities for Week 2

Sunday

Prayer time: Continue to seek God as a friend. Think of Him as a close companion by your side, a loving guide eager to point out the way, and a supportive friend always willing to buoy your spirits when you are discouraged. If you can begin to view God in this manner you will begin to catch a glimpse of God as He really is.

Activity: Read "Crossing Over."

Reflection: After reading of others crossing over, reflect on your own desires to enter into this experience. If you decide to go forward, your aim should be to start experiencing the Spirit-led life in small increments and build upward into more continual and constant dependence on God. Remember the process of change is gradual and setting unrealistic goals for instant and life-long transformation predisposes one to discouragement. It's better to sustain small changes than to try and make sweeping alterations that collapse in frustration.

Monday

Prayer time: Ask God to make you sensitive to His every instruction. I've watched people with cell phones, and they are very attuned to listen for its ring. Your task, beginning today, is to retrain yourself to listen for the still, soft voice of God. Ask Him to make you so sensitive that the lightest whisper of Jesus will catch your attention. Then ask God to give you a spirit willing to act on His instruction.

Activity: Today is exciting! Finally we move from theoretical understanding to practical implementation. To live a Spirit-directed life requires a mind willing to listen for God's voice, and while this sounds simple, most of us have trained ourselves to ignore the Spirit's prompting and so we have trouble staying focused. Use any clock or watch that has an alarm and set it to go off every hour. This reminder helps bring you back to having a receptive attitude. You may be amazed, as I was, at how quickly I could lose focus, become absorbed in my activities, and forget all about God directing my day. Try it for a few hours.

Reflection: How did you do? Did you sense any impressions in your mind? Don't be surprised if you aren't sure. You are not yet familiar with the Spirit's voice. In time, you will recognize Him as the voice of a close friend.

Tuesday

Prayer time: Continue to ask for special sensitivity in hearing God speak to you.

Activity: Choose an activity you do repeatedly throughout the day. If you work in an office, it might be answering the phone. A carpenter might choose the use of his hammer. The busy mother might choose each diaper change. Don't put a lot of effort into choosing. Just pick whatever the Spirit brings to your mind as you read this and use that activity as a call to prayer and dependence. Pause just a moment with each activity and ask God to direct your thoughts. If you will do this, you will find yourself starting to practice the type of dependence God wants to incorporate into all your activities all day long.

Reflection: Did you find using the activity as a prompt helpful or just a form? Why? What do you think might help you remember? Plan to try your idea next time.

Wednesday

Prayer time: Ask God to show you the special relationship He wants you to concentrate on today. It might be with your spouse, child, friend, or parent.

Activity: Today's focus is to allow the new sensitivity you have been practicing to have a practical influence with someone you love. Seek the Lord's leading whenever they come to your mind, but especially when you are with them. Make a concerted effort to filter your words through God before you speak them. Be especially sensitive to their needs. Perhaps there is a little something you can do to lighten their burdens.

Reflection: Did you notice a difference in how you related to them? Did they?

Thursday

Prayer time: Today ask God to show you that special area you struggle with. For example, maybe it is diet. Ask Him to demonstrate His power in your weakness.

Activity: After prayerful reflection, plan an escape route for your specific area of struggle. This means deciding how you are going to deal with your specific temptation before the temptation comes. If snacking is your problem, maybe you will decide to drink a big glass of water every time you feel the urge, thus replacing the bad habit with a good one.

Reflection: Did maintaining a dependent relationship with God alter the way you related to your specific area of struggle?

Friday

Prayer time: Think of your successes and failures this week. Ask God to give you understanding for each situation, so you can improve the next time.

Activity: Drawing on your prayer time, think again of those situations that were conducive to your Christian walk and those that weren't. Your activity today is to attempt as much as possible to place yourself in the best environment for growth.

Reflection: Have you started the process of crossing over? Don't become discouraged if it seems awkward. Instead, continue to experiment with God. A wonderful experience awaits you if you will go forward. May your experience grow and deepen into a consistent enjoyment of being attached to God and receiving His guidance.

Saturday

Reflection: As always, this is a day to recharge your spiritual batteries and secure the gains you've made in your walk with God. If you missed an activity this week, perhaps you might take today to make it up, but spend time listening to God today, not just in your quiet morning devotional time, but try to hear His voice during the busiest part of your day. May God continue to bless you!

CHAPTER 3

Attached and Receiving

"Abide in me, and I in you. As the branch cannot bear fruit of itself, except it abide in the vine; no more can ye, except ye abide in me" (John 15:4).

CHAPTER GOAL

The goal for this chapter is to take the experimental connection formed in the previous chapter and continue to make it a real and vibrant connection with God. Just as the branch must be connected to the vine, so must we maintain a living connection to Christ that we might be attached to Him and receive from Him wisdom and strength for the day.

Living a Spirit-led life requires us to *let go* of our control. It requires that we throw our dependence upon the guidance of God's grace in every situation of life and cling to Christ no matter how difficult or perplexing the circumstances seem to our human wisdom. Having once crossed over and experienced grace and cooperated with it, the great trial and difficulty of the Christian life shifts to maintaining this experience on a consistent and ongoing basis.

The new Christian and his family are a lot like my boys and me when we decided to take up a new activity. I told them, "All right, boys, since you're interested in rock-climbing, I'll teach you how to rappel. There is only one problem—I don't know anything about it, but we'll learn."

I had engaged in many adventure-sports in my life, but serious rock-climbing had never been one of them. So we got the very best books we could find on the subject and studied them until we thoroughly understood the theoretical performance of each maneuver. Then we purchased the very best equipment we could afford. We talked rappelling until you would have thought from their conversations that my boys were world-class climbers. At last, however, the big day came when we headed off to the cliffs to put our knowledge to the test of real life.

I didn't know a lot about mountaineering and wish you could have seen my anchor system; I was overly cautious. At last I had the ropes secured, so that even I thought they were solid. Then I invited Matthew to go first. He tiptoed to the edge and, looking down, decided to offer Andrew the chance to go first. Andrew hesitantly squirmed forward and looked over the edge. He said, "Not me! You go first, Father."

"Yeah!" Matthew agreed. "You go first."

So I walked over to the edge of the drop-off and looked down. Have you ever noticed that it seems twice as far down from the top as it does when you look at it from the bottom? Well, I got my equipment all set up and prepared to slide over the edge of the cliff. If only there was some way of letting you see that climbing rope. I'm sure the imprint of my fingers is still visible. I've never grabbed something so tightly in all my life. I went over that edge and actually enjoyed the trip down. After climbing back up the trail to the top, my boys and my wife all went down. We learned to rappel that day, but do you think my boys would have gone over that precipice without me leading the way?

Of course not, but that is what most Christian fathers and mothers do. We tell them the way they should go. We study with them and make sure they understand the principles. But we don't go over the edge. We don't lead the way, and then we wonder why they don't become Christians. Worse yet, the children see Mom and Dad floundering through life without a lifeline.

What would you have thought of the idea of rappelling off those cliffs without a rope? Preposterous, you say, right? Well, untold millions do that very thing every day. These are not worldlings, mind you, but good Christian folks like you and me, who attend church, believe the Bible, and love their neighbors. Just like my boys, they study dependence upon God and they talk as if they engage in such activities every day. In reality they can only talk a good game because they have little or no experience to back it up. Why? Because to swing yourself over the edge means that self and self-sufficiency must die. All our dependence must be placed upon something else. Unless you are willing to place your whole weight on the rope, you can never do more than look, act, and talk like a climber.

You see, true Christianity is more than mere talk, more than intellectual knowledge; it's a true and living connection with God. This type of true Christianity is rare, far rarer than you might think, and that's why I feel so privileged to introduce you to the Waters family. Long ago, before we ever knew we would be forming a ministry, God brought this unique family in contact with us. What set them apart from so many others was their commitment to follow God. This commitment was not set inside conventional limits. Rather it was an open and free giving of themselves to God, no matter what the cost. They would eventually become our partners in ministry, but they are much more to me than simply fellow laborers in the cause of God. They have continually inspired and challenged me over the years as they have sought an ever-deeper relationship with God. Hence, I was really excited when they agreed to share some of their experiences with you. Let's join Tom as he is working on some household tasks.

"I had just finished a small home repair and had a screwdriver in my hand. My next task was to wash the car, and I stuck the screwdriver in my back pocket, handle downward, and headed off for the car. My inclination was to pull the car up where the hose could reach then get the soap and other supplies. However, as I was walking, there was a quiet impression in my thoughts.

'Tom, put that screw driver away first.'

"Now, I always teach my children to put things away before starting another project, but the inclination of my heart was to do it my way. After all, what difference will it make if I move the car up first? Well, perhaps a lot.

"I remembered another time when I was getting ready to go backpacking and the Lord impressed my thoughts with the idea that I needed to make sure I brought my hat. *Of course I'm going to bring my hat,* I argued to myself, and I put off actually going and getting it. Only upon arriving at the trailhead, did I realize my hat was still at home—hours away! For most people this might have been an inconvenience, but for me it's another story. Let's just say that when your hair is starting to thin on top like mine is, you no longer have the same amount of protection you used to have, and I came home from that trip with a sunburned scalp. This experience, however unpleasant, did set the stage for me to give more careful consideration to the instructions I had just been given.

"*All right, Lord, I'll put the screwdriver away first,* I said. Placing the tool back in its spot, I realized that many items I needed to wash the car, the soap, the bucket, were right beside the tools. So I gathered them up and walked back toward the car. I had yielded my way to God and had found it wasn't as unpleasant as my flesh wanted me to believe after all. Opening the driver's door I jumped into the van and suddenly the full implications of what I had just done hit me. If I had done this same thing with that screwdriver sticking out of my back pocket, it would have gone right through the upholstery of the seat and not only damaged the car but given rise to a situation that would have tempted both my wife and me to lose our hold on Christ. I was so thankful I had chosen to yield to that impression."

I'll come back to Tom later, but did you see grace working in Tom's life? Did you see his response to grace? God's grace called for action. He had to believe it was from God, surrender his wishes and desires, and take the action to put the tool away. Then he had to stay dependent upon God, even when he didn't know why God had instructed him so specifically. In time he saw what God had known all along, but obedience, that is faith, came before there was a clear vision of the reason.

We may never fully understand why God asks of us some of the things He does or why He allows certain problems and trials. We can, however, depend upon Him as a loving father and trust His judgment and wisdom. We don't have to know the reason. We only have to practice belief in His guidance, surrender to His will—even when the way seems rough, even when His choice for us is the last thing we may want to do—and put our full dependence on Him to solve the problems with which we are beset.

Everyone who has ever tried to live the Christian life has encountered firsthand that dependence, as an intellectual truth, is a far easier thing to assent to than the exercise of dependence as a living, breathing reality during a crisis. Many people ask God's help as they muddle through life's problems, but this is not dependence. If the truth is told, most of us have seldom experienced dependence upon God. I say that because with untold millions professing Christianity, we have less power than the twelve disciples did. Had we learned the secret of dependence, we would not find ourselves so helpless.

The transition from the old self-directed life to the Spirit-directed life is never easy, but this is not because God in some arbitrary way has chosen to make the way difficult. It is because of our own heartfelt desire for self-government and the clamoring of our appetites, passions, and desires that the Christian yoke seems so onerous. Unless we choose to fully let go of such things to the control of a wise Father, we may find our attempts to live the Christian life a miserable existence. Our minds will intellectually desire to go forward in the path of God, while every other fiber of our being is straining to return to the old life.

It is what we pine for that truly shows where our affections are. Unless those affections are decisively removed from the worldly and placed upon the heavenly, our spiritual life will resemble a yo-yo, always moving up and down, but never moving beyond the ties that bind us to the hand of Satan. It is never easy to escape his bounds, for when we desire rescue and are willing to be dependent, he is aroused to resist us. Satan welcomes any religious practice that allows self to live, for in ourselves we are powerless, but should we start to depend upon God moving forward as He opens the way, then he is a defeated foe and knows he must lose the conflict.

Hence we must understand that in the trials of life that come to us, it is not the outward crisis that can defeat us, but the yielding to self that brings defeat to the soul. One of the hardest lessons for us to learn is to become totally distrustful of self. We may be sincere, but all too often we retain the reins of control in our hand while honestly desiring God's guidance. See if you can relate to my struggles as I earnestly set off to have God guide me on a wilderness adventure.

I had heard the persistent rumors of the trapper's cabin for quite some time. People seemed to know the general area it was in, but no one seemed to have actually seen it. It was just the type of intriguing story that piques your curiosity and makes you wonder if it is even real. I've always loved to investigate the unknown, so it wasn't long before I decided to make a personal reconnaissance of the area and really find out if the rumors were true.

I have found that if I am to get some special, one-on-one time with God, the wilderness provides a refuge, free from interruptions, phone calls, and the pressure of ministry, which is never fully out of mind even when set intentionally aside. I love these special days away in the wilderness. I refer to them as my Enoch time, after the Old Testament man who had a closer walk with God than almost anyone before or since. I come away from these days with a mind refreshed, spirit revived, and self humbled by the knowledge of One infinitely greater than I. So, it was in anticipation of such a weekend that I hoisted my pack and headed up the trail toward adventure.

I made my camp beside a little mountain lake, whose shore was an alluvial mix of gravel and boulders left by melting glacial waters. Crawling into my tent that night, I fleetingly thought of some of the men who have gone camping with me. Good men, who seemed every inch Christians, but they would spend their nights awake, unable to relax, fearful of the grizzly bears that roam these valleys. I'm not unmindful of the danger that these creatures present. After all, I have spent the last two decades of my life among them. My nonchalance is not born out of presumption, but rather out of a studied confidence that God controls every aspect of my life. It is He who led me to live in the wilderness, and I do not believe that He brought me to this point to provide an easy meal for an omnivorous beast. He controls my life and future. Hence, I sleep when others worry.

Rising early, I laid out my plans, asking God to help me find the cabin, and I set off on what was to be an extremely challenging day. I covered the whole valley that day, crisscrossing here and there, investigating every likely location, asking God for help, but I returned to camp empty-handed. My search was an absolute and utter failure. I was dead tired and disconcerted. I had asked God's help, but I had failed. Why? I made a fire and heated some water for peppermint tea, while the sun slid lower on the horizon. "Why didn't I find it, Lord? You know where it is." There was no answer, just silence.

Suddenly, as the sun's beams continued to slide lower, I saw something on the other side of the valley. No! It couldn't be! I grabbed for my binoculars and saw the outline of the overgrown cabin emerge from the woods. The sun glinted off the old roof and clearly distinguished its location in an area I had traveled though several times that day. *Why didn't You show it to me before, Lord? I was over there, not more than a few thousand yards away. Why didn't You show me then, Lord?*

Because you were the one running the search, Jim. You were in control. You were in charge of the expedition. I was the follower. You wanted My blessing on your efforts. It was only after all your efforts had failed that you were willing to listen—to let Me lead.

Holding onto God and letting Him lead in the problems of life, accepting His leadership and guidance, is a struggle for all of us. The tendency to run our own show, to act on our own and to speak without thinking or "filtering" is so inbred in us that it requires intentional effort to be open to the Lord's leading.

I've asked my friends Paul and Carolyn to share how a small task turned into a two-day nightmare. I can empathize with them in their struggle to remain in Christ, and I think you will too. Paul says,

"Carolyn and I were both working full time out on the front lines of Christian evangelism, when we were brought to the stark realization that desiring change in our own experience was not enough. The kind of relationship we wanted to experience with God wasn't just going to happen, but rather it would come about as we took time to surrender all to Him and did everything in our power to answer our own prayers.

"First we looked at our environment. We were living in a tiny travel trailer on a busy park in the Midlands of England. We had always been reasonably tidy housekeepers, but we realized that better organization of our limited space would make our cozy home easier to maintain. I'm not suggesting that we should work our way to heaven by cleaning our homes all day. I am, however, insistent that our environment affects us, mentally, physically, and spiritually. A well-ordered home is more restful to its occupants than the opposite. We were becoming increasingly aware of the shortcomings of our location. In the trailer park we couldn't walk more than a few feet without conversing with one of our neighbors, hearing their music, and on occasion their colorful language! Should we have children here, it would be hard to control their associations. Obviously we needed to move to a more rural location. In England, however, this is easier said than done, even if you've got the resources to afford country property, and we had nothing, only the desire and the belief that God would open the way."

Carolyn adds,

"Paul was right. We knew God wanted us in a better location, but we searched all over England, Scotland, and especially Wales, and came up empty-handed. It was hard to be patient with the delay. Our human spirit wants everything to happen right away, but God was leading. Paul's business prospered during those years of searching and our savings grew, but the type of property we were looking for was still out of reach.

"Expanding our horizons, we took a trip to southern Ireland, where we found a derelict cottage that we could afford and hopefully renovate. The stone structure was in such sorry condition that it would have to be gutted and the interior rebuilt. Still, we felt the Lord had opened the way and we returned to England, quite optimistic until we discovered that I was pregnant. I was shaken. This wasn't part of our plans. We wanted to move first, get the cottage renovated and settled. My health hadn't been the greatest, and I had looked forward to improving things before childbearing. I had planned to have children four years from now and here I was—pregnant. I was so unsettled because it wasn't my perfect plan. However inconvenient the timing, our plans went forward and by the time we moved, I was, even to the uninformed observer, obviously 'with child.'

"With our future home, the derelict cottage, uninhabitable for the foreseeable future, we decided to haul our recently purchased $2,500 trailer to Ireland and live in that temporarily. We hurriedly prepared a site for it near the cottage. The site, unsheltered from the constant winter winds, proved to be a poor choice. As much as we hated to uproot the household we had barely settled, the trailer had to be moved to the other side of the cottage, and the sooner the better.

"Enlisting the help of a local forester and a farmer who owned a tractor, Paul prepared to move the trailer the one hundred fifty feet to its new location. I took all the pictures off the walls and was on the verge of taking my china out of the cupboard when Paul stopped me. 'No need to move the china, my dear; it will be all right where it is for this short trip,' he reassured me.

"I was uneasy but yielded to his judgment. After all, he knew more than I did about moving trailers, and we weren't moving very far. And yet, both of us had the unshakable feeling that things were about to go as wrong as they possibly could.

"Originally Paul had planned to move the trailer himself, but when our vehicle proved insufficient for the task he had enlisted the help of the farmer who was one of the few local people we had made acquaintance with during our brief two months in Ireland. This last-minute change in plans was not to be without consequence. In the excitement of the moment Paul had forgotten there was a depression, a small ditch if you will, several feet in front of the trailer. The wheels on one side of the trailer would have to cross over this ditch, and Paul had planned to bring the trailer up to the edge and then, being able to see the exact location for the crossing, fill in the depression thus bridging the gap. The farmer, unaware of this problem, started to tow the trailer. Just as everyone was rejoicing that the tractor was strong enough and our system seemed to be working fine there was a huge *bang,* which brought everything to a pitiful halt.

"Being seven months pregnant and unable to be of much help, I had taken my penny whistle and walked up a small knoll to watch. It looked like everything was well in hand as the trailer moved slowly, professionally, it seemed, and then one side of the trailer dropped violently down and the whole structure listed to one side like a sinking ship. Even from a distance, I could see through the windows of the trailer, all those unsecured items becoming airborne as they were thrown viciously across the room, accompanied by the sickening sound of china breaking. I wanted to dash right down there and investigate the damage. Emotion surged through me. *Sure, Paul, my china will be just fine where it is,* I thought. And yet, somehow, amid the storm of feeling welling up from within me, I felt the restraining influence of the Lord speaking to my heart, encouraging me to stay where I was, and encouraging me not to act from impulse. So I stayed where I was a little longer and watched as Paul turned to investigate the problem."

Paul continues,

"Carolyn may have struggled to stay where she was, but I was wishing I was someplace, anyplace else! I couldn't believe what I saw! The wheels were down in that ditch, and my first inclination was to say, 'Why didn't you remind me, God?' but the fault was mine and mine alone. Both the farmer and the forester had other obligations and headed off to their respective jobs. It was clear to all of us that I would have to jack the wheels out of the ditch, and it would be time-consuming. The farmer promised to return in a couple of hours and help me complete the move.

"I was feeling keen regret for my own incompetence, mixed with frustration and abandonment. I wanted to say poor me and have a pity party. I walked around the trailer to look the situation over, but in reality I was struggling with the thought of how long and hard this was now going to be. My plans for the day were in ruins, my promises to Carolyn broken, my God had seemingly abandoned me to my own self-sufficiency or stupidity, and as I walked around toward the door just barely hanging on to Jesus, there was Carolyn."

Carolyn says,

"I'd walked down the hill, despair nipping at my heels. I so wanted to straighten Paul out. The temptation was almost overpowering! It was his fault our wedding china was broken. The longing to give vent to those feelings of anger and frustration could be felt like a physical need. Apart from God, we really are despicable people, but God is faithful. Even as weak and as prone to sin as we are, God was with us and He had provided a most unexpected way of escape. Paul's eyes met mine, and he quickly said, 'Don't even say a word.'

"In that moment of absolute truth, knowing what was in my heart, I knew he was right. He was not angry or defending himself, but was stating the simple fact that there was no way we could trust ourselves to speak just then. I nodded and held my peace, and despite the crisis we faced and the trouble we were in, we held on to our Savior and each other. Instead of blaming him, I found new sympathy and compassion welling up in my heart for my husband. He knew how bad I felt, and I understood how bad he felt about it. I turned away so he could get on with his work."

Paul continues,

"Carolyn was right. To get that trailer out of the ditch was going to be just plain old-fashioned hard work. With the two-ton jack I could lift up the four-ton trailer a few inches and pile rocks under the wheels then set it back down and then repeat the process, gaining a couple of inches each time. Despite the cold November air, I was sweating profusely, but I was ready when the farmer returned.

"By then another problem cropped up as well. We couldn't turn the trailer and move it the way I had envisioned. The only option was to haul it one-third of a mile down the drive to the road, where it could be turned, and then tow it back up the drive to its new location. I was very concerned about this new dilemma because I had just spent a lot of time beside those rear wheels, and I knew the rear axle was bent. The little wheels under those homes aren't designed for long-term towing, just positioning the trailer the last few feet. When the big trucks deliver them to their site they put a specially designed undercarriage under the trailer for transport. All I had were the wheels that were part of the structure, and they were never intended for the type of move I was anticipating, especially after they'd been dropped in a ditch. If that axle broke anywhere along the drive, the only home we had would be stuck right where it happened to be. However, there being nothing else for it, I gave the farmer the go-ahead and down the drive we headed. *Please, Lord, don't let that axle break!* I prayed fervently."

Carolyn adds,

"As I watched Paul walk beside the trailer, my heart was in my throat. My home, the only material security I had in this new country, was leaving. My emotions wanted to take control. To be honest, I just wanted to have a good cry! I couldn't watch any longer, so I fled to the shell of the cottage. It was cold, little more than the unheated stonewalls. But upon entering, I noticed the old bath stand we had purchased at a sale, intending to clean it up and paint it. God is so good! He gave me something to do with my hands while I was otherwise helpless. I started to vigorously clean the old metal, thankful for a normal activity. My home might be traveling slowly down the drive—maybe to never return—but there in that cold shell of our cottage, with my unborn child moving within me, God was allowing me to feather my nest. And for the moment I was able to enjoy a respite from the trials of the day."

Paul says,

"Because the driveway curves out of sight of the house, I was unaware of Carolyn's activity. I walked beside the trailer as it slowly limped along, silently thanking God for answering my prayers. The damaged axle had taken the strain valiantly. Now we only had to back the trailer into position on the new site I had prepared. Just a few more feet and this ordeal would be over, but it was not to be.

"The new site had a slight incline and backing the trailer up that slope was beyond the strength of the farmer's small tractor. The machine had done remarkably well, performing a task for which it was never intended, and yet as I watched those big wheels slip and spin in the mud, trying to force the trailer in place, all I could think was *Please, Lord, let this ordeal be over. I'm hungry, cold, and tired. I don't want any more problems.* I wanted so badly just to have the job over and done with, and now it was impossible.

"When self is thwarted, it is always a temptation to play the blame game—blame the farmer, blame the tractor, blame God—anything to make self feel better. Thankfully, self is not the only conduit of messages our minds receive, and God had not abandoned us. No, no, He was only taking us to a depth we had never experienced before. He reminded me that this kind man had helped us a good portion of the day and had done the best he could under the circumstances. So instead of falsely accusing him for his lack of machinery, I thanked him for his efforts and turned my attention to setting up the mobile home for our use that night.

"I had to figure out how to jury-rig the water and electricity to stretch the gap between where the trailer was and where I had planned it to be. I had the electricity hooked up and was finishing the water when I heard Carolyn's footsteps in the trailer above me—obviously surveying the damage. I hoped, for her sake, it would not be as bad as I feared."

Carolyn says,

"As soon as Paul got the lights on, I hurried to check out the damage. At first glance it looked very bad. My new range was lying on its side in the kitchen, but other than a few small dents, it looked fine. The china in the china cupboard had suffered some breakage, but again it wasn't as bad as it looked. There were only two plates actually broken. At last I got to the item that concerned me most. I had figured out long before that the object I had seen flying across the room in front of the window had been my prized keyboard. Dreading what I would find, I picked it up and stared in disbelief at its pristine condition. With a certain amount of trepidation, I plugged it in and, wonder of wonders, it worked! 'Thank You, Lord!' I breathed in relief."

Paul says,

"Entering our home that night was an experience I will never forget. Carolyn was relieved that the damage had been minor and superficial, and was doing what she could to make home 'home' again. It had been a hard day. We were hungry. I had worked hard all day, and Carolyn was pregnant. Our evening meal was a haphazard collection of whatever we had energy to put together. I longed to get cleaned up, but there was no hot water yet. The power had been off all day, and the water was little warmer than the freezing ambient air temperature.

"We knew we had been in a trial, a long drawn-out trial, but thank God we had not let go of Him, not even for a moment. We had been tempted, pushed, and harassed by the devil as he used our own fleshly nature to work against us, but we also knew we had both been *attached* to God Himself and *receiving* His power ... His sustaining grace to live above sin and self.

"After supper we collapsed into bed, exhausted but happy, and slept, albeit somewhat crooked in the unleveled structure, knowing all the time that tomorrow we would have to do it all over again as we tried to move the trailer the final few yards.

"Morning seemed to come around too soon. After worship and breakfast, I connected the phone line so we could call around for a winch. Locating one some distance away, we drove to the shop and rented it for twenty-four hours. It was a heavy-duty, hand-powered winch, a type I had never used before. I was soon to discover just how much hand power was required and realized that I faced a gargantuan task.

"Using various trees, I pulled the trailer toward its position. By afternoon I had run out of trees in a position I could use and decided that since there were some large bushes, I would try those. I asked Carolyn to watch them and let me know if, and more likely, when, they started pulling out.

"Applying pressure, I called to her, 'Are they moving?'

" 'No!'

" 'That's good because the trailer is!' As incredible as it sounds,

I pulled the trailer into position using those large bushes. And as an added blessing, a friendly little robin hopped from the trailer to the bush and perched there, completely confident, it seemed, that God was not going to let it pull out of the ground. We seemed to draw strength from his presence, a little reminder that God was with us. As the sun set on our second day of struggle, the trailer wasn't exactly where we had planned for it, but it was close enough!

"I crawled under the trailer to level it and attach the utilities. At this point it was just a struggle to keep going. I was so cold that my fingers had trouble making the connections. I was wet and muddy. In my weak and exhausted condition, it was a great temptation to feel very sorry for myself. The snow had started to fall, and the bitter wind still swept around me, even in this more sheltered location. It is hard to set aside our personal discomforts and force the mind to focus on God's love and care. But upon reflection, I knew things could have gone far worse. More important, we had both held on to God during a crisis. We knew Satan had been trying to destroy us and Jesus had sustained us in the face of his assault. In the light of this knowledge and with these thoughts in mind, I could endure a few more minutes of discomfort as the last of my tasks were completed."

Carolyn concludes,

"Why did Paul and I survive this trial, when in the past, smaller problems have set us off into selfishness and conflict with each other? We were the same people, with the same inclinations to self and sin that we possessed in former days. The difference in this situation was that both of us had made the choice to hang on to Jesus *before and during* the crisis. We've had our struggles since then and will face more in the future, but those two days have always stood out in our minds. For it was there, on those wind-blown slopes, there amid our first Irish winter, that we realized God could keep us in every situation of life."

God wants to sustain and guide you and me in every problem, every temptation, and every crisis of life! So why is it that so few of us allow Him to remain in control? It is because we want God as a convenience, as someone to appeal to, if things move beyond our control, but otherwise just a non-interfering entity. We don't know what we're missing! God is not like an earthly monarch or the social elite who hold themselves aloof from the common people. Christ showed that God makes no distinction of persons. Even the very lowest members of society found Him ready to associate with them. Today He desires, indeed longs, for you to experience His friendship too. God cares for us with a deep and passionate love that sees beyond how sin has degraded us and views us instead as what we may become through our union and communion with Him.

Do you remember dating that special someone and how you hung on every word they spoke? Each letter was read over and over, each assurance of love and acceptance cherished, while your heart beat a little faster and the day seemed brighter because of the knowledge that someone loved you? Well, what you and I have experienced on a human level is open for everyone to explore with the God of the universe. And unlike our fellow human beings, who do not always understand us and inadvertently hurt us through their callousness, God never fails to lift us up, to forgive when we have erred and to love us even when we are most unlovable. Words are not adequate to describe what is awaiting those who would experience God on a personal level. You need not feel that God is in some far-off heaven. No, God can and should be experienced by all as a constant companion, throughout our entire day.

Sometimes when life is hard or our way is difficult, we wistfully long for a friendship with someone of importance or wealth, a friend who would help us in our struggles. And yet, the wisest, the richest, and the mightiest Monarch that has ever been offers us friendship better than any the world can offer—better than knowing the president, better than friendship with the world's wealthiest man, or even the greatest sports hero. As incredible as it is, most of us ignore or reject His offer!

Often the rejection is unintentional. Sometimes, even those who claim to be Christians neglect their friendship with Him, whose name they have taken. That's a real shame because friendships add so much to a person's life, not only adding to our enjoyment, but also enriching our intellect.

Tom Waters certainly does this for me. We have spent an awful lot of time together, but he still surprises me with his insights and introspection. I'll let him tell you about a most profound experience he had during one of his own "Enoch" times.

"I don't know exactly why the urge comes at certain times, but it is almost as if I can hear the call of the wilderness. It really isn't audible, rather just a pulling at my heartstrings, an inbred desire to spend time in nature, communing with nature's God, my heavenly Father. I always tell my wife the mountains are 'calling' me. She just smiles and says, 'When do you want to go?' She knows the blessings I gain when I respond to the call. They rub off on her too.

"On this particular occasion I had felt the call for some time. Finally I told God that as soon as the snow had melted enough, I would go. It was still early spring in the mountains where we live, but I eagerly got out my maps and chose an area with a southern exposure. I'd never been there, but I anticipated that it would be snow-free when I wanted to go. This is an important consideration in an area that gets snow measured by the yard.

"The night before I left, I listened to the weather band radio, and the forecast was terrible! A big storm was moving in with wind and rain. *Well, that's it,* I thought to myself. *I'm not going out in this kind of weather.* Sure enough, the next day was overcast and gloomy. As my wife, Alane, and I took our early morning walk, dark angry clouds clashed with each other overhead. Scattered drops of rain fell, intensifying the feeling that these were the first warnings of the impending storm.

" 'Are you still going to take your Enoch time?' Alane asked as she surveyed the scene.

"Before I could answer 'No,' there was an impression in my mind from God saying, *Have you asked* Me *whether or not you should go?*

"*Well, no, Lord. I mean, I know it is going to storm and … do You want to me to go, Lord?*

"*Yes, Tom, I want you to go.*

"So I yielded my inclination to the Lord's will and said, 'Yes, honey, I am. I believe the Lord has something unusual planned for me on this trip.' Of course, I was thinking of the weather, but little did I know just how special a time God had in store for me.

"I got ready to set out after lunch. With only a three-mile hike ahead, I would have no trouble reaching camp by evening. As Alane looked over my camping gear, she voiced a concern. 'Honey, I don't think you've got enough food with you.'

" 'Of course, I've got enough food,' I replied. 'You're always so concerned that I won't have enough to eat. I have plenty of food. In fact, I have so much food that I'm going to take some of it out.' " Alane didn't say anything but looked on questioningly as she watched me unpack some of my provisions.

"I drove to the trailhead and started out under overcast but no longer stormy looking skies. I was thinking about what it means to be surrendered to God, I mean truly and totally giving myself to God, really letting Him take my life and use me as He desires. This was my goal, my aim, if you will, for my time in the wilderness.

"With those thoughts in mind, I was quite a way up the trail, when this *big black thing* jumped out of the bushes and startled me! I involuntarily took a step or two backward and reached for the pepper spray I always carry in case of bear assaults. As I regained my senses, I realized it wasn't a bear but a beautiful black Labrador retriever. My heart continued thumping as my brain tried to process the information that all was well. It was just a dog.

"The dog, just as shocked at seeing me as I was to see her, had also backed off a few feet, and now that we both realized there was no threat we moved toward each other. She was obviously someone's much-loved animal. Well-mannered and wearing a collar but no tags, it was baffling to imagine how she had gotten out into the wilderness. I hate to admit it, but my first thought about this lovely dog was, *Oh, no! This dog is going to be a distraction for me. I came out here to spend time alone with God.*

"Wishing that I could dodge the issue I told the dog, 'Stay,' and started on up the path. I was hoping its owners were hiking somewhere nearby and the dog would locate them, but it followed me. I had no idea what to do with the dog, so I prayed, 'All right, Lord, if for some reason I'm supposed to spend this time with that dog, then this is what I want to happen. I'm going to tell it to stay and then head up the trail. If it stays, then I know I don't have to worry about it, and if it comes with me then I know that this is part of Your plan.' Turning to the dog, I said in a firmer voice, *'Stay!'* I was instantly reminded of the times that I've tried as a parent to gain authority through the tone of my voice instead of exercising the authority God has vested in us as we connect to His strength. Well, for whatever reason, the dog stayed and I continued up the trail, happy that I had avoided that problem.

"Nearing the little mountain lake where I planned to camp, I rounded the corner of a hillside and found myself in snow—lots of it. It was obvious that this particular area did not benefit from the southern exposure, and I was quite stunned to find I had no trail to follow, and the snow was three feet deep. I knew I should be close to the lake, so I studied my maps and prayed that God would help me find the lake. Then I walked, tramped, and waded through that heavy snow until I was beat. After an hour and a half, I admitted defeat and stopped to rest. As I caught my breath, this *big black thing* leaped out of the woods and startled me *again!* I quickly realized it was the dog and in my mind I said, *OK, Lord, You must want this dog to be with me, but, Lord, would You be willing to just tell me where the lake is?*

"The reply wasn't audible, just the voice of my conscience. But it sounded in my ears just as forcibly as if someone had spoken out loud. The Lord said, *Yes, I wanted to, but you never asked. You only wanted My help, and I have been helping you, but if you want Me to show you, here is what you do. Follow the ridge along until you come to the stream and then follow it upstream until you come to the lake.*

"I sat there amid the trees and snow, amazed at the simple, straightforward, and logical directions I had received. Of course I could follow the stream up to the lake. It had just never occurred to me. So I followed the ledge and came to the stream in less than ten minutes. In another ten I was at the lake and ready to set up camp. Later I backtracked over the correct route and it only took six minutes from the spot where I had first gotten lost. I had floundered about for the better part of two hours, because I had to do it my way.

"Out in the open beside the lake, I could see the vast expanse of turbulent sky. What a specter it presented to me! Gusts of wind blew the lake water into waves and peaks, while clouds as dark as night boiled up and swept toward me, their canyons lighted with sheets of lightning, their rumbles of thunder echoing through the mountains. The storm, forecasted earlier in the day, was about to break, and I realized I must set up camp with all haste!

"Quickly I moved to set up my tent and as I did, I realized I had never set the tent up by myself before. I had always had another set of hands to help. Thankfully, the tent didn't give me any trouble. In that electrically charged atmosphere I hurriedly put the finishing touches on the tent. As I threw my pack inside and prepared to follow, the world lit up with an incredibly brilliant flash of lightning. The thunder was so close and so loud that the earth shook and this *big black thing* dived into the tent with me!

"Now, I was willing to let the dog stay with me that weekend, but I *was not* going to sleep with it. So I started pushing it out of the tent. The poor dog didn't want to leave me, and it took a while to push it backward until only its head was in the tent, but I couldn't make further progress. I zipped the door opening down around the dog's head and then with a last effort managed to extricate the head and close the opening. I settled into my sleeping bag as the full fury of the storm broke and the dog settled under the tent fly's overhang and got as close to me as she possibly could. She managed to push in the interior wall of the tent so far that my feet rested on her body.

"That night was one of the worst storms I have ever experienced— especially alone! The darkness was oppressive, and Satan seemed to draw near me, bringing all my old fears vividly to my consciousness. He reminded me that there was no other human being for twenty miles and if something happened, I was helpless and *alone.* My old fears of the dark and the wilderness pressed in around me. Over and over, I had to surrender these fears and feelings to God and ask Him to remove them. I knew deep down that Satan was fearful of my spending this quiet time with God and wanted nothing so much as to distract and discourage me. He knew all the right buttons to push, all the secret weaknesses I possessed, and yet my God was faithful! Before the storm abated, I had perfect peace and contentment through surrender to God.

"The next morning the dog was still there at my feet, right outside the door, just as close as I would let her get, and the Lord spoke to me in the quiet of my thoughts.

'Tom, you treat Me just like a dog! I'm always there. I've never forsaken You. You tell Me when I can come in and when I must leave. You ignore Me, and whenever you want Me, I am with you because I love you with an everlasting love.'

"I can't tell you the effect this had on me there in the wilderness. It was so vivid. He was right. That was how I treated Him in my self-management. But He loved me still, and I felt my heart respond with a longing that things might be different. I made a commitment to enter into a deeper intimacy in my communion with God. I wanted to gain a keener awareness of His presence, to recognize He is *always* with me, and to experience Him as my constant Companion and ever-faithful Friend.

"I looked at the dog, and she looked at me so longingly. I could see she was hungry—very hungry. Suddenly, it dawned on me that the Lord wanted me to share my food with that dog, and in my mind's eye, all I could see were my hands taking that extra food out of the pack, and inwardly I wailed, *Oh no, my wife was right! I'm not even going to have enough food for myself, and now I'm going to have to share with this dog!*

"I really didn't want to share. I had taken that food out of my pack after eating a good meal. Now I was ready to eat, and there was too little for the appetite I had worked up, let alone a surplus to share, but I knew that was what God was calling me to do. At last I had to choose. *All right, Lord, I'll share half of my food.*

'Tom, you don't need to share half your food. You weigh 160 pounds, and that dog can't weigh more than fifty. I'm not asking you to share half, just to share some of your food.'

"As is usually the case, surrender was not as hard as my flesh would have had me believe. So, feeling the peace that came from my choice, and appreciating God's proportionate sharing arrangement, I set out to prepare the two of us a meal. When everything was ready, we ate, but I must say here and now that I was impressed with the manners of this lovely dog. She was so hungry. I mean you could just see the longing in her eyes, but she didn't make any move to get the food until I offered it to her. What an example of self-control and an unselfish spirit. What a rebuke to my selfish attitude of the moments before, when I was wrestling with being willing to share.

"By Wednesday night, the beautiful dog had become my companion, and I was growing to know her. She had never growled or barked the whole time we'd been together, so it came as a shock that night to hear her start to growl, softly at first, and then with more urgency. I didn't need to be a dog expert to realize something was wrong out there. I squirmed out of my sleeping bag and unzipped the tent door. I could see nothing, but by now the dog was barking furiously, all the while looking down toward the lake.

"Because the ground slopes away toward the water I couldn't see whatever had her so stirred up. I raised myself up for a better look, and there by the lake was a powerful bull moose. It was wonderful to get a chance to see one, but the dog had awakened me because it viewed the moose as danger and had warned me. I couldn't help thinking of all the times God has done the same for me and all the times I have ignored or reasoned away His counsel. I determined yet again to make Him my priority and to have Him as my constant Companion.

"By the time I was hiking out on Friday, I was walking with the awareness of two companions. I had the God of the universe on one side and the dog He had led into my life on the other. I had walked up that trail just days earlier, occasionally praying to God as I went along, but now I was talking constantly with Him. When I had started out, I said, "Lord, I'd like to talk with You more consistently," and I had been struck by the idea that I should talk to Him just as I'd talk to Jim. So, there I was, talking out loud to the Lord while I hiked, and

He was answering back in the quiet of my mind. We had a wonderful conversation. Finally, I reached a point where I realized I had been doing all the talking and questioning for some time. I decided to ask God a question, just like I would have asked you, had you been hiking with me, and I had been doing most of the talking. "Lord," I began, "what do You want to talk about?" I'd never asked God a question quite like that before.

"*Heaven,* was the reply.

"Heaven?"

"*Yes, heaven. I have a mansion prepared for you in heaven.*

"Now, this is not news to anyone who has read the Gospels as far as John 14. For there, Jesus states, "In My Father's house are many mansions" and "I go and prepare a place for you," but the effect on me of personalizing that simple statement cannot be overstated. God loved me and had prepared a place for me! He had my full attention as He continued.

"*My son, you must learn to depend completely upon Me, learn to give all of yourself … to have all of Me. If you are willing—I will tell you moment by moment what that means—in every situation. Only when your will is swallowed up in Mine, when your only longing is to love Me with your whole heart, just as I love you, then you will find heaven begins for you on earth and you will have a mansion with Me in heaven.*

"As I reached my truck and lowered the tailgate to load my pack, the dog jumped right in. I shut the gate and told myself, 'This dog's owner drives a pickup truck.' I drove home, and we received an enthusiastic greeting, although I must say that my new companion received more than her share of the attention. Sure enough, there were problems and trials awaiting me, but something was different and my family noticed the difference right away. Why? I came home from the mountains vitalized with the conscious companionship of Christ. I was committed to being led by Him moment by moment and was radiant with the joy that comes from union with Him."

Tom was practicing the presence of God throughout his day. It is an experience open to anyone but is hard to obtain when our lives are too busy to hear God's voice. In the wilderness, it is easier to hear God because there are fewer distractions. However, you don't have to go to the wilderness to obtain a "wilderness experience." We can focus upon God's voice in New York City or Atlanta, *if* we are willing to put forth the effort to tune out the distractions. Anyone can listen to God and submit to Him, if they are willing.

I'd like to have you meet Janell. She was thirteen and a typical worldly teenager growing up in a "Christian" household. She hated housework, fought with her sister, and wore clothes that would attract the attention of young men, including what she referred to as a "modest bikini." Like so many other teenagers, she was deeply sensitive. Her desire to be a Christian was hidden beneath the veneer of moodiness and the flippant nonchalance of a human being not at peace with themselves or God. Hearing about the practical gospel in some of our sermons, Janell decided to allow God the opportunity to work in her life. I'll let her tell the story in her own words.

"I met Sally, Jim's wife, and while I'm sure she didn't intend it, the things she shared really shook me up. She had not just spoken *about* Jesus, but of her experience *with* Him. Sally Hohnberger had sweetness about her, and gracious warmth that drew my heart to her. She had the kind of life I wanted—a life my parents and others talked about but hadn't been able to gain. She spoke tenderly of her husband and boys, and how they were caring for the home and making the meals, even preparing for company that was due to arrive when she got home.

"I was struck with conviction. Her gentleness and tender words were such a contrast to the conflict and harsh, cutting language of our home. More to the point, I felt convicted about my habits in our home. I hated housework and avoided my duties, even simple tasks like after-meal cleanup. I was stung by the idea that boys, I mean *boys* could be better at something than I was. It was more than my pride that was hurt; it was the conviction that their family was truly Christian and my family and I weren't. I pointedly saw my need of change, although not a word of reproof had been spoken to me. Flushed with embarrassment and repentance, I made a decision to change and immediately went to help my mother with the work that needed to be done."

There is much more to Janell's story, but I'll stop her here for now because I want us to examine her life and see the simplicity of the gospel. She was won over to God, not by a mighty sermon in the pulpit, but by seeing someone who truly reflected Christ. She was convicted, and she acted upon the conviction she had. She didn't know the depths of biblical exposition or the terms of the theologian, but she possessed a willingness to live up to the little she knew, and that is all God demands of anyone. If she is to maintain that submission, she will have to continue to progress, step by step, as God brings more of His will to her attention. You and I have the same struggle. Will we do what God asks? If we will, then that trusting submission and childlike dependence on God will bring an inner peace and joy to our lives that is beyond any worldly security. I have never seen this better illustrated than in the life of my ministry partner, Tom Waters.

Our families had gotten together with several other families to spend a day of worship up in a remote mountain valley. First, I felt impressed to take my best ballpoint pen. Now there was no reason to take such an item on a hike. *That's ridiculous,* I thought, but I yielded to the divine impression anyway. As our group of vehicles arrived at the trailhead, I felt a sudden urgency that I must not be parked in. It was so strong that I knew I had to turn my truck around so that it was facing out. No one understood why I was so insistent, and I couldn't explain it myself. I just had to obey that inner voice, despite the fact that it inconvenienced a number of people, who had to jockey their vehicles about to accommodate me.

I wasn't the only one with strange promptings that morning. Alane, Tom's wife, had the impression to fill the little container of activated charcoal she carries in her fanny pack completely to the top. Even as she filled it, she remonstrated with herself. *This is silly,* she thought. *After all, you only need a little bit for a bee sting.*

The mountain valley was a beauty, surrounded by gorgeous mountain scenes, with one majestic peak overshadowing us nearby. It was a place of primitive beauty to draw our minds toward the Creator and make us sense the smallness of humanity and our need of a Savior. There, amid the grandeur of the mountains, we studied and discussed the lives of the Waldensian Christians, who in the Dark Ages had fled from persecution to the mountain retreats and the wilderness. These remarkable Christians had, for centuries, kept the light of God's Word and the experience of true Christianity from being wholly extinguished. At last our talk was over, and inspired by the mountain we had been gazing at all day, a sizable part of our group decided to climb to the summit of that rocky peak. I wasn't on the scene when things fell apart, so I'll let Tom tell what happened next.

"I was walking with my son, who was still fairly young at that time. Near the top, I realized the pace we were traveling was slower than most, so we stepped off to the side to allow others to pass by us on the narrow path. Unfortunately, I stirred up a nest of bald-faced hornets. These are very aggressive and will continue to inject venom until they are knocked off your skin or killed. At this point I was only concerned for my son, and I literally threw him up the hill to a friend to remove him from danger. However, it was just long enough for the hornets to work! I found that I had two nasty stings on my face. I'd never had a reaction to a sting before, but I felt swelling begin immediately in my face and throat and I knew from my medical background that I was experiencing anaphylactic shock and I could easily die up here on this beautiful mountain before help could reach me. I had to get down and *fast!*"

In the valley, Sally looked up at the group on the mountainside. She saw the sudden commotion and knew instantly something was wrong—dreadfully wrong. Leaping up, she grabbed for the fanny pack that held her first-aid supplies, but through divine providence, she ended up with Alane's matching one—the one with the full container of charcoal.

I had led the group up the mountain, and from my bird's-eye view near the top I saw Sally leap up and run toward the foot of the mountain. Then I heard the shout that Tom was hurt. I raced down the mountain path. God must have given wings to my feet because I reached Tom shortly after Sally did. He was a terribly distressing sight. His face was so grossly disfigured, I barely recognized him. His breathing was labored and his whole body was becoming hard and stiff with the swelling. Sally was already applying charcoal, and Alane soon joined her in this task. Tom used these frantic moments between gasps to instruct me how to use my pen to perform an emergency tracheotomy. I listened and willingly agreed to do it, if need be, but I wanted to hold off until there was absolutely no choice.

"Tom, you're not going to die!" I asserted. I knew God had put us together in ministry, and I knew what the Bible says, so I repeated it to him. "Tom, one can put a thousand to flight and two can put ten thousand to flight. God wants us, you and me, to put ten thousand to flight. He isn't finished with you yet!" I said this with conviction, for now I *knew* why I had been impressed to turn the truck around. I reasoned that if Tom were supposed to die in the wilderness, God wouldn't have made such preparations to rescue him. I knew God had prepared a way of escape, and I sought to reassure my suffering friend. Tom says,

"Jim's words were reassuring. Here I was, facing death, yet I was completely at peace. I had surrendered to God's will for me that day, and now in the midst of the crisis, I was still at peace, willing to let my life end there in the mountains, if it be God's design for me. This was no false bravado, but the result of a cultivated, surrendered relationship built over time. Now it was yielding its fruit of peace, while a storm of trouble raged. For you see, when death is staring you in the face, you can't lie to yourself and say that everything is fine and that you're ready to die, if you're not.

"After the group got me down into the valley, it was clear I was in shock. I don't want to be overly dramatic, but many people have died in far more civilized circumstances. They laid me down and elevated my legs, but Sally quickly ruled out this form of treatment. It might be standard treatment for shock, but after watching my respiratory state decline even more, as my swollen legs drained into my torso, it was clear I had to be moved. If my lymphatic system was to be stimulated to help with the swelling at all, I needed to walk. Jim and another friend got on either side of me, and I was half dragged, half carried while I stumbled and tried to walk to Jim's vehicle. Hurriedly placing me in the back seat, Sally and Alane climbed in on either side and worked to massage the fluids out of my upper limbs. I didn't know it at the time, but the swelling was so bad that both these women, who are registered nurses, feared that I had so much fluid in my soft tissues that it was robbing my cardiovascular system of the fluids it needed to circulate oxygen to my traumatized system. We made it to the doctor in time, where I was stabilized and soon recovered.

"I am here today because of the efforts God made in my behalf to save my life. I stand awed by the love He has for each one of us, and I am ever so grateful to the many dear people who learned how to be *attached* to God and to *receive* His messages, so that my life could be spared. God could have worked a mighty miracle without human involvement, but He chose to use human agents to effect His plan for my life."

Attached and receiving is a way of life, my friends, in fact the only way of life. If you will cultivate this experience, you too will have a story to tell of God using you in a mighty way. Never again will your life seem out of control or purposeless, for the God of the universe will be leading, directing, and guiding you each day. "Trust in the Lord with all thine heart; and lean not unto thine own understanding. In all thy ways acknowledge him and he shall direct thy paths" (Proverbs 3:5, 6).

Activities for Week 3

Sunday

Prayer time: Ask God for His wisdom as you read. The implementation of these principles will vary with the individual, and you need wisdom from on high to go about the task in your life, as He would have you to.

Activity: Read "Attached and Receiving."

Reflection: Which experience most epitomizes your relationship with God? How would you have reacted to the life-and-death crisis in the wilderness? Imagine yourself in the different roles. If you had been a rescuer, would you have listened to God's direction, even when it made no sense? If you had been Tom, could you have calmly accepted death because you trusted God's judgment? Did you catch a vision of what true dependence on a power outside of us can be like?

Monday

Prayer time: In seeking after God this morning, remember Tom's experience. Talking to God is rewarding, but listening to God and hearing what is on His mind can hold even greater rewards. Make an effort to spend some listening time with God this morning.

Activity: Today's activity will require you to not only be sensitive to your own spiritual condition, but also honest in your personal assessments. You see, after we learn how to surrender to God, the problem we face is one of consistency. You may leave your private prayer time and suddenly realize that virtually from the moment you got off your knees, you left God behind. Your task today is to see how long you carry the presence of God from your worship time throughout the day. Your desire should be to see the time you stay connected to God on the increase, but don't get discouraged if you seem to lose hold on Him quickly. The moment you are aware you have lost Him, stop, get reconnected, and try again. You are working to overcome the habit patterns of a lifetime, and as much as we desire change, in most cases it is not an instantaneous experience.

Reflection: Is it awkward to try and remain consistently dependent? Have you already found some rewards of living in a surrendered state?

Tuesday

Prayer time: How did you do yesterday? Now go to God and ask Him how you did. Ask Him what you can do to sustain His presence with you for a longer period of time.

Activity: Now it is time to implement whatever God shared with you in your prayer time this morning. The whole purpose of this book is for you to learn dependence upon God. I don't have the wisdom to guide you, but He does and He will, *if* you will let Him. If you are not sure what He is asking, go back to Him for more direction. What if He hasn't given you any new direction? Then act on what you already know to be His will. God doesn't need to give you direction in those areas where you already know His will for you.

Reflection: Did you find that having to depend upon God for direction made you a more sensitive listener to His voice? If so, imagine how sensitive you could become if you grew to distrust your own judgment and wisdom and cultivated total dependence instead.

Wednesday

Prayer time: Continue your efforts to hear God's voice in a deep and personal way. Consider the time you are spending with God each morning as a date with a special person. Remember you are not looking to develop religion but a relationship.

Activity: Today we want to start becoming distrustful of self, so ask God to make you sensitive. Try and find several situations today that you usually handle without even thinking about it, activities you consider to be "no-brainers," like answering the phone, taking the stairs instead of the elevator, or even responding to a simple question from a spouse. Take these and ask, "Lord, what would You have me to do?" See if His ideal for your actions is different than what you've been doing.

Reflection: Did you find that God's ideals for even simple actions were higher than you previously considered? God has shown me in the past that He is concerned with the tone of my voice, my attitude, and even my body language, because through all these things I convey a message about my heavenly Father far greater than my words will ever do alone.

Thursday

Prayer time: Ask God for the courage to cross your own will. Dependence upon God is the most wonderful thing we can experience, and yet for many it is the hardest thing to stay within the boundaries of the new experience because it so crosses their own will to remain submissive before another—God, yes, even God. It requires courage to subdue our self-will and choose to do what is best when we don't always feel like it.

Activity: OK, you've had some hard work this week, so today's assignment is of lighter nature, although certainly not unimportant. Today we need to learn to enjoy the Lord. Too many of us strive to achieve, and because we have not yet achieved the full depth of the experience we desire, we redouble our efforts and then weary in well-doing. There is nothing wrong with setting a high goal, for God would have us achieve far more than we can imagine, but the Christian experience is to be one of happiness and peace during our journey heavenward and not just when we reach our destination. Think of the most loving and understanding parent you have ever seen. God is many times more loving and understanding, although just like good parents He has standards that must be upheld. Hence, as long as you are willing to do whatever He is asking of you right now, at this moment, rest assured that you remain in Him and He smiles upon you. Strive to come closer to Him today and enjoy the knowledge that already, just weeks into seeking Him, you have come a long way from where you were and He is pleased with you. Remember, "he which hath begun a good work in you will perform it until the day of Jesus Christ" (Philippians 1:6).

Reflection: Are you able to picture God as a loving father rather than as a severe judge? Remember our attitudes have a tremendous effect upon our actions. It is impossible to love someone who terrifies us. If you feel you cannot approach God, then come to Him confessing these fears. Jesus said, "I will draw all men unto Me." Even the fact that you are reading this book, that you have an interest in God is proof He is drawing you in a very personal way. He longs for your companionship. Are you willing to allow Him close enough to form a friendship?

Friday

Prayer time: Be sure to bring your real-life problems to God. If a fight you've had with a friend troubles you, lay the situation at His feet, seeking His wisdom. If you have been hurt, bring these feelings too. Someone once described those who bear their troubles and grief alone as a man who was carrying a huge burden. As this unfortunate man struggled along, another traveler driving a wagon invited him to ride with him. After clamoring up into the wagon, he gratefully seated himself, all the while still holding on to his burden. The surprised driver exclaimed, "Why don't you put down your burden?"

"Oh," the man replied, "it would be too much to expect you to carry both me and my burden."

Let us act with more wisdom than the poor man had.

Activity: Today's theme is action. For a long time I would take Jesus with me right up to the point that my real work of the day began, and then I would set Him aside so I could get things done. After I learned to start involving Him in every activity, I ran into the opposite problem of hesitating to act when He directed me, because I retained my lack of trust. Work today at whichever of these two problem areas you find yourself in. Ask God to make you sensitive to include Him in all your plans and activities. Then leap out in faith and trust Him when you hear His voice. The only thing that builds trust is to experiment and see if God can be trusted.

Reflection: Have you been able to make any progress in these areas today? Trusting God does seem to come hard to us and that should be surprising, considering all the times we've trusted ourselves and fallen flat on our faces. Can you resolve to allow Him more control of your life from here forward?

Saturday

Reflection: Enjoy a day off from activities and try to take some special time with God. Often the weekend affords us time to go out in nature, where the majesty of creation points the way to the Creator Himself. I hope you have had a blessed week of growth.

CHAPTER 4

Less Attempted, More Achieved

"Let us therefore fear, lest, a promise being left us of entering into his rest, any of you should seem to come short of it" (Hebrews 4:1).

CHAPTER GOAL

To see as never before that to achieve more than superficial Christianity requires a total commitment. This commitment may cost us many things, which the world and even our fellow Christians view as good and desirable, but nevertheless keep us from a deeper walk. God has opened the way for every one of us to obtain what we long for, if we will learn that less attempted is more achieved.

It was a beautiful fall day in southwestern Virginia. The quiet crunch of the gravel under foot and the gentle caress of the breeze created a pleasant tranquillity felt by all—all, that is, except Steve.

"I just can't make it work for me!" he blurted out in frustration. "I've listened to you in person and on tape. I believe in your message wholeheartedly. I want the experience you talk about, but I just can't get it! And I don't even know why," he ended with a sigh of exasperation. Steve had a problem that no pleasant day or tranquil environment could cure.

What do I say, Lord? I prayed silently.

When I am called to counsel with souls crying out for help as Steve was, I am often deeply troubled because in and of myself, I possess no wisdom or knowledge that can satisfy the longing that has just been expressed. It makes me fearful because I know that I am dealing with eternal realities. Someone's salvation is at stake, and I need the guidance of the Lord more at this point than at any other time. As I silently petitioned God for wisdom, I felt a sudden inspiration. "Tell me about your life, Steve," I said, "everything that has gone on for the last few weeks."

For the next ninety minutes Steve described in detail his home routine, job commitments, and other obligations and activities. It was a valuable, eye-opening exercise, which left me with no doubt as to where the problem lay. "Steve," I gasped, "you're trying to swim with ten men on your back. I couldn't live the Christian life and maintain your lifestyle either. No wonder it doesn't work! You don't need a better understanding or more knowledge. You need to radically alter your circumstances! Right now the deck is stacked completely against you."

Steve is hardly alone. I've met with hundreds of "Steves." They're good men, honest men, pillars in their community and churches. They earnestly desire to seek and serve God and yet the very essence of Christianity escapes them. It is not by chance that these honest seekers find their way so muddled. The enemy of souls has worked for years to create an environment hostile to the development of true Christianity. He had succeeded beyond his wildest dreams, and the fact that he has been successful in the United States—a country known for its religious freedom—demonstrates just how subtle are the dangers you and I face.

Never has there been a society that is both so economically prosperous and so enormously stressful. Duties, obligations, and commitments chase one another wildly through our days, leaving us disquieted, exhausted, and prone to give way to irritations, impatience, and fretful self-pity. For most of us, life has increasingly begun to resemble a merry-go-round that spins faster and faster with every passing day until we are moving so fast that we fear to jump off. And worse yet, just like that playground toy, no matter how fast you go, you get nowhere!

Today's churches are suffering from this same dilemma. They are stalled—not moving forward. Instead, there is a steady decline in true spirituality, while the form of Christianity is ever increasing. Ministries and outreach have increased in direct proportion to the decline in introspection. Proselytizing has supplanted piety. Personal religion is steadily disappearing from the churches, while public religion flourishes. Never have the lives of the members been busier and less satisfying, filled only with the empty forms of religion, rather than the genuine article. The churches are attempting *more* and achieving *less!*

Some time ago a minister called me to complain about my messages. He hurriedly dispensed with the formalities and got right to the point. "Jim, I just moved into a church where you have given three seminars over the last three years and I want to tell you … I'm troubled!"

"Why?" I queried.

"Well, many people in the church really loved your messages, and a number of the families have tried to apply what you preach in their lives and now they don't come to *all* my meetings! They don't attend *every* evangelistic effort of the church! When we ask them why, they say they are working on their families. They don't seem to fully support church programs anymore, and it's all your fault!"

"Are they critical or negative?" I asked.

"No. They're beautiful people."

"Are they living up to biblical standards?

"Yes. They're upholding the standards."

"Well, what are their families like?" I pressed him further. "Do they treat their spouses and children properly?"

"You just don't understand, Jim. They are wonderful families— the top families in the church. That's why I need them at all my meetings."

His entire focus was the programs of the church, and now that he had members who were making their spiritual lives and their families a priority, he didn't like it. Those families don't have time for all his programs now because they are following God's program. Programs aren't bad or wrong unless they steal our time from or cause us to neglect what's really important. We must have something to share before our outreach will be effective. Many a minister has become so focused upon the "gospel work" that they seem unable to recognize the *true* work of the gospel when it shows up in their own congregation. It's quite natural for them to rise up and oppose it because it hinders their programs.

God's plan for His people is continual growth. Christianity is not a one-time achievement and then Christians are ever after enabled to rest content with their accomplishment. No, true Christianity is always in a state of growth, very much like the growth of a human infant. When a baby is born, it is helpless and totally unable to care for itself. And yet we love to care for babies and provide for their needs, even clean up their messes. We think everything about them is lovely. But if after four, six, or even ten years, they haven't advanced, haven't grown, and still require the same amount of care, do we still think the situation is lovely?

How is it then that we seem content not to grow as Christians? The average Christian is almost totally indistinguishable from their non-Christian neighbor. Religion has become superficial. There is no dying to self, no entering into grace, and no recognition of Christ at our side through His spirit. Those who claim to follow Christ are tied to the same systems of employment that everyone else is. Employers frequently demand sacrifices of home life if the employee wants to get ahead at all. And those who claim to be Christians willingly sacrifice the home on the modern altar of success, just as the heathen used to offer their children as human sacrifices.

The same troubled marriages and the same lost and rebellious youth that plague the world also mark today's Christian households. I travel and speak at lots of churches, and I'm telling you that the families in the church are in deplorable condition. It is largely the result of trying to live up to everyone else's expectations for us. We have put on yoke after yoke offered us by the world, by our friends and family, and, last but not least, the yoke of earning a living. Together, they have piled burden after burden on us until life is little more than a crushing load. Worse still, we have added yokes of our own making by our unwillingness to deny our desires, and now the heavy chains of debt drag at our heels until we are ready to collapse!

The church should be a refuge, but Satan has learned to turn what should be a blessing into a curse. On top of the worldly yokes has come the yoke of church offices, obligations, and board meetings. Then there is the yoke of school commitments for yourselves, your children, or both. Finally there are the yokes of maintenance for homes and cars as well as civic duties, carpools, sporting events—and the list goes on and on and on in a never-ending cycle of demands on our time, which unfortunately is not never ending.

Christ calls for us to take His yoke upon us and learn of Him. His yoke is easy and His burden light. I told Steve he had ten men on his back, but that was just figurative. In truth he had too many yokes, and he was drowning under the load. What about you? Some of you are trying to swim with eight; others are going under for the third time with fifteen wrapped about your neck. So, how are you going to get them off?

One way or another the yokes are going to have to come off, if you are to have any hope of achieving what you desire from the Christian life. There is one method of removing yokes that I guarantee will work for every one of you—persecution, torture, and a prison cell. When you are jailed or imprisoned for your religion, I guarantee the yokes will fall off. I know this because of a remarkable man named Noble Alexander. A friend loaned me his book, *I Will Die Free* (Pacific Press, 1991), in which he tells of the twenty-two years he spent in Cuban prisons for his faith. He endured the most inhumane treatment one human could devise to torture another, and yet his faith grew. It is a remarkable story, and when I returned it to my friend I asked him if he knew what had become of Noble after his release and immigration to the United States.

"He's a pastor somewhere up in New England," my friend responded.

"I'll guarantee you that he has lost the depth of his experience," I commented.

"How can you say that, Jim? That man stood for his faith in a way that you and I have never had to do."

"I know that, and while he probably hasn't let go of Christ, I still think that now that he is in this country, he'll have lost that special experience he had in jail."

My friend didn't agree with me, and of course I had no way to verify my theory, but I asked the Lord to help me cross paths with Noble because I wanted to know if what I thought was true. I was speaking at a church in New Hampshire, when the pastor exclaimed, "Jim, you'll never believe who's coming to church today!"

"Who?"

"Noble Alexander."

"No!"

"Yes! He told me he wants to hear you speak."

"That's great! I've got a question for him."

"Oh, what are you going to ask him?" he probed. After I told him about the discussion with my friend and explained my question, he asked rather dubiously, "You're not really going to ask him that, are you?"

"Why not? People say I'm fairly aggressive!"

Unfortunately, events in his own church prevented Noble from coming in person, but we talked later that week by phone. I told him about reading his book and the admiration I felt for him and the experiences he had gone through. Then I told him about my conversation with my friend. "Now, Noble, I want you to take your time before you answer that question."

"I don't need time to consider that question. I often long to go back to my experience in prison," he quietly replied. I didn't know it at the time, but in the next year two other men would confirm Noble's experience in their own lives. One had also been a pastor in Cuban prisons, and he also agreed that he had lost that special spiritual experience here in the United States. The second was a man who found the Lord while in prison, serving a twelve-year sentence. "I was free in prison," he told me. "In prison there is no wiggle room! When you get out, there is a lot of wiggle room!"

That confirmation, however, remained for the future, and I pressed Noble further. "Why, Noble? Why is it so easily lost here?"

"Jim, you know *why*. The fact that you even *knew* to quiz me to the depth you have, tells me you already know the answer."

" Noble, I want to hear it come from your lips. I want to be able to tell people that I have your permission to say that *you* said it." And I asked him three times in our conversation to verify his permission to share this. He said, "Jim, America is the hardest place in the world to gain the experience with God that you preach about. When I was in prison God was very real to me, and my need of Him was very real. I was focused! But here I'm constantly distracted and constantly pulled off. Staying focused *here* is work!"

"Welcome to America, Noble," I said.

There is another option, friends. It's called voluntary confine-ment—not solitary confinement—voluntary confinement. This is not some type of monastic living. The monasteries of old were by and large a pitiful failure at bringing people into a saving relationship with God. No, we don't want to cut ourselves off from the world as much as we want to limit the world's, and yes, it may be, that we must limit even the church's infringement into our lives. To do this it means that I'm going to learn to say No gracefully not only to the bad things that want to steal my time but also to the good things, so that all I have time for is the very best! John the Baptist, Moses, Enoch, and our Lord Jesus Christ Himself all practiced voluntary confinement. I must practice voluntary confinement until I have slowed my life enough that I can be still and know, and I mean really know that He is God. Even more important than that, I want my life freed enough from the hectic pace of this age so that I can sense His presence by my side.

God believes in "less attempted, more achieved." In John 15:2, Christ Himself says, "Every branch in me that beareth not fruit he taketh away: and every branch that beareth fruit, he purgeth it, [less attempted] that it may bring forth more fruit [more achieved]." When you prune a tree you get rid of the dead branches, but you also want to remove nonproductive limbs, and then you want to remove the excessive foliage that hinders fruitfulness and saps the tree's energy.

But isn't the foliage good? Don't these limbs produce some fruit? The answer is yes to both questions, but to have your tree produce at peak performance means you will have to prune away even things that are good so that your tree can bring forth the best possible fruit. Can you catch the parallel in our lives? If we want to be Christians and really prosper, we are going to have to remove not only the bad in our lives, but also many things that are good. The good is often what prevents us from achieving the best and truly reaching our goals. This is where so many sincere people fail to obtain that experience with God for which they long. As they come out of the world, they leave the bad behind and the churches have so many "good" things for them to put in the place of the bad that most never question whether the good is keeping them from the very best. Yet in many, many cases this is exactly what happens. We are so stressed and so burdened, not with the cares of this world, but with our attempts to minister to the world, that we have no time to perfect a true Christian character. The temptation is everlastingly before us to think that because we do good things, we are good people and we often fail to understand that the good is the worst enemy of the best. Our goal is not to become good people, our goal is to become like Jesus; and that, friend, is the very best. The problem we face is that the good is harder to eliminate from our lives than the evil.

Let me share with you a modern parable. I love tomatoes! Forgive me if they are not your favorite food. Feel free to mentally substitute any item of food you like so you can enter into the following experience with me. You are excited because we have been invited to a restaurant and not just any restaurant, but a famous, world-class institution that specializes in serving the biggest and the best tomatoes—ever! When we arrive, the service is friendly, the atmosphere most pleasant, and the china place settings exquisite. Our anticipation builds as we order the famous tomato platter. In an incredibly short time, the service personnel bring us huge platters garnished like pieces of art, and nested daintily on a bed of beautifully ruffled kale is a *scrawny, two-inch* tomato that you could have found in any grocery store. Imagine your disappointment and then utter outrage!

Well, that's what you and I are to the world—a bunch of little tomatoes! Noah, John the Baptist, Paul, and a host of other Bible characters were big tomatoes. They delivered just as advertised, but you and I are little tomatoes. We go to the world and tell them all about our world-class restaurant and then they look at us, and I have to be honest, they are not impressed.

How do you get large tomatoes? I well remember the time I went to visit a friend, and we found his wife in the garden picking off tomato blooms. I didn't know a lot about gardening back then, so I asked her, "Doesn't fruit come from those blooms? Why are you picking them off?"

I remember her laugh as she explained, "Oh yes, Jim, you're right, the blooms do form fruit. But you see, Stanley loves big, juicy, tomatoes! So I make sure the plant doesn't try and set too much fruit by picking off extra blooms. That way all the energy of the plant can go into making the tomatoes it does set into the very biggest and best."

Can you stand another restaurant story? As I travel the country and the world I have eaten in many restaurants, most of which are fairly undistinguished. So I was delighted one day during my travels when my hosts informed me that our lunch plans that day were to eat at the largest vegetarian restaurant in the world. "Everything is organic, nothing is artificial, and it's all good for you," they expounded excitedly. I walked in, and right before my eyes were three different salads. They looked so good I think I could have made a meal out of just the salad, but it didn't end there. After the salads there was a buffet line of several side dishes, beautifully coordinated and presented. And I don't know how they did it, but when I got to the entrees, all three were my favorites! The breads and rolls were exquisite, all fresh from the oven and artfully arranged. Their aromas wafted across the room. Next I found myself gazing at six tempting desserts.

"I feel like I'm looking at the finalists in a beauty contest. How can I choose? They are all beautiful!" I told Sally. And I hadn't even gotten to the organic juice bar. Every juice was 100 percent natural, freshly squeezed. I could taste it before I even poured it.

Now, suppose I take my tray and load it down with two salads, three side dishes, a handful of rolls, two main dishes, three desserts, and two juices. This is great, right? I mean, it is all good food, the very best the world can provide. What happens if I take all that good food and stuff it down? Don't you feel sorry for my stomach and my digestion? As good as all that food is, if I take too much or too many different kinds, my system cannot assimilate it and the results are bad, real bad. If I am to benefit from this wonderful vegetarian restaurant with all its organic natural food, I am going to have to practice voluntary confinement.

Life is just like a buffet line, and it's overflowing with good things. How can we say No to these good things? It's called voluntary confinement—you can't have it all and survive. You have a multitude of choices before you because life is just like that restaurant. In this book I have shared some practical steps for knowing God better, but as good as those things are, if we don't make the proper choices, we're going to fall flat on our faces every time. The first three chapters in this book are the keys to the Christian life. This chapter is the solution to finding the time needed in our busy lives and hectic schedules to become true Christians. So how are we to accomplish this?

We must bring life down to the irreducible minimum. Most of us look at our lives, and we see a whole list of things we must do. Then we somehow try to shoehorn them into our day. A better way to go about it is to find out what the irreducible minimum is and then to shape our schedule around it. In my experience, the irreducible fell into three categories. First and foremost, I had to have time to be a Christian, time for worship and contemplation as an individual. Then I had to dedicate the time needed to maintain my marriage with Sally and to love and play with my children. Lastly, we all had to set aside time for work, either in the home or out of the home, so that the family could be maintained. And that's all. Everything else had to go.

In many ways it was difficult to let go, but in the end scheduling was a whole lot easier, and suddenly life was a whole lot more fun!

"Wait a minute," you might say, "I didn't see any time on the schedule for church offices, outreach activities, sports, no time for—well, for half the things I do each day!" And you're right! There isn't! No matter how many good activities pull at your heartstrings, the only ones that are truly essential are making sure you and God are one, caring for your wife and children, and taking care of the work necessary to maintain your physical needs. Everything else is an extra, even outreach to others. Our lives have become so unbalanced that it may feel very strange to try and put things back in their proper order. However, if yours is not all it should be, then all your good activities and all your outreach toward others will, in the end, cause no lasting benefit. Philippians 4:5 says, "Let your moderation be known unto all men." The problem is that we haven't been living moderate lives and now we are reaping a bitter harvest of lost young people and shattered marriages within the Christian church.

Reordering your life is hard but worth it. Pruning and reducing to the irreducible minimum will teach you how to live in such a way that the peace and harmony of heaven will be present in your home. And some of the activities that have to be eliminated now may be reintroduced later as the Lord leads and we get the hang of using voluntary confinement in every aspect of our lives.

Here are some practical questions that will help to direct your thoughts as you think about cutting back. How much do I really need to earn? Must I earn enough to be a conspicuous consumer? How can we cut back? Simple things like setting a budget and sticking to it help, but if you are in over your head with a mortgage payment that requires an excessive amount of your income, then you may need to move and downsize if necessary. My good friends Barry and Pam found that Barry would have to cut back his hours to give his family the time they needed and to give him the time he needed with God. Because Barry was an efficient worker, his employer agreed to his unusual request for him to work shorter hours, something unprecedented for his profession. The Lord showed them ways they could cut back in order to get by on less income. God blesses choices made on principle and designed to bring families closer to each other and closer to God.

Too many have romanticized the idea of heading off into the wilderness to build their own home. They seem somewhat shocked when I tell them, "I hope you never have to go through the experience of building your own home." It would be different if you were a builder by profession, but I've known too many people who set off with the best of intentions, never realizing to just how huge a task they have committed themselves. The really good reasons for moving are to provide your family with an atmosphere more conducive to perfecting Christian characters and possibly to reduce your expenditure for housing also. James and Donna have been kind enough to share their story in hopes that it will prevent others from making similar mistakes.

James and Donna have three children, Trever, Allison, and Seth. Like so many parents they looked at the way their children were growing up and desired something better. They decided to move from the Great Plains to Montana, planning to build their own home and live the Christian life they were learning about. I'll let them tell their story.

"After our house sold, we moved to Montana, where our goal was to look for land and hand-build a log home together as a family. I was going to take a year off from full-time work in order to build, although I would supplement our income by doing some substitute teaching.

"Through a realtor, we located twenty beautiful acres and started building our home. We had to have some place to live while the house was being built, so we constructed a 750-square-foot garage. Over the next four years, we built our dream house. I went back to work, but always the house was our consuming passion. Over the years the project grew. We incorporated design changes that others recommended, which seemed reasonable at the time, not stopping to make sure it was what God wanted for us. Even though we had come to Montana to find God, we found Him being pushed aside in the business of life.

"After *four* years of building, the interior was finally complete and only some finish trim work and decking remained to do outside. The home was lovely. It was self-sufficient, with its own generator and battery storage system. The wood cookstove was set up to provide all the hot water as well. We triumphantly moved into our beautiful 3,200-square-foot home, but all those changes had cost more money than we planned. Instead of reducing our debt load, we had done the opposite! The amount we owed for the house was now into six figures. This wasn't what we wanted!

"Worst of all, none of us were happy with the new house. After we had lived in the garage for four years, the new house felt too large. We didn't like being so far away from everyone else in the family. We had spent more than four years and thousands of dollars to build a house that nobody liked when it was done. But, most important, we had lost the vision and desire for what we really needed—learning how to walk with God and maintain that vital, living connection. That was gone! Would we ever be able to get that first love and focus back?

"We had lost our vision, but thankfully God hadn't, and He provided us a second chance. He impressed us to sell the house and use the equity to get out of debt and buy a much smaller, newly built home on five acres where we could finally focus on our goal of walking with Jesus, rather than just building day in and day out. We had learned how to work together through our building, but now the Lord wanted to teach us how to play together and to just enjoy each other.

"Today as we strive to apply the principles of yielding our wills to Christ, dying to what self wants, learning to listen to God's voice, and seeking to maintain a living, vital connection with Christ, our family is experiencing the joy of the hard choices we had to make in order to start over. We praise God that He redirected our efforts and goals."

It is easy to get sidetracked when making large changes, as James and Donna did. Satan doesn't care how he distracts us; preventing us from seeking God is his only aim. If he can use "good" things to keep us away from God, it suits him all the more.

My friends and coauthors, Tim and Julie, currently live near the edge of one of the most populated areas of the country and yet, if you were to visit their home you would find it tucked away in the woods with all types of wildlife, including bears, as regular visitors. Tim still works in a highly urban area, but by working a nontraditional schedule, he commutes the longer distances without the hassle of traffic. Anyone looking to limit the amount of time that must be spent in employment will benefit from the lower housing costs away from the urban centers. It doesn't matter as much whether you choose a quiet home in suburbia or a wilderness cabin in the mountains. What matters more is the state of mind and heart that motivates such a choice. Many have moved out away from civilization and yet their religion consists only of their pride in what they have left behind. Such fanaticism is not Christianity. Yet, another family might move to an equally isolated setting, leaving just as many comforts behind and in that setting breathe the very atmosphere of heaven because they are wholly motivated to seek God. Country living is an advantage to the Christian; for then he is not as constantly exposed to evil. But it is only a tool, used of God, to help us gain a living connection with Him, not the end product.

Some may think I am advocating that we should work only enough to maintain our families at a poverty level, but that is not my goal. Fathers and mothers set the tone of the home, and if they gain a connection with God, they can lead their children into that connection as well. If they are overstressed, it is nearly impossible for them to take the time they need to seek after God, and the whole household suffers. Some families, because of their circumstances or past choices, might have to spend fifty hours a week working to meet the needs of the home, while others, because they may lack debt or because they have a large earning potential, might only have to work twenty or thirty. The Holy Spirit will make it clear to your heart what you should do as you present your individual case before Him.

The world has seduced us with the idea that the busier we are, the more important we must be. I once overheard a conversation between two women that went like this:

"Susan, I haven't seen you in ages. How have you been?"

"Well you know ... busy, busy, busy."

"That's good," her friend responded.

I tell you, it was all I could do not to jump into their conversation. "No it isn't!" I wanted to shout back. We have been seduced into believing an error. The devil loves having us stay over-committed because it not only keeps us from God, but it discourages us. Most of us are like Steve, who was trying to swim with those ten men on his back and if you don't get them off, you are going to fail in the Christian walk. You will drown before you ever learn to swim. If you have been finding it hard to put into practice the first three weeks of this program, there is a reason. You probably need to attempt less so you can achieve more.

Very seldom do I travel and speak alone, but the other summer I went to the Midwest to speak at a conference there, and because I was not far from my mother's home I decided to take a week and spend it with her. She is getting older now, but what a blessed time we had doing things together, shopping and eating out. That weekend I decided to spend the day at my old church—the very first church I was a member of as an adult. These dear people had helped me with the transition from knowing next to nothing about God and Christianity to eventually becoming their head elder. What a reunion I had with those dear folks!

After the church services, everyone gathered around and invited me over to their places. I enjoyed them, talked with them, caught up with them. It was great! I stayed with them longer than I normally would have because I just didn't want to leave. I got back to my mother's house rather late, and she was already in bed. So I said my prayers and settled in, all nice and cozy. I was just on the edge of dreamland when the Lord spoke to me in the quiet recesses of my mind and said, *No you don't, Jim. I want you to sit up. I want to have a talk with you.*

But, Lord, I'm tired.

Just sit up, Jim. I want you to review the events of the day you just went through.

Well, Lord, I don't have to do that. They're in my mind, plain as day. It was great!

I want you to go back twenty years, and I want you to view those same lives, those same faces and marriages.

That really got me to thinking, and you know what I saw? They were the same! Those people I loved hadn't changed, hadn't grown in more than two decades. Suddenly the tears started, and I said, *Lord, they're missing it, aren't they?*

Yes. That's what I wanted to show you, Jim, and you didn't tell them. You just enjoyed the social gospel.

Now I'm not being negative, and I'm not being critical. I am sharing with you what God showed me that night, and He showed it to me for a reason. When an infant is born, it is completely helpless, and we love to care for its needs. We gladly clean up the messes, dress and bathe it, but if five years go by and it hasn't changed, hasn't matured, hasn't grown, we don't think that situation is quite so beautiful. What about *twenty* years going by without changes and growth? Now look away from my old church and turn your focus inward. Have you changed in the last five, ten, twenty years? I mean, really changed?

God says in Psalm 55:19, "Because they have no changes, therefore they fear not God." Have you been growing and changing as a Christian or have you remained at the same place you were years ago? If you are not satisfied with where you are, if you've made some progress but would like to be further along, even if you find you have slipped backwards, don't give up now. It is time to attempt the least you have ever attempted so that you might achieve more than you have ever experienced.

Activities for Week 4

Sunday

Prayer time: This chapter will require honest introspection, which often crosses our will. Ask for a humble and teachable spirit that God may be able to show you what He wants you to accomplish.

Activity: Read chapter 4, "Less Attempted, More Achieved."

Reflection: Consider the words you have just read. Did you see a reflection of the life you now lead?

Monday

Prayer time: Are you learning to listen to God's voice? Seek to have a solid connection today as we examine our lives and seek solutions to the problems we face.

Activity: Take a sheet of paper and just keep track of your day's activities from morning until night. While this is not a glamorous task, it is going to be very useful.

Reflection: Did you find yourself so busy that even keeping track of your activities was a pain? If others could see a day in your life, what would they think?

Tuesday

Prayer time: Ask God for wisdom to see areas that need attention and change in your life.

Activity: With your list in front of you, take a few minutes and examine your day. Was it a constant chase after unfinished business? Did you have any breathing room or were you stressed all day? What are the ten men on your back that keep you from swimming?

Reflection: What would your life be like if these distractions were removed? What would you be willing to do in order to be free from them?

Wednesday

Prayer time: Implementing change can sometimes seem as stressful as the things you are trying to eliminate. This is entirely human for we tend to cling to the familiar, even when it's a less than wholesome situation. Seek for courage to move out of your comfort zone if that is what God is asking of you.

Activity: Take a new sheet of paper and try to bring your life down to the irreducible minimum. Make a list of all those things that would have to be eliminated or cut back to bring your life down to this ideal.

Reflection: Are you willing to part with those items that are on the "eliminate" list?

Thursday

Prayer time: Remember that the purpose of changes is to obtain a special experience with God. Ask Christ to make you aware of the meaninglessness of those things on your "eliminate" list from yesterday.

Activity: Make your list practical today. Look at reordering your life and see which items can be eliminated immediately and which ones are unbreakable commitments, such as legal contracts. Others, such as social and church commitments, are social contracts and can be broken, even though it's difficult. To end these, you may have to face some misunderstanding, but fear not, many misunderstood the Savior's motives as well. Lay out your new schedule, as you would like it to be, even though you realize it may take some months to free yourself from everything holding you back. Seeing your life reorganized toward your goal will be an encouragement to you.

Reflection: Almost without question some will not understand your new program and goals. Plan how you are going to deal with these situations ahead of time. It can be very disconcerting to have a dear friend criticize you when you hoped for their support, and to a certain degree everyone who really chooses to follow God must tread the path alone.

Friday

Prayer time: Seek comfort from your loving heavenly Father and gain encouragement from His approval of your plans. Lay everything before Him and know that He will lead you.

Activity: Today you should take action on any activity that can be eliminated immediately. This means you may have to write some notes of resignation from the school bake sale committee or the church board. Don't expect that everyone will be gracious, but remember you are gaining something more important than their disapproval. Keep in mind that no true Christian would want to hinder you from gaining a closer walk with God.

Reflection: You may be hesitant or uneasy about the things you have cut from your schedule and even more concerned about those that you are planning to remove in the future. Remember we are not planning to leave a void, but to replace these activities with those that will help us achieve our goal of learning to walk with God. Think about what you would like to do with those free moments. At first you will just be freeing up little periods of time, but treasure the moments and use them wisely and you will build a life you are going to love.

Saturday

Reflection: Enjoy a peaceful day. If you really went forward in this week's activities, you may feel wrung out and tired. Christ invites you to "come ye yourselves apart ... and rest a while" (Mark 6:31). Rest in His love and know that while change may be hard, it will bring a sure and happy harvest.

Part 2

Empowered Marriage

CHAPTER 5

Lost and Found

"*Nevertheless I have somewhat against thee, because thou has left thy first love. Remember therefore from whence thou art fallen, and repent, and do the first works*" *(Revelation 2:4, 5).*

CHAPTER GOAL

To catch a vision of hope for your marriage, no matter how hopeless things may seem. At one time you loved each other, and somehow things are not what they used to be. Your love can be restored if you find what was lost.

Outside the car window, endless cornfields rolled by. The neat orderly rows seemed to march solemnly away from the road, with only a clump of trees here and there disclosing the outline of a creek or a patch of ground too stony for even the most determined Midwestern farmer. Alane, still a newlywed, contemplated the scene in awkward silence. Only the muted sounds of the car and Tom's breathing betrayed the fact that she was not alone, and the pain welled up again. Her voice quivered with emotion as she turned to Tom and asked, "Why don't you talk to me anymore?"

Tom's hands tightened on the wheel. His jaw stiffened. Frustration surged through him. The angry thoughts tumbled and tripped over each other in his mind. *Not again! It is always my fault. She gets upset no matter what I say!* He needed an outlet, something to vent his exasperation on and impulsively his hand formed a fist and he hit the window.

Later, when Alane described her feelings to me, she said, "I knew he would never hurt me, but when I saw his display of anger, I was frightened. I was frightened because I truly felt my marriage was crumbling, and there was nothing I could do to pull it back together. Why was this happening to me? How could something that had started so wonderfully become so miserable in just a few short months?"

Let's meet another couple, Denny and Brenda, who live in Hawaii. If they had known Tom and Alane, they would have understood their plight. Here's their story:

Brenda says,

"When Denny and I married, we thought our dreams had come true. Each of us had survived failed marriages, but we thought we could make it this time because now we were Christians. We felt God had brought us together, and that having paid our dues, and learned our lessons from our failed unions, we were on our way to wedded bliss. How little we knew of the future. Our first year was a nightmare.

"Denny worked long hours as a truck driver, and I was an insurance agent. We were both busy, but I still harbored dreams of greeting him at the door after a long day at work and sitting down to eat together. I knew he went to his ex-mother-in-law's house after work each night to see his children and sometimes stopped at his mother's to eat. Somehow I just expected that these things would change now that he was married to me. When they didn't, I was shattered. I tried to be understanding and keep my cool, but I would inevitably greet him in a way that made him not even want to come home."

Denny says,

"That's right. All I needed was a nagging, unpleasant wife to come home to after a long day. She knew I had obligations from my previous marriage, and I expected her to understand. I was already doing these things before she came along. It really bothered me to have her complain, especially when I was only doing what I thought was right and staying involved with my children."

Brenda says,

"Of course I didn't understand! And he didn't even seem to care for *my* feelings. We communicated poorly, with arguments and harsh words. We fought often. He would compare me with his ex-wife in the things I said, and tell me I sounded just like her. You can imagine how much I liked that! Then I would spout back and tell him that if we both said the same things, it was probably because they were true. There were other differences too. I wanted a family. He already had four children with *no* plans for more. Many times the word *divorce* entered our conversation that first year, but both of us were too stubborn to admit defeat, too proud to listen to people say, 'I told you so.'"

A friend of mine had a relationship problem too. Edwin sat at his daughter's birthday party amid the boisterous sounds of happy children and realized with a rueful yearning that he did not truly know this child who had lived with him for seven years. In his heart he longed to be a true father to his children, but where was he to find the time? Every moment was consumed in the practice of medicine and in teaching the art to other up-and-coming physicians. His failures at home were just too depressing to think about. At the hospital, he was Mr. Wonderful. There, he was a success. Describing it in his own words, he said, "Work consumed me, and I didn't resist."

What happened to my dear friend? He had diagnosed the problems of hundreds of people; yet when it came to his own failures at home, this brilliant man was seemingly unaware of his own problems. And he is not the only one. Many people fail to see the obvious, and because it is the path of least resistance, they just continue on, ignoring their spouse's true needs until it is too late. My coauthors were that way. Tim would work sixteen hours a day for weeks at a time, making lots of money and leaving his lovely young bride lonely at home with two young children. Let's join them on one of those rare days that Tim is actually home.

"I was enjoying a quiet evening when Julie called my name. Something in her voice caused me to look up. I could see she was dead serious and clearly nervous about whatever she wanted to discuss. Her demeanor caught my attention, as she came to me and stated with simple eloquence, 'I'm in trouble. I've developed feelings for another man.'

"I can't say I was shocked. After all, I had been ignoring her, but she just isn't the type one thinks of as carrying on an affair. As a busy mother with two little children and deeply religious, she seemed almost baffled that it had happened to her. There had been no overt adultery, but in a real sense this was worse. I had lost her heart, her feelings, and her love. Where does one go to get those back?"

That's a good question. How do you get your partner's heart back after you have lost it through neglect? At some time in their existence, every one of these couples had each other's hearts. They possessed wonderful relationships that they were sure would stand the test of time and last forever. Yet, something went wrong in their relationships. That same thing has gone wrong in my marriage, and the same problem probably already exists in your relationship or is likely to in the near future.

In the United States 50 percent of all marriages fail and of those that survive, few are of the caliber and quality we dream of when we take that big step to become husband and wife. If we want to avoid becoming a statistic, we must identify what is going wrong in our relationships. For almost all of us, the answer is depressingly simple. Let's look at the lives of the couples just mentioned and see if we can pick out a common thread.

Tom and Alane

Alane says, "I was the nurse recruiter for a large Midwestern hospital when I met Tom. I excelled at what I did in a quiet and understated way, but it hadn't escaped the notice of my superiors, and I enjoyed their approval and commendation. Tom was the robust, fun-loving, flirtatious evening supervisor of radiology. Even though we were in many ways opposites, there was a strong attraction.

"As I got to know Tom, I saw mirrored in his heart the same longing to serve God that I had in my own. Granted, our understanding as to how to do that was more limited in those days, but I was certain Tom was the one God had chosen for me."

Tom says,

"Alane had qualities unmatched by any woman I had ever been interested in. I had dated other women, but there was something about her, the way she carried herself, and her commitment to serve God, that not only attracted me but also lifted me up and encouraged me to hold myself to a higher standard than I might have without her influence. Here was the godly woman I could have a proper courtship with and the kind of marriage I'd always dreamed of. I knew God had put us together and that married life was going to be bliss!

"Well, it wasn't bliss. When we returned from the honeymoon and got back into the work-a-day world, I found out that marriage isn't always a bundle of laughs. It's a lot of hard work. My natural tendency was to gravitate back toward the same activities and the same friends I had had in my single days. I found myself still acting single. I didn't even understand it back then, but Alane had made me her life, and she was only a part of my life. I was very outgoing, and I still wanted to go out and have fun. I wasn't doing anything improper, but I might tease someone a little or greet a lady friend with a hug, and while the world might look at such things as innocent, Alane didn't think too favorably of these activities. Can you blame her? I mean, here I am a newly married man, who had just pledged my life to building a marriage and home after heaven's order, and yet I was still drawn by my old single mindset.

"Now, when Alane, the woman I had been attracted to because of her high standards and principles, objected to my behavior, I resented it. Do you think I chose to take responsibility for my actions and reform my life? No, of course not! I blamed her. It was her problem that she couldn't accept these things. *She ought to loosen up a little,* I thought. I hadn't led a principled social life in the past. And even though I had committed to a higher standard and had high ideals when I married Alane, when I got together with my old friends, it was the same old story. I wanted to act like I had always acted. I couldn't do that when Alane was around, so I started to discourage her attendance at my softball games and other activities because I didn't want to be inhibited by her presence.

"I started criticizing Alane's shortcomings. Often I didn't intentionally set out to be hurtful, but in putting her down, I felt better about my areas of struggle. This turned out to be a two-edged sword because it became my habit to pick on her, and she started taking even simple suggestions as critical comments. It got so bad that I couldn't even suggest we make the toast darker because she would interpret this as a personal put-down. The more she overreacted, the more I tended to withdraw and in turn the more she felt rejected and ignored. The cycle escalated without us even realizing what was happening and the stress between us built exponentially."

Alane continues:

"Tom is right when he said the pressures were building. I had entered marriage with what I thought were reasonable expectations. All I wanted was to make Tom happy and for him to love me. I wanted him to desire my companionship and to appreciate me for the unique person I was, but despite my best efforts the opposite was happening.

"Tom, who had always been my sunshine while we were dating, increasingly became quiet and withdrawn. I'd try to talk to him, but he'd become even quieter. I felt so hurt and so rejected. I longed to share my feelings with someone, anyone, but I couldn't. Often I'd long to pick up the phone to call my mother, but I would never actually do it. How could I? I already knew she felt our courtship was too short and the marriage premature. I had worked hard and long to convince her how wonderful, mature, and sensitive Tom was. If I called now, I would be humiliated and have to admit that maybe it was a mistake, yet in my heart I knew it wasn't. I believed that God had brought us together, and while we might be having some adjustment difficulties, it didn't change the fact that Tom was the one for me.

"Unfortunately, I had no idea what to do with our uncomfortable situation. Things between us certainly didn't get any better. They got worse, and I learned to stuff down the hurts. Of course, they didn't stay stuffed down but built like water behind a dam. Desperately needing someone to confide in, I thought of my friends at work but quickly ruled that out. I remembered ruefully how one of them had come to me while I was dating and said, 'Let me tell you who the *real* Tom Waters is.' She had told me all about the flirtatious man I was involved with, but I wouldn't listen. 'Oh, no,' I said, defending him, 'that's not the way he is.' No, there was no one for me to share my hurts with, and as Tom criticized me, my feelings of rejection moved on to despair.

"At times these feelings would overwhelm me so much that I would cry uncontrollably, huddled on the floor in one of the spare bedrooms that we used as an office. I became increasingly nervous around Tom. I felt like I could never do anything right. I was so skittish that if I was in the kitchen doing something and he walked in, I'd often slip and cut myself with a knife or burn myself on the stove.

"I tried so hard to get Tom to love me. On Sundays I'd fix him breakfast in bed. I was always up before he was anyway, so I'd make everything just right and bring it to him on a tray, complete with flowers and candles. He loved the attention and always told me how wonderful I was, but I began to take even these words of genuine praise and turn them into a negative. 'The only thing you like about me is that I'm a good cook,' I'd complain angrily. I wasn't living up to his expectations very well, and this was one of the few areas in which he was trying to be positive. But because I didn't know how to surrender my feelings to God and have Him remove them, my only ways of coping were to curl up and cry or to strike out with sarcastic criticism. I hurt so much and wanted so badly to solve our problems, but in the end I was just hurting myself by pushing Tom further away.

"This was how my life was during those first months of marriage. I didn't cry every day, but several times I retreated to the office room floor or my bed and cried until I was exhausted. I felt so unloved and unappreciated.

"The only constant in my life was work, and without that little bit of normal life, I could have been in real trouble. I also seemed to be able to 'snap out of it' at work, and this annoyed Tom."

Tom says,

"She's right! Her work performance did aggravate me, not because I didn't want her to do well at her job, but because she seemed so different at the hospital. On her days off she was like some weeping baboon, and then she'd go off to work and be instantly transformed into little Miss Professional. Why couldn't she act this way at home? 'Come on. Snap out of it!' I told her, but it never worked. In fact, nothing worked until the day we had our breakthrough.

"We'd been having one of those days, and Alane had retreated to the office room floor, while I retired to the basement. *Here we go again,* I thought as I sat there contemplating our few short months of marriage. Things seemed so bleak. I'd tried everything I knew to get Alane to change, and she was still a basket case. While I claimed to be a Christian, I really didn't know anything about how God talks to us, so I was shocked when the thought came clearly to my mind, *If you don't stop picking on your wife, you're going to destroy her.*

"I was stunned both at the vividness of what I was sure had to be God talking to me and even more so at the message. I sat there and contemplated what I had just heard. *Well, if I can't pick on my wife ... You mean ... it could be* my *fault, Lord?* This was entirely new to me because I had developed such a poor view of Alane that I naturally assumed that whatever problems we had in our marriage were hers. This was a totally different view of things, and suddenly I had a whole lot more to think about, but God wasn't done with me yet.

"*Tom, you need to write down ten things that are positive about your wife.*

I thought about that for a while, and the only thing I could come up with was that she was a good cook! I couldn't write that. That drives her crazy. *Lord, help me! I can't think of a thing.* Gradually, bit by bit, as I allowed my mind to be free to the Spirit's influence, I started to see the positives, but then I faced a new problem. My personality is such that I would have liked to take my list up to her and say, 'Here are some things the Lord had me write down that are positive about you.' Now, you can imagine how therapeutic that would have been! Thankfully, even though I didn't really understand how to let God lead and direct in my life, He made it clear that this list was not for me to share, but that I had to incorporate it into my attitude. I realized that I needed to concentrate on Alane's good points. I had been madly in love with her just months before and by constantly looking at the negative, I had come to the place of hardly being able to notice anything positive. I knew that, from this point forward, when negative thoughts came up, I would have to give them to God and think about one of the positive attributes from my list instead. I spent a long time with God in the basement that night, and when I came up, it was with a different perspective of my wife, our marriage, and myself."

Alane says,

"I don't know how long Tom was downstairs in the basement, but it was a long time. I was sitting on the office room floor, my elbows resting on my knees, my head down between my legs, totally exhausted, having cried out the last of my energy. He stood in the doorway and spoke words I'd never thought I'd hear. 'Honey, I'm sorry. I'm sorry for the way I've been treating you. I haven't been treating you right. I love you.' Immediately I burst into tears. I had wanted so badly to hear those words, and I was glad to hear them. And yet it was almost painful, and the tears gave vent to my mixed emotions. I'm sure he must have wondered what was wrong with me! He had uttered frustrated apologies before like, 'I'm sorry I hit the window. I mean … I'm just frustrated—that's all. I just want this to stop!'

"Now he came over and reassured me that he loved me, helped me up from the floor and hugged me. And while I couldn't express it at the time, I knew something significant had happened and all those stifled feelings of love and contentment with Tom started to ooze back to the surface.

"For the next couple of months, we rebuilt our relationship from the ashes of the past. I was just beginning to feel happy and content when I got pregnant. I didn't want to be pregnant. I hadn't planned on children for five years, and here we had been married just eight months, the first six of which had been extremely trying. I remember lying in bed, so sick that I couldn't even think about getting up and breaking the news to Tom with—you guessed it—more tears! He was so wonderful when I told him, not disappointed at all.

"I would never have chosen in my human wisdom to have a baby at that point in our lives, and we certainly weren't trying, but God in His wisdom knew that this was just the thing that would motivate Tom to become the husband I needed him to be."

Tom says,

"Alane is correct. I was excited and motivated! When I was growing up my parents had kept babies for the Children's Aid Society, and I vividly recalled how those poor children were marred by their homes, where emotional upsets and tension were the predominate characteristics. I knew that I could not afford to have my wife upset if I wanted the prenatal influences on my child to be pleasant and soothing. I learned not to react to Alane as I had in the past, but to build her up and encourage her. When she got insecure and fearful that I loved the baby more than her, I responded with love and assurance, rather than saying something like, 'Don't be silly. Snap out of it!'"

Alane continues,

"It was wonderful! As Tom learned day by day to let God guide his actions and words, he was suddenly transformed from Mr. Insensitive to Mr. Wonderful! He took me to his ball games now because he *wanted* me there. He wouldn't even sit in the dugout with the other players, but would sit with me on the bleachers, snuggling me close in the corner of his arm. I felt so loved and wanted that I started to bloom and prosper as the woman God had called me to be. From that point forward, our relationship has continued growing and expanding. Yet, none of this ever would have taken place without the intervention of a loving heavenly Father, who had placed us together and was unwilling to let us sacrifice our marriage on the altar of stubborn pride.

"Today we stand with a marriage that is second to none. We used to have areas we couldn't talk about; areas we had learned were better off left alone if you didn't want a fight. Now there is nothing we can't discuss, and what a freedom it is to have nothing between us. We love each other today in a better and deeper way than we could even have dreamed of when we first married. And we look forward eagerly to our future, not because we know what tomorrow holds for us, but because we know we will face it together with the One who is changing us completely!"

Denny and Brenda

Brenda says, "No one knew about our arguments except our neighbors, who couldn't help but hear. They knew what kind of marriage we had. Denny was a deacon in our church, and I taught in the children's division. Because we had no children living with us and no plans for any, we took mission trips and enjoyed outreach activities in faraway countries, never questioning whether we had anything to give in a spiritual way. Then suddenly it happened. I was going to have a baby! I shared the news with Denny, whose response was, 'Oh, no! What have I done?' It took him two months to finally accept it and support me. It was a difficult time. I longed for Denny to share my excitement. Pregnant or not, I left for a pre-planned, three-week seminar in Washington State."

Denny says,

"Brenda is right. It was a difficult time. I was beside myself. I was already paying child support for four children, and the last thing I was ready for was another one on the way. While Brenda was at her seminar, I read an article by a man named Jim Hohnberger. After reading it, I said to myself, 'This man understands the true meaning of the gospel that will save us from ourselves.' I so wanted to meet him and talk to him. And then I saw that Jim was going to be a speaker at meetings in Washington State in just a couple of weeks. That's where Brenda was! I contacted Brenda to see if she was willing to stay on the mainland another week and attend the meetings with me. She was. Somehow I managed to finagle time off from work. As you can see, I was desperate! God worked it out, and we were able to attend the meetings and meet Jim Hohnberger.

"Jim's ideas were completely new to us. He talked about his home life and how his family was putting into practice the principles he shared. The most amazing thing is that the principles worked. He told us that we were not to wait on our partner to pick up the message and to do the changing, but we were to live victorious Christian lives ourselves—right now! Well, this was the beginning. We both started to let Jesus change us by abiding in Him, and stopped trying to change each other. Of course, success came slowly and is still coming, but it has changed our marriage tremendously."

Brenda says,

"When Denny and I started off into old habits of arguing, I would ask the Lord what I should say. When nothing except what my flesh wanted to say came to mind, I learned to keep silent. Denny became more and more the man I needed. He began spending more time with me without neglecting his duty to his children. At last we began to treat each other as if we loved each other, and it was wonderful!

"Jim and Sally's family stopped by and had a meal with us as they passed through Honolulu. I was amazed as their two teenage boys got up immediately to wash the dishes after dinner. What we saw in their family was what we wanted for ours! It was working in their home. Their boys were proof. We asked more and more questions, and they shared more and more."

Denny says,

"The problem was that as Brenda was learning all these wonderful things, she wanted to change everything at once! This was too much, too fast for me. It took Brenda a while to realize this wasn't something she could nag me into, rather, she needed to encourage me to be the godly husband and father God was calling me to be, so that we could advance together. It was hard for both of us.

"As we started to order our home after principle, we found our fellow church members thought our ideals were too hard or wouldn't work in their situation. After all, they said, they couldn't expect their children to do such things, of course implying that we were more than a little off to expect such behavior from ours."

Brenda says,

"It was only after our son was two years old and memorizing his Bible memory verses, sitting nicely until he finished his entire meal, and generally demonstrating self-control rather than the typical 'terrible twos' behavior they had warned me about, that people suddenly started to ask how we were raising him. Some of those same ones who thought we were crazy were now complimenting us on our son's behavior. Our family has increased to two children, and our home is so totally transformed that people have a hard time believing us when we talk about how bad things were in those early days.

"All during this time, I longed to move to the country, but God had other plans. We were living in a tiny apartment behind Denny's father's garage, right in Honolulu. It had originally been designed only as a playroom, and it was very cramped, with hardly enough space for us, let alone children. As time went on, we began to understand that God wanted us to change and gain the experience of walking with Him right where we were. More than seven years later, we are still living in our 'playroom,' but with Jesus, it's like a little bit of heaven. We are convinced that the time is near when we will be moving away from the city, but God has been good to us here, patiently teaching us to apply what we know in our present circumstances. All He has ever wanted from the start is our hearts—completely and totally that He might reign within, and then in His timing, we know He will move us to the place that is best for us."

Edwin and Maria

Maria says, "Edwin was so wonderful. Even though he was a busy family-practice physician, I would come home after working the evening shift as a nurse and find little things that he had done to help me. During our first year of marriage, we scarcely saw each other, but I still considered myself blessed to have united my life with such a kind and thoughtful man.

"Eventually I found flaws in my seemingly perfect companion. On weekends when I was off, I coveted time alone with him. I began to resent friends and church members, who seemed to compete with me for his time and attention. He was an elder in the church we attended and had many responsibilities. We stayed for potluck after church every week, had afternoon meetings, and were often the last ones to leave.

"His attention was wanted by so many, and he did not resist, even though I was always longing for more time with him. One afternoon after church, I began feeling more and more angry. It was hours after potluck, and one person after another wanted to talk with him about church business or other matters. It was so hard to wait patiently for him to finish and come home with me. I tried to busy myself talking with the other women who were there that day, but what I really wanted was my husband. At last I lost my patience and decided to do something to get him out of there and home with me.

"He had been having a lengthy conversation with another elder from our church, when I walked up to him, tried to interrupt politely, and informed him that I really needed to go home, intimating that I wasn't feeling well. I asked if we could leave now or if he preferred, he could give me the car keys and find a ride home later ... never dreaming that he might choose the latter. The friend he was visiting with offered to drive him home himself, which Edwin accepted. I took the car keys and left feeling extremely hurt and angry.

"The negative feelings I had been harboring all afternoon overwhelmed me as I drove home alone. I was determined to teach him a lesson. When I got home, I called my parents who lived some forty minutes away. I wanted to be gone when Edwin arrived, and I did not intend to leave a note. I asked my father if he could come and pick me up as I wanted to come and visit with them and Edwin needed the car. Sensing that something was wrong between us, even though I had not shared what happened, he denied my request, wisely suggesting that I stay home and work things out.

"When Edwin finally got home, I was cold toward him and noncommunicative. But as it was not in my nature to hold my feelings back for long, I soon exploded, expressing my hurt and anger."

Edwin says,

"Maria certainly did explode and it is consistent with my temperament to be more passive than active in relationships. This might be because I grew up with a mother, sisters, and cousins who were direct. I preferred the passive role because it was easier to know what a person felt or wanted if I just listened, and I did not have to work very hard or discuss things at length. I wanted to be understood but really did not put forth a lot of effort to make it happen. I wanted to be liked, so I would be a peacemaker rather than confrontational. I would 'go with the flow' rather than act on principle. Taking a stand was not the thing to do, if it meant disturbing the peace. Compromise was the name of the game. Since it was very important to me to be loved and accepted, I sought to meet my friends' demands on my time. This was the first time that Maria had become very upset with me. She was certainly direct. So I apologized and did what I could to restore the peace."

Maria continues,

"I thought things would be different with Edwin from that time on. As the months went by and I started working the day shift, I discovered that my hunger for intimate fellowship and communication with my husband was not to be easily satisfied, even though we now had every evening together. He still seemed very thoughtful, often performing little acts to help me in the home, but he never seemed to want to take time to just sit and talk with me enough to satisfy me."

Edwin says,

"Before Maria and I got married, I could and would read for hours, or put on music and listen for hours. I had an active imagination and often sought to feed it with exciting stories—especially science fiction. If someone called on the phone, I would respond graciously, but rarely did I initiate a call. I preferred friends who accepted me as I was and who did not try to change me. I could flip between being an introvert or extrovert. When by myself or with family, I would do my own thing, but when I chose I could also be the life of the party. During those early years of marriage, I used to wear my Walkman radio or take along a book to read when we attended social gatherings, which I would take out if there were a lull in the conversation.

"Maria encountered the same behavior from me in our home. I did not mind housework. I often did the dishes for her, vacuumed, or cleaned bathrooms on occasion. I would often get into trouble with my male friends, because their wives would point out my helpfulness as an example to them. Maria's friends always envied her. Because of this, Maria grew to tolerate my lack of communication. She wanted to communicate. I wanted to read. She wanted to spend every opportunity sharing. I wanted to become absorbed in listening to the news, reading *Newsweek* or *Time* magazine, watching TV, or working on the computer. I made it quite difficult to be intimate. I preferred stimulating, exciting input, not giving output."

Maria says,

"Although I never felt satisfied, in time I came to accept Edwin's behavior as 'normal' for his personality. I reasoned that he had plenty of good qualities to outweigh those that I did not like. I still considered myself happily married, but sought deeper friendships with other women to satisfy my need for sharing."

Edwin says,

"Maria may have found an outlet for her need to share with her friends, but I found my need for more stimulating input slowly growing, too. I traveled frequently on business and would stay up late to watch movies on HBO, Showtime, or Cinemax in the hotel. The movies were exciting, enticing, and pornographic. I did not resist. At first I just watched movies in the hotel, but then I started to view them at home after Maria and the children were in bed. Occasionally, if a movie came on too late to stay up for, I would tape it for later viewing. Movies became my desire and secret life.

"And then it happened! One day Maria wanted to show a close friend a video of something. I had carelessly left a video that I had taped, unlabeled among the other videos. She chanced upon this tape with her friend there, popped it in to see what it was, and watched what I had taped."

Maria says,

"When I realized what Edwin had done, I was shocked, hurt, and embarrassed! When he got home I confronted him. We had never enjoyed deep and honest sharing of thoughts and feelings, and this was no exception. His explanations didn't satisfy me at all. In the preceding months I had often tried to discuss spiritual issues with him. I felt the need to have God's presence be more real in our home and in our lives. Edwin had always responded as though he was with me and shared my feelings. Now I wondered if it was all a farce. I felt so betrayed and felt as though I could never trust him again.

"However, even then, unaccustomed as I was to discerning the Holy Spirit's voice, I perceived that God was asking me to be calm and patient with my husband, and to lay my burdens on Him instead. So I tried to withhold censure, to pray for him, and to give him space to work through his feelings."

Edwin says,

"I could not provide Maria with a satisfactory answer for my behavior. She was appropriately distressed and ashamed. I became very depressed. I decided to seek counseling. I actually enjoyed talking with the counselor. She would ask questions and listen nonjudgmentally. I began to see that the reason I became depressed was that there was a major inconsistency between what I said I believed, and what I did. We talked about my passive role in relationships, my need for love and acceptance, my reluctance to confront, my peacemaker role, and my desire to please my wife with helpfulness. The counselor suggested that I was a 'caretaker,' neglecting my own needs, and encouraged me to do more for myself. So I began to do less of what I had done naturally—the helpful little things in the home. The dishes that I had often done for Maria now always sat in the sink waiting for her to do them."

Maria says,

"While Edwin was seeing the counselor, I often felt bewildered. I wondered if after counseling was over, I would find myself married to a totally different man than the one I had known. The one thing I had always been able to depend on during our years of marriage was his desire to help me when I needed help, his willingness to share my burdens when I was busy, rushed, or tired. I had especially appreciated that and now that we had little ones, I felt I was on my own."

Edwin says,

"Maria was baffled by my behavior, but everyone else thought I was wonderful and told me so. My patients would affirm me, people at church would affirm me, and naturally I sought more of that attention! I was always available for others. As time went on, Maria became more and more dissatisfied. And I became more passive in our relationship. I had not made spiritual matters a true priority. I had stopped looking at pornography, but our communication did not get better. I, too, became more dissatisfied with how things were going. I loved my wife and did not want to leave the relationship. I just wasn't happy. That year stands out in my memory as the worst year of my life.

"But to continue on with the story, our spiritual lives do not exist in a vacuum. They are part of real life filled with 'real life' problems, and one of our problems was money. While I made a good living as a physician, we were going deeper and deeper in debt. We knew the Lord did not want us in debt, but we were not quite sure what to do. One morning when Maria was out jogging, she noticed a small house for sale in our neighborhood. *Maybe this is the Lord's answer to part of our debt problem,* she thought. We decided to pursue it and several weeks later we were moving from our 3,000-square-foot home into this little 900-square-foot house with garage. The little house only cost half of what our large one had!"

Maria says,

"Edwin went along with my idea of downsizing the house, but our parents and our friends thought we must have lost our minds. Whatever they thought, the little house proved a blessing to us in many ways. It was so much easier for me to maintain, and it taught us in a simple way that less really was more. All the things that wouldn't fit easily into the house were stored in the garage. As the months passed, I was struck with the thought that I couldn't remember what was in the garage. It was so stuffed that I couldn't even go out and check. We hadn't needed all those things after all. We didn't even miss them."

Edwin says,

"I had noticed for some time that Maria was seeking a closer walk with God. Although I, too, longed for something better than we possessed, I didn't share the same spiritual hunger and I felt her leaving me behind spiritually. As usual I went through the motions and didn't let her know I was discouraged and distant."

Maria says,

"Edwin acted like he was on board with the changes I desired and certainly he didn't mind the loss of the larger house payment. I may not have been aware of all Edwin's struggles, but I did know all was not well. I longed for my husband to be the spiritual leader in our home. He had started to lead out, but looking back I realize that I was one of the biggest obstacles to Edwin's leading because I would criticize his efforts and try to make him lead the way I thought he ought to.

"We had started a Bible study group with some of our closest friends. One of the topics we chose to study was country living. It seemed to us that God's ideal for His children is not in a heavily populated city, but rather in rural areas, where the works of creation greet the eye and can lift the thoughts heavenward. Our friends felt impressed to step out in faith and put their house on the market. The Lord blessed them and opened the way for them to move. Within months we helped them load the moving van.

"I longed to be in a country setting too, and as my yearnings increased, Edwin agreed to put the house on the market, but he was skeptical and logically I couldn't fault his reasoning. We had only been in our little house a year, and Edwin was sure we couldn't recover our money so soon."

Edwin says, "Maria was so eager to move to the country, but I wasn't convinced it was the right time for us. However, houses were not selling in our neighborhood and rather than refuse and disappoint her, I figured we could put it on the market and I would be safe for a while. So we listed the house on Sunday, but I refused to have a sign on the lawn. And I certainly wasn't going to tell anyone at work that I was planning to move to the country. That was for sure! Tuesday, a realtor brought a client to see our house. He couldn't have picked a worse time. We had just had a heavy rain and the roof started leaking badly! The people came and went. They couldn't miss seeing the problem for themselves. *They won't be interested,* I thought.

"Maria called me at work on Wednesday. It seemed that the people who had viewed the house *were* interested. Their realtor was coming that evening with an offer. I'll be frank. I was less than happy with the news! I wasn't ready for things to move *that* quickly! I arrived at home just as our realtor pulled up. I told him we were not selling unless the buyers offered a specific price and would take it without the roof being fixed! Maria was uncomfortable with my bold assertion. She felt I was making it impossible for the house to sell—and I was!

"A few minutes later the buyers' realtor arrived and proceeded to name the exact price I had just quoted to our realtor. The client didn't even want the roof fixed because they planned to tear it off to build a second story. My realtor's mouth dropped open, as did my own. I could not believe my ears. I gave up. The Lord was in this. There was no way I could fight against it anymore. I learned not to challenge God, unless I am ready to act when He answers heartfelt or even half-hearted prayers if they are according to His will."

Maria says,

"Edwin may have been dismayed, but I was thrilled. We moved to a lovely old house in Michigan. The house was in great need of repair and remodeling, but it was set on forty quiet acres of lovely woods and hills. The presence of the Lord was more easily felt in this location, but soon we were too busy to take full advantage of it.

"After Edwin and I moved, I longed to make real changes in our family and put into practice the principles of true Christianity. As the months passed I felt we were not making any real progress, and I couldn't put my finger on the reason. We attended a family camp meeting sponsored by Restoration International. The meetings were wonderful, and I came home inspired, ready to succeed, but still we seemed only to take small steps."

Edwin says,

"Maria may have been inspired, but I sure wasn't. I had, in my mind, placed the speakers up on a pedestal and in so doing unconsciously placed the experience they spoke of out of reach for mere mortals like me. Hence, Maria was once more striving on her own, and as usual I didn't share what was really going on in my heart.

"Late that year we faced the prospect of losing a child to what was initially thought to be malignant melanoma. God was merciful, and the original diagnosis was incorrect, but it did bring into sharp focus what was most important to us.

"I had become involved with many things in our new location and now I realized I needed to let them go and refocus on my family. It took a crisis to get my attention, but now I knew what I needed to do. I resigned from the board of the local hospital, I resigned from committees, and I resigned from all those activities that used to keep me away from home in the evening. I wrote in my journal, *'I am convicted I have some serious spiritual growing to accomplish. At the present time I have been called of God to serve in my home. I am not called of God to serve in the community or even in the community of believers at the present time. I shall not trifle with God. I cannot serve in any outreach program until the Lord gives me permission to do so. This is contrary to my inclinations for I dearly love doing it, but I am determined to serve the Lord. I have set myself on this course and will not be dissuaded, even at the expense of losing love and acceptance from those I regard highly. This is my struggle.'* My resignations were not all graciously received, and it was a very difficult thing to do, but I knew then and I know now it was the right thing to do!

"We attended the next year's family camp meeting, and what a joy awaited us in the coming year. I confessed my feelings of spiritual inferiority, and for the first time Maria learned what I had been struggling with. Suddenly I desired more than anything else to obtain the experience with God I longed for."

Maria says,

"Wow! After that camp meeting, it was like I had a different husband. Edwin was suddenly engaged in all our efforts, and our family grew by leaps and bounds. He sought more and more to protect his time with us. He resigned from his father's family business and stopped doing national TV programs. As a family we tended to spend a lot of time outside the home, visiting friends. It seemed that our children's greatest longing was to spend time with their friends, rather than spending time with their family.

"One evening we were driving home after having spent the day with friends. I watched the sleepy children settle into the car for the trip home. I realized that we had not spent much time together as a family that day. They had enjoyed their friends, and we had enjoyed ours. I wondered what thoughts had gone through their minds that day. I felt as if I was a stranger to them. Had Christ been a part of their thoughts at all?

"As Edwin and I discussed this thought later, we concluded that although friendship with other families is a blessing we needed to spend more time nurturing friendships within our own family. We started making sure other more pressing matters did not interrupt our family time in the evenings. As we made our children a priority, their attitudes shifted and our family started to draw together. Months later we decided to visit some friends one evening and our oldest inquired, 'What is going to happen to our family time if we go tonight?' I knew she loved her friends and in the past would have jumped at the opportunity to spend time with them. I was delighted to see her becoming protective of our family time."

Edwin says,

"In the summer of 1997, we spent time camping in New Mexico. My family was captivated by the beauty of the forested mountains and frequently tried to envision living in that environment. About this time I felt the Lord was calling me to take a sabbatical from medicine to be with Him and my family. I wasn't sure what I would do, but I was ready should the Lord open the way for me. The following year we made another trip west to explore the possibilities. We visited with realtors and talked about properties. I could see my wife and children were excited and participating in the process, yet I felt like this move required more faith than I had. And as usual, I wasn't ready to admit that to anybody.

"It was the day before we were due to leave for home. We had been camped near a lovely lake surrounded by hills. Maria wanted to see the sunset so she suggested we drive deeper into the forest and find a better spot. We proceeded farther and farther, traveling a loop that would eventually take us back to the main road. As we drove we found ourselves traveling through increasingly larger patches of snow. Then we came to a little hill and got stuck. *Oh, no,* I thought. *Here we are, stuck in the middle of a national forest, miles from anywhere, with no help until spring!* My family thought it a great adventure, but I was not happy!

"We settled in for the night, warm, well fed, and sheltered, but stuck. I did not sleep well. I struggled most of the night trying to think of a solution and remonstrating with myself for going down a road without knowing the conditions.

"As morning dawned, I started talking with the Lord, but what sticks out in my mind most is the question He asked me, *Do you trust Me?*

"When God asks a question like that, you cannot lie. *No, Lord, I guess I don't.* It broke my heart. I called myself a Christian, was born in the church, a missionary's child, a preacher's child. I was an ordained elder, I had preached and taught, but the bottom line was I didn't fully trust God. I had to be in control.

"That confession of unbelief was the beginning of a deeper walk for me. As the morning dawned, we had breakfast, dug out our car, and drove out of the forest and then back home. A week later, while I was having my private devotional time with the Lord, I pondered with anxiety the prospects of moving. What would my employment be? What about a home? Where? When? How? The fear of the unknown loomed before me. I wanted to have faith, but I didn't. My inclination was to postpone any decision until I had every option fully researched, and thus leave no room for a faith-based choice. Again that familiar question echoed in my mind, *Do you trust Me?*

"I made my decision, regardless of my feelings. And before I could change my mind, I announced to my delighted family that we were moving to New Mexico. We now live a few short miles from that memorable spot where we were stuck in the snow."

Maria says,

"Edwin and I have no regrets. We have lived in this remote setting for over a year now, and the trials and problems we have faced here have been harder than ever. These trials have fostered the life of dependence on God that we longed to have. It's been wonderful to explore the forests together. Our hilltop home overlooks a canyon where elk graze and bugle in the fall. We have befriended a hummingbird that comes in and out of our window and eats from the feeder set for him on our table. The children delight in these activities and many, many more. By God's grace we have rediscovered each other, and our children love being together. Together we are learning to walk, moment by moment, surrendered fully to the will of God. He took our marriage—a good marriage by worldly standards—and made it far better. He reshaped it after heaven's order, and we will be forever grateful!"

Tim and Julie

Julie says, "I mopped furiously, hoping to ease the tension. My nerves were frayed. I couldn't sit still; I had to be doing something. There was a deep pit in my stomach, and I knew I had to choose. Which man did I want more—the one who made me feel beautiful, loved, and interesting or the man I had pledged my life to, the father of my children?

"How did I get in this mess anyway? My mind drifted back in time to my first pregnancy. It was such a peaceful, glorious time. Tim treated me like a princess. I was his 'baby,' and he doted over me with never-ending attention. I soaked it up like a sponge. He cooked me tempting meals and searched high and low for anything that would appeal to my queasy, morning-sick stomach. He finally hit on animal crackers and passion fruit juice. Our friends at work teased us unmercifully, but it was all in good fun.

"Having Ellen was a wonderful experience. We both talked about it for days and agreed that it made our wedding day pale by comparison. Tim was such a good daddy. He gave Ellen her first bath because I was so nervous and afraid of breaking the tiny little thing. I can remember cozy evening worships with Tim playing his guitar, Ellen cradled in my arms, and our cat jealously claiming her spot on my lap. Life was good, except for one thing—finances.

"I had wonderful dreams of being a full-time mommy, and for a year we struggled along trying to make it work, but we fell further and further behind. Soon it became clear to us that I would have to return to work somehow. I knew it had to be, but in my heart I was resentful and bitter. I wanted to blame Tim. I knew it wasn't entirely his fault, but I wanted to blame him anyway.

"There wasn't time to sulk for long. I found a good position, and soon it became just a fact of life. The more pressing issue was Ellen. We were adamant that daycare was not an option for our child. I had worked in one previously and was duly unimpressed. Finally we hit on the idea of working opposite shifts. I would work days and Tim would work evenings. And thus began four of the longest years of our life. I went off to work early, and Tim would take care of Ellen and the household things all day. When it was time for him to go to work, he would bundle Ellen in the car and drive nearly an hour to the hospital where we both worked and meet me at the main door. We traded places and then amid a flurry of goodbyes, he would head off to work, while I drove the same long miles he had just traced back home. We had it all figured out, or so it seemed.

"I was always tired after a long day and the extra commuting. It was easy to find fault with what Tim had accomplished or not accomplished all day long while I was gone. We would talk on the phone so we could keep in touch as to what was going on. But it seemed like all the little problems and difficulties that married couples face just got pushed aside or swept under the rug because there was never time to deal with them. I would hope for time on the weekend, but the weekends were packed with church activities and household chores so we could do it all over again Monday morning. Pretty soon we began to feel like roommates or ships that pass in the night.

"Things did improve financially and four years later, it seemed like my dream was about to come true. We would have another child, and I would stay home. *Now things will be different,* I thought. *Now I will be happy.* This pregnancy went well too. I wasn't as ill, but there was a lot more stress. Tim didn't have time to dote over me, and our relationship had deteriorated a lot in the preceding years. Disagreements were common and vocal.

"Things were better with me home. I had more energy, but I found out right away that staying home wasn't all it was cracked up to be. I had two children to care for, a house to manage, and all the cooking to do. At work, I knew what was expected. The schedule was all planned out for me, and they appreciated my hard work and diligent efforts. At home I had to juggle everything alone, and nobody really cared how hard I had worked. To make matters worse, I was lonely. Tim worked a lot. He felt the financial responsibility keenly and when he wasn't working, he was busy with church meetings and programs. The meetings seemed endless. I spent my evenings alone with tired, cranky children. There was no one to lift my burden or speak an encouraging word.

"Things seemed very bleak indeed—that is until a friend of ours stopped by. He was interesting and pleasant. He enjoyed children and took time to play with mine. We talked about religion and life and eventually ourselves and our feelings. The conversations deepened, and his visits became more frequent. It made me a little uncomfortable because Tim wasn't home, but I enjoyed the company so much. Tim knew, so I figured it was all right. He started doing little favors for me and fixing little things that bothered me.

"For some time the friendship grew. Things looked the same on the outside. We didn't do anything differently, but he became more and more a part of my life. I couldn't think about anything else. My heart seemed to have a mind of its own.

"Circumstances were such that we didn't see each other for a while and when we met again, I could tell he had missed me. There was warmth and friendliness in his voice that I knew was just for me. My heart beat faster. It was a little scary, but oh so wonderful. That evening as he left, he said, 'I have feelings for you.' It was a brutally honest moment, and the only thing I could say was 'I know.' A slow smile spread over his face as he contemplated my response. I turned away not knowing what to do. I knew I was in trouble.

"I was guilt ridden. Things had gone too far, and yet I wasn't sure I wanted them to stop. I loved my husband, but I was 'in love' with someone else. My marriage was very unfulfilling. Tim had no time for me. My friend did. He made me feel loved and special. My conscience bothered me so much that I finally decided to confide in my husband.

"Tim was wonderful ... so understanding, so in control. At first he thought it was just a silly 'crush.' But as I shared more and he realized who and what was involved, the big picture began to materialize. He soon saw that unless things stopped, we wouldn't have a marriage much longer. He took time off work to deal with my friend and tell him the relationship had to stop. Then he came to me and said, 'Julie, you have to choose. I won't make you stay.'

"I wanted those good feelings the other man provided, yet I wanted my home and family too. I was afraid that I had gone too far down the wrong road—had sinned too much, that God wouldn't want me back. I was stuck in the valley of indecision. Bible texts flooded my mind, like, 'If we confess our sins, he is faithful and just to forgive us'; and "him that cometh unto me, I will in no wise cast out." I knew they were true, but did they really apply to me? Could I live with myself if I decided to go? I knew that if I chose to stay all I would have left would be an empty shell of a marriage. It looked pretty uninviting. I finally chose to stay with my husband and family . . . because it was the 'right' thing to do."

Tim says,

"When Julie chose me over the other man, I didn't understand that the reason she had chosen me was partly her fear that if she abandoned her marriage, God might not forgive her, and that every fiber of her being longed for the fulfillment the other man seemed to offer. Worse yet, because we lived in the same area, she had to see him at least once in a while, if only in passing.

"I naively thought that with the other man out of her life, we could resume our old life and go on. I quickly found that we couldn't pick up the old marriage—it had died long ago of neglect. We somehow had to rebuild a new marriage and a new relationship. We, or at least I, had no idea how to achieve this, and we spent a lot of time stumbling around in the dark trying to do the impossible.

"I longed for someone to counsel with, but there was no one. I was the head elder of our church, and I had worked intimately with the pastors. I knew that they possessed a religious experience with no more real transforming power than that which Julie and I had.

Along the way, I had obtained some taped sermons from a man named Jim Hohnberger. Something in his practical messages appealed to my heart. More important, he shared from his own experience and failings. We managed to book him for a weeklong series of meetings scheduled in the fall. If things hadn't improved by then, I decided to seek out his counsel. After all, he was from out of state and maybe he wouldn't be too shocked by an affair in the elder's family.

"Things did get better for Julie and me. We treated each other more civilly and started talking again, but we were the same old people with the same old natures. She kept wishing I would change and meet her needs. And to be honest, I wasn't satisfied with her either. When things didn't go right, it was so tempting to bring up the past. We became desperately aware that our religion offered us nothing. We longed for something better, something that would change us. We had tried and tried, but everything we did seemed to fail. There had to be more to Christianity than what we'd found. We finally resolved that if we couldn't make it work for us, we would just throw it out altogether. Maybe this new speaker would have something to offer. We could only hope."

Julie says,

"Tim had no idea how I struggled in the eight months following the affair. I truly wanted to 'be good' and do right, but my heart longed for the friendship I had left behind. It was like there was a big hole in my life. Everything reminded me of him. I cherished the memories and the feelings they generated. Little things would trigger them, and I seemed to have no power to shut them out. I longed for someone to talk to, but I didn't dare. No one knew, and I couldn't risk the embarrassment.

"Tim had been so strong at first, but I soon discovered how deeply hurt and angry he was inside. I hurt, too, because I knew I was to blame. He feared I would still change my mind and that we would never 'fall in love again.' Jealousy and despair alternately raged. He wanted me to change and be the woman he always wanted me to be, and I wanted him to love me just the way I was. It was a terrible tug-of-war."

Tim says,

"Yes, I was angry. I didn't want to go though all the work to repair the damage. It crossed my will. I think deep down I was troubled by something else. I was troubled by the knowledge that it could have been me. In our years of disconnected living, I had looked lustfully at women. It was only the lack of opportunity that had prevented me from the same fate, and something in my manhood was offended. I should have been the one out there having the affair, rather than playing the role of the jilted lover. So I would lash out, put Julie down because it made me feel better about myself at a time when my self-esteem was at low ebb.

"By the time Jim Hohnberger came to speak I was ready for *anything* that might improve things. I went for a walk with Jim and started our conversation with the following statement. 'Jim, we're desperate! If we can't find a way to make religion work for us we are going to abandon it completely.'

"Jim looked at me, and he did something I never would have expected. He smiled, and said, 'I'm glad to hear you say that. That's exactly where Sally and I were when we left for the mountains.'

"We walked to a mountaintop and looked out over the valleys below. As the hawks soared and a warm fall breeze shook the leaves, Jim shared the fundamentals of walking with God. Nothing he shared was new to me, but he made it practical and for the first time I could see how Christianity was supposed to work in the real world. When he heard the story of our troubled marriage, he simply said, 'You need to move. Don't make provision for the flesh. Don't leave your wife in the situation where she is constantly tempted by the other man.'

" 'We don't have the money,' I protested.

" 'Save it,' he replied."

Julie says,

"I don't know what Jim told my husband on that walk, but I was skeptical. I went along anyway. Anything had to be better than what I had. What did I have to lose? I feared leaving the only home we'd known for seven years, yet part of me was glad to leave the memories. Finally we made the decision to go. We started saving and by the following spring, we had enough cash and we left.

"It *was* easier to forget and go on in the new place. God had picked a lovely wooded spot for us. The home had a resort type feel with a huge whirlpool tub and a fireplace, little things that tended toward intimacy and sharing. A lot of healing started to take place. I had no friends around to visit with, so I started turning to my husband for companionship. We began to enjoy each other again. I tried to throw myself into the children. Things were really getting better. I was thrilled."

Tim says,

"Julie is right. Things were much better, but the process of change was gradual, not the overnight transformation I longed for. It took years to build a new relationship, but today our marriage is so much better than what we knew before. Our family has been knit together, and we would rather be together than anywhere else. Julie is more the woman I need today than she was when I married her fourteen years ago. We found we couldn't repair the old marriage. It had to be thrown out and replaced with a brand new relationship. Now we aren't just partners, but best friends, and home is a place where all of us are learning to walk with God. And that special relationship with the God of the universe is the only thing that makes all these other blessings possible.

"This does not mean that we are finished products. No, we have not achieved all that we desire, but our feet are set on the path. And while we may trip and fall many times, we look forward to the future as God reveals more and more of His plans for our lives and we follow the path laid before us."

I relate to one degree or another with every one of the couples that have shared their stories, and I imagine you have as well. When it comes to love, the stories are all different, but they are woven with a common thread. Have you seen yourself, your spouse, and your marriage in the couples portrayed? I know that when my marriage was not what we wanted, we were filled with a longing, not necessarily for a new or different partner, but for the ability to make our marriage into what we had dreamed about. Every one of the men and women in this chapter has stood at that point. They all share the common thread of becoming desperate enough to try a new way, to risk doing something different.

So before we examine the tools, the keys, if you will, to reviving your marriage, you must decide for yourself if you want to change things. To change things for the better is going to require that you make some sacrifices and exercise a lot of self-denial. Are you willing? Great marriages don't just happen. I hope I have been able to let you catch a glimpse of hope, a vision of the promise that can be yours, if you choose. Picture yourself in the following story and choose your destiny for yourself.

While waiting to pick up a friend at the airport in Portland, Oregon, I had one of those life-changing experiences that you hear other people talk about—the kind that sneaks up on you unexpectedly. This one occurred a mere two feet away from me.

Straining to locate my friend among the passengers deplaning through the Jetway, I noticed a man coming toward me carrying two light bags. He stopped right next to me to greet his family.

First he motioned to his youngest son (maybe six years old) as he laid down his bags. They gave each other a long, loving hug. As they separated enough to look in each other's faces, I heard the father say, "It is so good to see you, son. I missed you so much!" His son smiled somewhat shyly, averted his eyes and replied softly, "Me too, Dad!"

Then the man stood up, gazed in the eyes of his oldest son (maybe nine or ten) and while cupping his son's face in his hands said, "You're already quite the young man. I love you very much, Zach!" They too hugged a most loving, tender hug.

While this was happening, a baby girl (perhaps one or one-and-a-half) was squirming excitedly in her mother's arms, never once taking her little eyes off the wonderful sight of her returning father. The man said, "Hi, baby girl!" as he gently took the child from her mother. He quickly kissed her face all over and then held her close to his chest while rocking her from side to side. The little girl instantly relaxed and simply laid her head on his shoulder, motionless in pure contentment.

After several moments, he handed his daughter to his oldest son and declared, "I've saved the best for last," and preceded to give his wife the longest, most passionate kiss I ever remember seeing. He gazed into her eyes for several seconds and then silently mouthed, "I love you so much!" They stared into each other's eyes, beaming big smiles at one another, while holding both hands. For an instant they reminded me of newlyweds, but I knew by the age of their kids that they couldn't possibly be.

I puzzled about it for a moment then realized how totally engrossed I was in the wonderful display of unconditional love not more than an arm's length from me. I suddenly felt uncomfortable, as if I was invading something sacred, but was amazed to hear my own voice nervously ask, "Wow! How long have you two been married?"

"Been together fourteen years total, married twelve of those," he replied, without breaking his gaze from his lovely wife's face.

"Well, then, how long have you been away?" I asked the man. The man finally turned and looked at me, still beaming his joyous smile. "Two whole days!"

Two days? I was stunned. By the intensity of the greeting, I had assumed he'd been gone for at least several weeks—if not months. I know my expression betrayed me and I said almost offhandedly, hoping to end my intrusion with some semblance of grace (and to get back to searching for my friend), "I hope my marriage is still that passionate after twelve years!" The man suddenly stopped smiling. He looked me straight in the eye and with a forcefulness that burned right into my soul, he told me something that left me a different person.

"Don't hope, friend … decide!"

Then he flashed me his wonderful smile again, shook my hand, and said, "God bless!"

With that, he and his family turned and strode away together. I was still watching that exceptional man and his special family walk out of sight when my friend came up to me and asked, "What'cha looking at?"

Without hesitating and with a curious sense of certainty, I replied, "My future!"

Activities for Week 5

Sunday

Prayer time: When dealing with deeply personal areas it can be hard to separate emotion from fact. Too often we tend to justify self rather than look honestly at the cause-and-effect in our relationships. In this time with God seek a willingness of spirit that He may reveal to you just the message He has for you in this chapter.

Activity: Read "Lost and Found."

Reflection: What is your marriage like? Do you think it is hopeless, that it can never be fulfilling? Is it just too badly damaged to ever become like those mentioned above? If so, you are right. Apart from God you can't fix the problems in your relationship, but with God it can be better than you have ever hoped.

Monday

Prayer time: If ever there was a time you needed practical guidance it is today. Few things exert so much influence on our spiritual destinies as our marriages. Seek the wisdom of God for your situation.

Activity: Consider the marriages you know, be they friends, family, or whatever. Are they the type of marriage you want? What are the things missing from your union?

Reflection: Consider your spouse. If she or he had to answer the above question about what is missing, what would they say? What could you do about it?

Tuesday

Prayer time: Seek God's objectivity as you examine the problems in your home. Don't justify your position or play the blame game. Look for solutions.

Activity: Remember your dating period, the feelings and romance. Does it bring a warm smile of remembrance to your face or a grimace and pain over what your marriage has become?

Reflection: Do you think it is possible for couples to rekindle the flame of romance? Do you think it is possible in your marriage? Do you wish it could happen?

Wednesday

Prayer time: You are forming a relationship with God, just as you formed a relationship while you were dating. Special time spent together and honest sharing are the keys to make your devotional life more than formality. Make sure you are seeking to know God as an individual and not just going through a routine.

Activity: Chances are there was some special thing you did as a couple that helped each of you to tell the other that they were the most special person in the world. Do you continue with those activities or have they fallen away, victim of your busy lifestyle?

Reflection: If you were to start up those old special activities, how would you feel—awkward, delighted, or both? How would your partner react?

Thursday

Prayer time: Think today of the state of the union you have with God. Is it strong enough to stand through the trials that life tends to bring, or is it a fair-weather friendship? Ask God how you can strengthen it.

Activity: When you think back over the conflicts you have had in your marriage, I think you will find that the most bitter and hurtful exchanges have always centered upon one or both of you demanding your way. What have you learned thus far about self-surrender that will help you in the future?

Reflection: Would you be willing to surrender your way if God impressed you to, even if your partner's attitude and deportment were selfish?

Friday

Prayer time: Ask God to grant you the freedom of thought to really see what your marriage might become through His power.

Activity: Plan out the way you would like things to be in your marriage, and I don't mean saying, "Well, I want my way all the time and then I just know I could be happy." No, what I want you to plan out is what you envision a true Christian marriage could be with all the loving words, the unselfish actions, and the passionate, other-directed love that is so missing from most relationships.

Reflection: Are you willing to pour yourself out in order to obtain the marriage you long for?

Saturday

Reflection: Take some time today and observe your partner. Try and see the positive things that attracted you in the first place but that you may have lost sight of. Hope and dream for the future. The spark can come back between you. Join me tomorrow as we look at kindling the flame.

CHAPTER 6

Kindling the Flame

"Keep me as the apple of the eye, hide me under the shadow of thy wings" (Psalm 17:8).

CHAPTER GOAL

Learn to take practical steps to begin, once more, to pursue your spouse. Everyone who has ever been in love has won someone's heart at least once, and you can do it again. It doesn't require youth or good looks to answer the plea of your partner's heart.

After Sally and I sold our house and business in Wisconsin and moved to the wilderness, we learned so many lessons that it astonished us. In that real-life environment, the application of principles to our spiritual life was not only more clearly understood, but also more easily implemented. Our life in the wilderness was so satisfying on every level—physical, mental, and spiritual—as well as conducive to growth in our marriage and family that I have trouble finding adequate words to describe it. But of all the lessons learned in those first years, perhaps none had a broader application or a more practical appeal than those taught by our old cookstove.

Our log cabin needed a real cookstove, and while we desired the best, we could only afford a used stove. After some searching, we located a used Majestic cookstove that was nearly eighty-five years old. I know that very few of my readers have ever used a wood cookstove, so let me explain. In my opinion the Majestic we found was, in its day, a top-of-the-line appliance with its beautifully trimmed chrome.

The casual observer might not have agreed with this sanguine assessment if they had seen that old stove when we got it. It was covered with grime, baked-on grease, and plain old-fashioned dirt and rust. It took me a month to get it back in shape. First I had to scrub off the grime. Then I went to work on the rust. I brushed, scraped, ground, sanded, and polished that old stove. We repainted the areas that needed it and had a water jacket made for it so it could provide our hot water. At last it was installed in our home, glistening in its new paint and polished chrome. While I didn't know it, that stove was destined for greatness.

It was just a cold piece of steel, but with a fire kindled within, it heated our entire home. The food it cooked was spectacular, and un-limited hot water was available from this tireless servant. I constructed a drying rack above it, and the old Majestic became a food dehydra-tor. In the bitter cold Montana winter, you could come in from many degrees below zero and stand beside it as waves of heat encircled you like the arms of a friend. When my feet got cold, nothing beat prop-ping them up beside its warmth. I couldn't even guess how many times we came in from some adventure in the snow and hung our wet wraps by the stove, which uncomplainingly had them warm and dry by the time we were ready to head back outdoors.

That old cookstove became the single most important tool in our wilderness home. We couldn't eat, bathe, or even stay warm without it. Yes, that old stove performed admirably, but that does not mean it made no demands. I soon learned that of the five types of wood that grew around me in Montana, the stove was much more efficient with one than with all the others. I strove to provide it with the wood that helped it function best. From the needs of the stove I began to understand that my relationship to the girl I had married was a lot like that stove. If I wanted a marriage functioning at peak performance then I had to provide the very best fuel for the fire of that special person I had married.

Thus began a twenty-year odyssey of reexamining my marriage. Along the way I have been privileged to counsel hundreds of couples and gain an understanding of the different fuels their marriages needed to succeed and thrive. The principles I will be sharing are Bible-based and practical. While I came to understand most of these principles myself, I would be remiss if I did not acknowledge the work of Gary Chapman, who has done a masterful job of presenting these principles in his book *The Five Love Languages* (Northfield Publishing, 1992).

Love does not, will not, and indeed cannot survive for long without expression. This is a truism, despite the tendency of modern movies and literature to romanticize unexpressed and unrequited love. Unexpressed love is a tragedy both to those deprived of its benefits and, most of all, to its holders. I remember hearing of a man who traveled to a hot, arid country. He noticed that many of the popular songs had to do with water, and he asked an acquaintance about it. "Yes," he replied, "we do tend to sing and dream about what is most rare. Is that why all of your songs are about love?"

Most of us would hate to admit it, but love, at least the fulfilling, long-hoped-for, soul-feeding type of love is at least as rare as rain in a desert country. Most of us look at our partners, and there is so much we wish we could change. Oh, some of our spouses are trying to feed the fire within our hearts, but how many of us long for the right wood? Some provide us with Douglas fir when we'd rather have spruce. Others feed us, but it is unseasoned—green and unpalatable. We tend to turn wistfully away from what might have been, from the true longing of our hearts. We look at the positives in our spouse and try to convince ourselves that these matter more than the right fuel. We sputter and smoke through life, struggling to maintain the fire when it could be so much easier with just a little of the right combustible substance.

Most of us are truly trying to kindle the flame, or at least we did try until we gave up in frustration. Why is it that we fail? Because we lose the perspective we had when we were courting. All of us know there's more than one way to say I love you, and at some level we know that this special person we are interested in responds best to one of those ways, those fuels, if you will. When you are first getting acquainted you intuitively try every available wood to feed the flame of your partner. Some go over better than others, and soon we learn what they like and enjoy, but somehow after we marry them, we stop those special attentions and inadvertently slip into old habit patterns of thinking and acting. We often try to feed our partners' love fire with the type of fuel we desire for ourselves. Unless they happen to respond best to the same things we do, which is extremely unlikely, we will find them growing dissatisfied and unfulfilled in the relationship. So how do we discover our spouse's special area of fulfillment?

There are what Dr. Chapman described as five love languages, and what I have called the five universal pursuits. Every single one of us responds to one degree or another to all of these; meaning that we can enjoy and appreciate any of them, but there is one that just suits us better than all the others, and that is the language of our heart. So what are these pursuits? We will discuss four in this chapter, saving the fifth for later.

You know, I was always told that some day the honeymoon would be over and after a year or two our marriage would lose its spark and become like everybody else's marriage. As time went on, my experience confirmed the words of these prophets of doom. But when I discovered the principles we will discuss in this chapter, I found the feelings I had toward my Sally during our courtship that had died of neglect, my neglect, were rekindled. I found that married love does not have to become cold, formal, boring, and sedate. Today I feel the flames of love for that girl I married more than I did when we were dating, and you can experience this too, by discovering what your spouse needs and then putting forth effort to see they receive it. It works both ways—for husband and wives. Your partner is longing for you to provide the right fuel. Will you do it? Husbands, are you groaning and thinking, *What am I going to have to do now?* Do you need some extra motivation? I'll share a secret I have learned through experience. It is impossible to out-give a woman! The more you give her, the more she returns in ever-increasing waves of love. It is an investment in her happiness *and* yours, and it will pay dividends far beyond any earthly investment.

As we look at these five universal pursuits, let's be sensitive not only to recognizing the one that we respond to, but also especially sensitive to the unique fuel that special person we married longs for. However, there is a caution I must share with you about these principles, and unless it is adhered to, you will never gain the full depth of what you desire. The caution is this. We can go out in our human power and provide what our partner desires, and this *will* yield a result for the better. But if we are sensitive to the Holy Spirit's leading in our life and are responsive to His guidance on when and how to apply this knowledge, we will experience a marriage far beyond our wildest dreams. Your home may actually become a little bit of heaven on earth, where peace and harmony reign. I am beginning to experience this with the girl I love, with my Sally, and since I know her so well, let me begin with her and the fuel she needs.

Sally thrives on encouraging words and compliments. These words cost us so little and yet they can do so very much, especially when they are uttered under the Spirit's guidance. So often we think that it is some big thing our spouse needs to feel fulfilled, but the rule in all of these areas is "little attentions, often." That's the way it is with my wood stove, and that is the way it is with those we love. We are focusing here on our spouses, but these principles work with our children, our parents, and our family and friends equally as well. To give sincere compliments requires that self be dethroned and that we develop an attitude of gratitude toward others. For example, even today, as I wrote these words, Sally put a new cover on the photo album we take with us to speaking engagements. These albums get a lot of handling because people are naturally curious about our home and lifestyle, and the old cover was looking a little worn. So Sally replaced it with a new cover. It was simple, attractive, and most of all conveyed the essence of who and what we are. She put herself into the project, and it looked nice. When I came in and saw it, I could have responded in different ways. I could have said "Thank you," which Sally would have appreciated, but it would have been the wrong type of wood. Worse, I could have said, "About time you put a new cover on that. I thought the old one was going to have to fall off first." This is the verbal equivalent to throwing water on that fire. But as I saw what she had done, I sensed the Spirit's impression in my thoughts to praise Sally, to acknowledge her efforts and encourage her. So I said, "Wow! That is great! Honey, it is really attractive and will definitely draw the people's attention. You were really creative!" If only you could see a video of her reaction to my words. It was wonderful. Her whole face lit up, and she was so pleased and encouraged. Another day she had made a blueberry pie for me, and when the meal was over and I sat back satisfied I told her, "Honey, that was scrumptious. That really hit the spot!" When someone hears words like those, it lifts their spirit. While you may say, "Big deal," it is probably because you haven't been practicing encouraging words and come to understand that these little words *are* a *big* deal.

Simple courtesies like "Please," "Thank you," "You're welcome," and "Excuse me" are socially required among strangers but too often ignored at home. Who is more deserving of politeness than those we love the most? Do we really want to send the message that strangers are more deserving of our efforts? I've seen families where this message is coming through to the wife or the children loud and clear, and this is ruinous to relationships.

When I clean up our sport utility vehicle and spend time making it look nice by polishing it inside and out, Sally often comes out and says, "Wow! Look at that baby shine!"

She has said that many times before, and encouraging words are not my special area of need, but I still enjoy hearing her say that. I still like to know that the time and effort I expend are appreciated. Many people long for this acknowledgment. It doesn't have to be false or exaggerated praise. Most people just want to have their efforts acknowledged.

I have a preacher friend who came to me because his wife never, and I mean never, commented on his sermons, and he longed for the feedback. She never realized that her interest in him was his heart's desire. When we were dating most of us willingly shared what we thought and felt as we explored and got to know the other person and tried to let them know who we were. Our spouses don't stop being interesting people after we marry them. I am still finding out things about Sally I didn't know, little stories, hidden talents, as well as feelings and concerns, and all this is after thirty years of marriage. Makes me look forward to the next thirty!

Sally is special in so many ways I could fill this book with things she does that I appreciate, but one area that really stands out is the way that she takes care of herself. She is always dressed nicely; she doesn't just hang out in sweats. She looks good and put together. This costs her time and effort. It's not as though she has a shortage of things that demand her time either. She does this just for me, whether or not company is coming, because she wants me to know that I'm just as important to her as any company. I make sure she knows I enjoy these efforts. A woman wants to know that her husband finds her attractive, that she still catches his eye. I don't mean this in an overly fleshly or carnal manner, but she wants to know he is still interested in her.

I have developed several ways of letting Sally know this. I may have a beauty attack when she comes in the room. *What* is a beauty attack, you may be asking yourself? Well, when she comes into my sight, she is such a vision of loveliness that I am overwhelmed. My hands clutch at my chest, and I stagger about before collapsing on the floor, and the only way she can revive me is to come over and provide some mouth-to-mouth resuscitation! She gets such a kick out of it; I've even done it when we had company. This kind of "play" keeps our marriage vibrant and alive. Couples should have fun together, and if you can enjoy affirming each other, all the better. The excitement of courtship is not supposed to end at the marriage altar, but to continue growing and deepening each year.

Too many women are not encouraged and praised for their intellect, and this is so important. She may think differently than you do, gentlemen, but that does not make her an airhead, as so many men seem to want to accuse their wives of being. I look for those times when Sally provides just the right idea or just the right comment, and I praise her. "Where did you ever come up with that idea? I wouldn't have thought of that in a thousand years! You're really something!" And you know, that is not empty praise. God promised man a helpmeet, and Sally is a helpmeet to me, bringing a beautiful balance into my life. She looks so pleased when I say this, and you know, she should be, because I am sincere and honest in complimenting her. This brings up another point: we should be sincere in these areas or we will not provide what our spouse is longing for. You can, and I do, exaggerate a little in a flirtatious way, and this is acceptable in the context of flirtation. Flirt with your spouse, wink at them, share a secret look, hold hands under the table, or exchange little notes. Even a wave across a crowd conveys so much love. It says, "You're special, and I notice you even when everybody else is in the way." Your words can flirt as well. "Wow! You sure catch my eye!" Don't neglect those cute pet names you developed for each other back when you were dating. Dust them off and use them if they have sat idle, because shared secrets build intimacy.

When we received the invitation for our twenty-five-year class reunion, Sally looked it over and then her gaze met my eyes. "Honey, you know there were more than 660 in our graduating class, and not one of them could hold a candle to you. I got the very best one!" Let me tell you, that did something for me! After all these years those words really do enhance our relationship.

Sally takes real delight in her gardens. There is nothing she likes better than to take me on a tour of the greenhouse or the vegetable and flower gardens. Now I've seen them every day, but I go with her. I could say, "Yes, that's a nice tomato plant," but I don't. I say, "Look at that tomato! Look at how those tomatoes are coming along. Fantastic! I can't believe the size of those strawberries—I mean, they're bigger than golf balls! Incredible! You've done a tremendous job!"

Encouraging words are so important, especially when these are the primary fuel we desire. Remember Edwin and Maria? He longed for approval and allowed himself to engage in all sorts of activities and jobs, neglecting his wife's desire for his time, anything so long as people approved and affirmed him for the great job he was doing. Yet, even though he was fulfilling his need with praise from others, he really desired praise from Maria, which was not forthcoming. Edwin was filling his need elsewhere, but in the process he found that he was miserable. Only when he and Maria started to fill each other's firebox with the right fuels did true happiness and fulfillment enter their experience. They had tried on their own to build a successful marriage but had found themselves powerless—battery-less toys. It was only as they submitted to God that self was hidden in Christ and they were willing to take the steps necessary to fulfill their partner.

The attitude of gratitude and encouragement is a foundational principle of God's character. God is an encouraging God. He says:

"I will not leave you comfortless: I will come to you" (John 14:18).

"I have loved you, saith the Lord" (Malachi 1:2).

"I will never leave thee, nor forsake thee" (Hebrews 13:5).

"Lo, I am with you alway, even unto the end of the world" (Matthew 28:20).

"Fear thou not; for I am with thee: be not dismayed; for I am thy God: I will strengthen thee; yea, I will help thee; yea, I will uphold thee with the right hand of my righteousness" (Isaiah 41:10).

Even our Lord Jesus Christ needed affirmation, and the Father provided it in these words. "This is My beloved Son, in whom I am well pleased."

Heaven is not a place of stodgy, self-righteous attitudes but rather the origin of a great stream of love and encouragement flowing out to the universe for the benefit of every living creature. The words God spoke to His Son He desires to say to every one of us. "This is My beloved son; this is My beloved daughter—in whom I am well pleased." God encourages us ever upward, always onward with the thought that yesterday's triumphs can be the steppingstone for still greater victories today, and His ideal for us is almost beyond our poor ability to contemplate. Like a parent with a timid child He is there telling me, "You can do it, Jim. I know you can. Take My hand and depend on Me; I will show you how." With such a God to lead and direct us, showing us the pathway of encouraging others, how can we refuse to provide what others long for?

Perhaps it has been so long since you said such things that you don't know how to start. Many people are afraid they'll sound silly or fake when they first try to speak encouraging words—especially if they have been used to using harsh and unloving words. But even the most verbally inept of us can write a note.

A note of encouragement is such a blessing for those for whom conversation is a trial. Some are articulate on paper but in conversation just can't think fast enough. But, provide them with time for reflection and writing and a masterpiece of encouragement can flow from their pen. Unlike the spoken word, the written note is often read repeatedly and treasured by its recipient more than a casually uttered phrase. Recently I received this note from Sally:

Dearest Jim,

You are the treasure of my life, the heartbeat of my day, and the joys in moments.

Love,

Sally

On the other side of the note was a heart with the words, "You're my man," with a smiley face. Her note was in every respect equivalent to my having a beauty attack.

Pet names are expressive of your special intimacy, but pet expressions can draw hearts together also. I often tell my wife she is the missing color of the rainbow. My son picked up on this and started telling his girl that she is the missing star in the heavens. A compliment paid in an unexpected way or in front of other people, especially with the element of surprise, can be delightful.

While backpacking I saw one of my sons provide a vivid example of this. We were crossing an open meadow filled with little wildflowers of various hues, but one was almost white with just a hint of pink. Noticing this, he called his girlfriend over to him and said, "Look, even the flowers blush in your presence." Then the flowers suddenly weren't the only things blushing in that mountain meadow. How true are the words of Scripture in Proverbs 18:21: "Death and life are in the power of the tongue." In your marriage and my marriage, death and life are truly in the power of the tongue.

I had just finished speaking and walked out of a church in a beautiful parklike setting, enjoying the day and the friendly people I had been privileged to meet. Down by the pond I saw a circle of boys, and they seemed to be poking at something with sticks. My curiosity was aroused and I walked down that way to see what was going on. I found that a turtle had come up out of the pond, and the boys, being boys, had poked at it with those sticks. The turtle had pulled back into his shell, and at that moment I was struck by how many "turtles" I have met in churches all over the world. So many spouses and so many children are in their shells, hiding from the stick wielded by their supposed loved ones. When we use harsh, cutting language with our spouse it is just as if we were poking them with a stick. Phrases like, "That's stupid"; "Can't you think first?"; "Can't you do anything right"; or expressions and body language that cuts them off, discards them; or verbal threats to end the relationship wound and hurt the other partner and might well be described as throwing water on the fire.

We can burden our spouse with troubles and trials. Sometimes a man will come home, and his wife dumps all her trials and burdens upon him, and he is almost crushed before he has even removed his coat. Proverbs 12:25 explains, "An anxious heart weighs a man down, but a kind word cheers him up" (NIV). Some of our loved ones long for a kind word. For some it would make all the difference in the world. You see, love is not so much getting what we want, as much as doing for someone else what they need.

Remember Alane shared how she felt and how she reacted when she felt unloved? She just pulled into her shell and cried and cried. It was not impossible to repair, but it required of Tom to surrender his idea that this was all Alane's fault and learn to listen to God's guidance.

I have visited, counseled, and stayed with so many couples that aren't stoking the fire. Many of them consider themselves good Christians, and perhaps they are not throwing water in the stove but they have allowed the flames to die of neglect. If you want to let the flames of love die out in your marriage it is really simple—just do nothing. It is guaranteed to work every time. Just tell your spouse, "Not now,

I'm too busy. Can't you see I've got important things to do?" You can see the flame start to sputter and die right on their countenance.

Often the manner in which we address others is much more important than our actual words. I remember as a child my father sitting at the head of the table and casually saying to my mother, "Bernice, throw me a piece of pie."

"Henry! Think of the children and your example."

"Bernice, throw me the pie!" he said with emphasis.

We'd never seen Mother ever do something like this, but she picked up that whole pie plate and threw it with great aim—in his face. There was a silent, expectant air as we all held our breath to see if it was going to be OK to laugh. My father just sat there in stunned silence as apples and crust dripped off his face and onto his shirt. "Well," he said, "guess I got the pie." And then he started to laugh, freeing the whole family to give way to the humor of the situation.

If you doubt the validity of these encouraging words, just take a week and say nothing but encouraging things to your spouse. You will be amazed at the difference it makes. If you find that encouraging words are that special way your spouse wants to be loved, then extend this experiment for a lifetime.

Another way that we encourage or reinforce the love we share is the giving of gifts. No, I don't mean on holidays or special occasions, but the giving of what one of my friends refers to as "just because" gifts. A gift is a visible token that says to the receiver, "You were in my thoughts today." In the gift is embodied the love that cared enough to pick out something just for our special someone.

I have never outgrown the thrill of receiving a gift, especially if it comes from my wife or sons. They know me so well that their gifts, more than any others, convey their thoughtfulness as they choose an item that would enhance my lifestyle or the enjoyment of my recreational pursuits. For example, Sally knew I wanted a certain knife and tool combination for backpacking. I hadn't requested it, but when she saw it she picked it up for me. She had read my desire, even while it remained unvoiced and she had gone to the trouble to make it a gift "just because" it would please me.

One day I felt the impression of the Lord that I should give Sally a "just because" gift. Now we live where a trip to town is at best a three-hour round trip, not counting on the time spent shopping. How was I to give her a gift that day? I got out the picture of the blouse she had been eyeing in the catalogue, and I put it on her desk with a note: "Order it. Just because." I had given her the gift even though I didn't have it in my hand.

Gifts can be very low cost. When Sally and I dated we didn't have the money to lavish gifts on each other. Poor college students rarely do. In fact, we saved the funds we had so we could get together on the weekends. Instead of buying gifts, we would make homemade cards and eat homemade picnics.

Not that long ago, Sally and I were with some friends, driving down a back-country road, and suddenly the roadside came alive with a profusion of wildflowers. I pulled over abruptly, causing everyone to ask if something was wrong. I didn't take time to reply; I just hopped out and returned with a bouquet for Sally. "Flowers for my flower," I said, basking in the warmth of her delighted smile.

Sometimes the gift is not just an item. It can also be the gift of doing the unexpected. A call from the office to your spouse might require you to give them a minute or two of your time, but it may be the highlight of their day! Julie fondly remembers the time her family gave her the gift of the unexpected.

"I had been busy all day and hadn't had time to plan anything for family time, so when Tim and the children suggested going to the state park not far from our house for our family time that evening, I was more than willing. Arriving at the park with its beautiful lake and peaceful setting, I started to unwind and relax. When the children wanted to drive to the other side of the lake and see the campground, I gladly went along to take a tour of the mostly empty campground. There were a lot of nice private campsites. In fact, the one that was taken just ahead of us looked exceptionally nice. Tim must have thought so as well, because he slowed slightly to look at it too. 'Those people have a tent that looks just like ours,' I commented.

" 'Yes, they do,' he said as he pulled into the parking area, and I suddenly realized it *was* our tent. The children and he had secretly set up camp for the weekend. What a special weekend surprise, made even more special by a skunk that decided our camp was a great place to visit and walked about our feet just inches away. What fun we had watching it forage for food in our garbage!"

When a couple is in love, it is obvious to everyone about them. Why? It is more than the look in the eyes, more than the utter joy they take in each other's company. It is also the tender touches: the protective arm about each other; the hugs that are a taste of heaven; the kisses they hope will never end; and the hands that are held at every opportunity, that so mark this phase of courtship. The problem is that most of us gradually leave this phase behind, but we do not outgrow our need of touch.

An infant that only has physical needs met but is never held, cuddled, and played with will be severely hindered in development and likely die before long. All because tender touches are not an option, but an absolute need for every human being, no matter what stage of life in which they find themselves.

Sally loves tender touches. We hug and kiss frequently, but there is much more than hugs and kisses involved. At times I have come up behind her while she is typing on the computer and I can see she is getting tired. Her energies have started fading and she looks like a plant in the garden that needs a good drink of water. So, I gently massage her shoulders and arms. Before long she, just like those plants that get a drink, perks right up. My energy has flowed into her through the medium of my touch and the knowledge that she is loved. Sometimes she can see I am stressed, especially if the day has been filled with lots of counseling or public speaking. She can just tell by the way I turn my head that I am getting a headache or a kink in my neck. She takes over, and soon the problem is resolved under her skillful hands.

Traditional touches are very important. Hugs and kisses at hello and goodbye bind the heart and can be much more than mere form. I have watched many a man kiss his wife goodbye out of a sense of obligation after he sees me kiss my wife, and believe me, the wife knows he's only doing it to save face in front of me.

I vividly remember one such wife, who tried so hard to give her husband the message that tender touches were important; they were her type of universal pursuit. She saw me sitting with Sally and how we held hands during prayer, how I always kiss her hand before I let it go. I can't walk beside Sally and not want to hold hands, and when we are near each other, my arm naturally finds its way around her. This wife watched this as they visited with us, and soon I saw her scoot closer to her husband, and you know what he did? He moved farther away. I watched as she chased this dumb ox in a subtle manner across the entire sofa. Still he didn't get the idea! You could just sense her frustration. Her husband was the type to say as he was leaving, "See ya." If she was really fortunate he might even say in the same tonal inflection, "Love ya."

I felt so bad for this poor woman that I invited her husband on a walk and explained what it was that his wife wanted. Then I sat back and watched the next day. He had his arm around her; there was real warmth in his words toward her; and she was swooning for him. She was so happy and so fulfilled with just those little gestures that I thought she would burst. These little things mean a lot, and if you have neglected them, you don't know what you are missing.

I would, however, add one word of caution. If you've let these attentions die of neglect, and the only time you engage in these activities is when you two are physically intimate, your partner may not respond the way you would like them to at first because you have trained them that any such activity is a prelude to something more. They may notice these new attentions on your part and get the wrong message. Time and consistency will quickly win them over; don't despair.

At last we come to my favorite personal pursuit—the one that tells me above all others that I am loved, and that is acts of loving kindness. When someone goes out of their way to help me, they are telling me they love me. When someone serves my needs, they are reaching my heart. I have had people share a meal with us, and after watching Sally, they think she must be an abused wife. Not in the physical aspect, but because she is constantly serving my needs. Sometimes I will be eating a meal and glance toward the refrigerator as the thought of something extra I'd like floats through my head. Sally will notice my glance and be on her feet to get whatever it is before I can get up or even get the words out. She serves me because she loves me, not because she is forced to. She loves serving me and enjoys the love it calls forth from my heart toward her.

Now, just because it is not her favorite pursuit, do you think Sally never wants loving service? Of course she does. My son and I went out one evening and dug potatoes from the garden and washed them up for her, not because it was our job, but because we knew she needed help, and she was thrilled. Serving others is not only Christlike, it is in many ways the essence of Christianity. When we realize that we must have a living and vibrant connection with Christ to help our own spouse or our children to find God, then we realize that one of the greatest acts of service we can do for them is to maintain our own relationship with God. Often in the context of loving others, we will do for them what we might not do just for ourselves.

Actions might be as simple as fixing a leaky sink or painting the bedroom on your day off. It might mean making his favorite pie or just seeing that his clothes are clean and pressed. None of the simple acts that we use to serve others are glamorous, but they don't have to be to win the affection of one who responds to them. For someone like me the motivation and the love shown are more important than any other factor.

So did you find yourself or your partner in any of the subjects covered? If so, you know what to do to provide them the special fuel that will enable them to keep the flame of love burning brightly in their hearts for you. Are you willing to do that? Will you take the steps needed so that when others see you, they think you are a newly wedded couple?

Marriage was given to you by God to provide you with pleasure and fulfillment as nothing else can do. Marriage was provided for Adam and Eve before sin entered the world, and God desires your marriage to be as happy as that very first one in Eden. I challenge you to pursue this week's activities below as an experiment in exploring how to fulfill your partner and yourself. May God richly bless you as you work to kindle the flame.

Activities for Week 6

Sunday

Prayer time: Ask God to give you a clear mind to recall what was so special about your relationship that you knew you had found your one and only when you married.

Activity: Read "Kindling the Flame."

Reflection: Did you see anything familiar, perhaps something from your dating days, that was once so important but has somehow been lost sight of?

Monday

Prayer time: Ask the Lord for some extra inventiveness to plan, as well as for empathy for your partner.

Activity: Today is the day for planning the week's activities. Every day you will try to concentrate on one of the universal pursuits about which we have been reading. It may take some extra ingenuity, but it will also be fun to see your spouse's reactions.

Reflection: Did you find it hard to focus on your partner's enjoyment this way?

If so, why?

Tuesday

Prayer time: Ask the Lord to be with you in your first attempt. To do today's activity well and see the results you desire, will require you to look differently at situations and to try and read your partner's response, which may very well be nonverbal.

Activity: Today's assignment is to use affirming words in any opportunity that presents itself. If you notice the day slipping away without a spontaneous opportunity, it may be that you are out of the habit of looking for them. But ask the Lord to help you create an opportunity before the day is through.

Reflection: Was your partner pleased? Shocked? Or just not sure what you are up to?

Wednesday

Prayer time: Take the opportunity to mentally prepare yourself for your partner to view you with a certain amount of suspicion. Yesterday was unexpected, but today will be the second round of new or at least long-forgotten attentions. Human beings are so unused to real loving attentions that they tend to think anyone using it is simply manipulating them to achieve some personal goal. Seek to let self die so that you may stay in Christ even if misunderstood.

Activity: Today is a day to give some kind of gift. People in the world expect to be given gifts for traditional reasons. Today is a "just because" day. It can be an inexpensive token, a dozen roses, or even a homemade card. What matters more than the money spent is the message—just because "I love you! You're special to me. You still catch my eye." These kinds of gifts mean far more than the expected birthday and anniversary gifts. Although, if your partner responds well to this pursuit, certainly make use of the traditional gift giving as well. A gift is a compliment in many ways. A woman who gets flowers at the office has been paid the ultimate compliment. The man who opens his lunch to find a love note can't help smiling. While fellow workers may tease about the flowers on her desk or the heart-shaped sandwich in his lunch, every jealous comment reinforces the value of what was given.

Reflection: How did it go today? And why? Which one of the two universal pursuits did your spouse respond to best?

Thursday

Prayer time: Ask God for the wisdom to pick just the right activity to please the one you love. Ask God to make you willing to be a servant just as Christ was. You may feel discouraged if they haven't responded to your first attempts. Don't despair. It took Christ a long time to reach the disciples' hearts too.

Activity: Today we move on to acts of service. If your partner likes this type of ministering to their needs, they will like almost anything you do for them, from picking up the dry cleaning to washing the car. But try to pick something that they especially want done.

Do remember that not every effort to perform an act of service is a true help. If someone tends to be sloppy, you might clean up their desk as an act of service, only to find out you discarded some very important papers.

Reflection: Well, how did it go? Have you found your partner's special pursuit? Perhaps it is still ahead of us.

Friday

Prayer time: In seeking God today, think about what it was like for Adam and Eve when God walked with them in the Garden. Did they hold His hand, hug Him in joyful greeting, kiss Him goodbye? These are questions without answers right now, but they reveal our attitudes toward these aspects of physical affection.

Activity: Today's activity can be tough because too many couples have allowed physical intimacy to become the only tender touches that are exchanged. Human beings must have physical contact if they are to be happy and thrive on any level—physical, mental, or spiritual. We are social creatures, and even the wildlife about us uses tender touches. They groom each other, scratch places that others can't reach for themselves, but even more important, they use tender touches to reassure each other. Seek to discover a tender touch that will reinforce your partner's sense of value, not make them feel suffocated. Perhaps a back or foot rub would be a good nonthreatening choice.

Reflection: You have tried four of the five universal pursuits. Have you discovered the one you personally like best while trying to please your partner? Have you discovered your partner's favorite pursuit? If not, next week should be intensely satisfying as we deal with the last universal pursuit.

Saturday

Reflection: If you have found your partner's preferred activity, spend some time thinking about how you can continue to meet his or her needs.

CHAPTER 7

Swing Time

"Come now, and let us reason together" (Isaiah 1:18).

CHAPTER GOAL

Communicating in a new and different manner will be challenging, but we can learn to leave arguments behind and enter into the experience of reasoning together.

"Father, you know I'm supposed to complete a woodworking project as part of home school this year," Andrew announced rhetorically, giving me a worried look. Of course I knew about the requirement; I had been the major force behind incorporating it into our school program. It was that worried look that concerned me. That look belied a struggle going on in a twelve-year-old mind, and his next words vividly stated the problem.

"I don't want to make another birdhouse or any other 'baby' project. I want to make something large and challenging."

A dusty memory suddenly rose from the depths of my mind, and a picture of my grandmother's front porch clearly displayed itself in my mind. I could see the adults gathered on lawn chairs in the cool evening hours. The little ones were playing with toys on the spacious wooden floor of the porch. I usually brought my trucks, and there at Grandma's feet I would listen to the merry talk of aunts and uncles and the endless click of Grandma's knitting needles, as the old porch swing creaked with her gentle rocking. The picture was so warm and reassuring. I told Andrew, "Why don't you make us an old-fashioned porch swing like the one at Great-Grandma's house?"

I wish you could have seen his face as the worry vanished and he exclaimed, "Really, Father?"

"Sure, go ahead. I think we might even have the wood. When you finish it we'll hang it out front between those two trees," I encouraged him, pointing to the spot I had mentally picked out. But I was talking to his rapidly disappearing back as he ran to get his plans ready.

Andrew threw himself into that project, but it wasn't easy. He had to use his inventiveness to solve a number of problems, and some of the things he came up with were quite ingenious. Soon he had a swing that was both attractive and comfortable. When he finished we purchased some chains, and he was enormously pleased as it sat proudly between the trees, a testament to his tenacity and his growing skills.

However, now that it was done, what were we going to do with it? Once more, memory came to my aid. My parents were a traditional family with my mother staying home and my father working. What was not so traditional was that unlike his coworkers, who stopped by the taverns on their way home, my father always came home at the same time every night. I used to wonder what made him different but never really contemplated it in depth. It was just one of those adult mysteries, I supposed. My father was so punctual about coming home that you could almost set your watch by his arrival. At half-past four he would come in from work, and Mother would greet him at the door, usually with some type of beverage. And then during good weather they would sit on the porch and talk for the better part of an hour until suppertime, when the whole family would gather. The mystery was explained years later by my mother, who one day felt I was old enough to learn something important.

"You know why your father comes straight home and doesn't stop to drink in the bars like the other men he works with?" she queried.

"I don't know," I replied, realizing Mom was going to let me in on a secret.

"Jimmy, he's here because he always has something to come home to."

I never forgot that little bit of wisdom. And when we moved to the mountains, I sensed Sally always wanted more of my time to just talk, but as I didn't work outside the home, the traditional evening visit of my mother and father didn't fit our lifestyle. We decided to try setting aside a half-hour at noon to share whatever was on our hearts. We would set our work aside, no matter how pressing, and go out and sit on that swing and relax together. Soon we were both looking forward to it, and "swing time" was born.

If you gain nothing else from this book besides the subject of this chapter, your life and your marriage will be markedly enriched. Some of you may have found that you or your spouse really didn't find any of the four pursuits in the last chapter fully satisfactory. That is because a sizable number of us want *time* with each other more than anything else. And just because you may have found that one of the other pursuits is your primary desire does not mean this one can be glossed over. No matter what your heart desires and responds to most, no relationship can long be sustained without an investment of time.

I just want to share a word of caution. Before you go and set up your own swing time, I have found that too many of us don't really know how to effectively communicate with each other. Nothing kills the desire to spend time together more than experiencing it as an unpleasant, stressful time rather than something that binds our lives together in bonds of sympathy and understanding.

Let me tell you about Marvin and Sue. Sue called me one afternoon about a month after I had spoken in her church, and she was disturbed. "We heard your sermon on swing time, and we really liked the idea. So we started having swing time too, but after two or three weeks my husband won't do it anymore. Can you call him and talk about it?"

"No, Sue, I can't do that. If he is willing to talk about it, ask him to call me, and I'll be happy to discuss it with him. But I won't do it without his permission."

A few evenings later I heard from Marvin. "Jim, I am sick and tired of swing time! It has turned into lynch time! Every time I come home and we try to talk, she digs up something from the past and has my head in a noose before I know it. I'm tired of it. So I stay at work in the evening and don't bother to come home early."

"Marvin, you're within your rights to feel that way, and you are not alone. It is a common trap. When couples haven't communicated for some time, one or even both partners has a long laundry list of all the issues that were neglected when there was no communication at all. In many ways, our marriages are like a sink that has gotten clogged up and needs to be unclogged to restore a free flow, but all the garbage that has backed up can be very distasteful and the longer it sat there, the less we want to deal with it. That is why swing time, like every other aspect of the Christian life and family, must be guided by the impressions of God upon the heart. Your wife has all this stuff backed up, and when you showed willingness to deal with it, she was so thrilled that she started dumping on you. She is not used to asking God what she should share, anymore than you have been. She just tried to deal with things the best she knew how and made a mess of things as we humans are apt to do when we control our own affairs."

Marvin didn't say anything for a minute and then slowly admitted, "I guess that makes sense, but what about swing time? I don't mind talking, but I can't stand it the way we're going about it."

"Marvin, swing time is like any other period of discussion. The Bible says there is a time to speak and there is a time to keep silent. Both of you are going to have to learn which is which. You guys took the first step to effective communication—setting aside a time to talk—and that's good. Now comes the harder part of refining that time into a period of growth and enjoyment for both partners. This doesn't mean that you will never discuss difficult subjects, but that you will approach these hard things in God's timing and work together for a solution, rather than trying to pin the blame on each other."

"Wow, do I ever hear you! I was beginning to feel like Sue was judge, jury, and executioner."

"I understand completely, Marvin. Sally and I have had to work through many of the same issues. Let's get Sue back on an extension, and we'll see if we can get you guys back on the right track with something that really has the potential to transform your relationship." When Sue got back on the line, I went over what I had shared with Marvin and then continued, "Every relationship we have, be it in our marriages, our friendships, or even with our business associations, all will reflect our ability to effectively communicate. Whatever we practice at home tends to carry over beyond the marriage into our other relationships. For years, you two have stuffed down the hurts and ignored the conflicts between you, and I bet you do the same when others have hurt you or when you have a clash with someone in the office or the church as well. It is time you transform this bad habit into one of effective communication. The first step is to go back and revive swing time. But you're not going to go about it like you did before, are you?"

"No," they chorused.

"Good, then you have taken the first step. Use the time not only to discuss problems but also to choose to admire each other, to simply chat, to plan vacations, to dream like you did when you were dating; and when you do hit a difficult area, approach it like peeling an onion. Just take one small layer at a time, instead of trying to do it all at once. Each layer may have its share of tears, but you'll find that each layer you work through brings you that much closer to getting rid of the root or core issue."

"We tried that," Sue complained, "and it only made Marvin upset and angry."

"Well, if either of you find an area too painful or you find yourself beginning to get angry and wanting to force or compel the other to see it your way, it's time to table the discussion for another day. Never allow your feelings to have sway. Instead, strive to make this time pleasant for your partner. Even when the hard topics have to be discussed, reaffirm that you would rather be going through these hard things with them and not with anyone else."

"I hear what you're saying, Jim. But it's awfully hard in the heat of the moment to do that," Marvin confessed.

"You're right, Marvin. You can't do it on your own, and this brings us to the second principle in effective communication, which is an absolute must, especially when you are dealing with an area of conflict. Commune with God before you begin communing with each other. Ninety percent of the problems we have between husband and wife arise because we don't filter our words through God for His approval before we utter them. We are driven by emotion, passion, or impulse in the heat of the moment, and as you two have discovered, that very thing destroys swing time with its open communication. We have to learn, as it says in James 1:19, 'Let every man be swift to hear, slow to speak.' The golden rule of doing unto others as we would have them do unto us is an absolute must, especially with that special person we married.

"Filtering means more than just words. We can communicate volumes with attitudes and body language. We need to make sure we come into situations of communicating with others submitted to God, with self subdued, and our aim being to seek the will of God, no matter how much it crosses our desires. As it says in 1 Samuel 12:7, 'Now therefore stand still, that I may reason with you before the Lord.' Here is the key to effective resolution of a conflict. Reason must carry the day, and both parties must hold self and deportment in check as if they were in the presence of God, for though unseen He truly is present with us."

"Jim, that seems like a pretty lofty ideal. Are there really other couples doing this?" Marvin quizzed me.

"Yeah," Sue agreed, "I don't know of any."

"Yes, there are some," I assured them, "but you're right, not many. Thankfully those about us are not our example, and if the truth is told we don't want their kind of marriages either. The ideal we are striving for is to be Christlike in our conversations. 'The words that I speak unto you I speak not of myself: but the Father that dwelleth in me,' says John 14:10. Everyone can think of times when our words caused a problem in a relationship with someone we loved. Christ sometimes had to say hard things, but I have found that the times when I want to say hard things, to set someone right or straighten things out, are the very worst times to do it because my flesh is controlling me. And often when God asks me to deal with something hard, that's the very time I least feel up to the challenge of conflict. We cannot trust our feelings and must have the guidance of an all-knowing God whose timing is never wrong and who desires nothing but our happiness."

"Jim, I've tried to approach Marvin with the right spirit, but I never get to complete my thought or point before he's interrupting me. Then I get angry, and all my good intentions seem to go out the window."

"You're not alone, Sue. This is our third rule for effective communication. Each one needs time to express their concerns without interruption. Now anyone can sit and let someone else talk on, but it's a lot harder to be a good audience and show you are honestly receptive to what they want to say. There have been many times when I interrupted Sally or cut her off completely without actually saying a word. I didn't have to say anything because my body language clearly told her how I felt. By my impatient fidgeting, I conveyed the fact that I couldn't wait for her to hurry up and finish. Other times, my eyes betrayed me. If Sally didn't see any empathy or could tell that I was already planning my rebuttal, she'd clam up. Let me share a story.

"One day after Sally had gone off to town, she came home all excited and pleased with herself because she had purchased three pairs of blue jeans for the boys for twenty-one dollars each. Now, in our family Sally has always been the spendthrift. She is always more willing to part with a dollar than I am. The reason she was so delighted with her purchase was that the jeans were marked down from the list price of twenty-six dollars and she felt she had gotten a bargain. However, I wasn't so charitable in my judgment. I didn't even give her a chance to explain fully. I thought to myself, *There she goes again. She knows we can get jeans just as good for fifteen dollars a pair in the catalogue. What a waste!* I calculated it all out in my head and could clearly see she had lost eighteen dollars on the deal, the equivalent of another pair of jeans. Sally was trying to finish her presentation, but I stopped her and said determinedly, 'You can tell me anything you want, but it wasn't a good deal. You're taking them back.'

" 'But—'

" 'Forget it, Sally. Nothing you can tell me is going to change my opinion, so you might as well not waste your time.' I was right, wasn't I? I could see she was flustered and frustrated, but I just let it go. I knew she had made a bad deal, and I wasn't concerned about whatever silly impulse had urged her to purchase them. The problem in this situation was not, contrary to my opinion, my wife's shopping, but the fact that Jim *was not* listening. I wasn't hearing her out. I had interrupted her by making a decision before she had made her case, and once I had done that, I saw no logical reason to listen any longer.

"The next morning in my quiet time, the Lord brought the situation to my mind. While my opinion about the purchase hadn't changed, I realized I hadn't given Sally adequate time to express her reasons. Now I felt bad about it because I knew I hadn't treated her with the respect she deserved. I went to her that morning and confessed that I had cut her off and I wanted her to have the chance to say what she wanted. This has always been a trial for me because Sally expresses things in a much less direct manner than I do. I have a struggle because I need to provide her the opportunity to express things her way, in her personality. My natural tendency is to say, 'Come on, get to the point!'

"So, Sally, finally seeing I was earnest about letting her talk, explained, 'I know we could get them cheaper from the catalogue, Jim, but we need these for the month-long trip we are taking in just a couple of days. We would have never been able to get a catalogue order up here that fast unless we paid for express shipping, and if we did that they would cost more than the ones I bought in the store.'

" 'Why didn't you tell me that?' I queried. I mean, I'm reasonable. It made perfect sense when she explained it. Why hadn't she just told me that the day before?

"Sally just looked at me, a knowing smile playing about her lips, and in the quiet of the moment I could hear what she was saying: 'Because you wouldn't let me.'

"Now, Sue and Marvin, even though this wasn't a 'swing time' conversation, you can see how the same principles of communication apply. In Isaiah 41:1 God says, 'Let them come near: then let them speak.' If the God of the universe who, unlike Jim Hohnberger, never makes a mistake in judgment, invites failing human beings to come near and to speak to Him, God must have tremendous faith in the power of this communication principle. It's as if He's saying, 'Let them speak and do not interrupt them, even if they don't share in the most graceful way.'

"Jim, I can't believe you did that to Sally! I can't tell you how many times Marvin has done that to me. You really do understand, don't you?"

"Unfortunately I do, Sue, and it doesn't stop there. My son Matthew was a talker from the time he could first make sounds. When he learned words, they poured forth from him in an endless supply of childish prattle. It was so tempting to ignore him or shush him up. After all, I didn't have time for such nonsense. At least I thought I didn't. It's no wonder that when kids get to be teenagers, they won't talk to us anymore. If we establish a pattern of noncommunication early in their lives, it's just a natural outgrowth. If you have shut off a free flow of communication in your marriage or your family, it will require extra effort on you part to reestablish them, just as I had to go back to Sally and apologize for cutting her off.

"The other thing to remember in this category is the need to understand what is really being said, rather than just listening to the specific words that someone is using. Some people do not express themselves as clearly as others do, and we must give them the freedom to be who they are by listening for the intent of their conversation and not picking on their specific words. We do this in everyday conversation without thinking about it. If someone asks me to crack the window, I know that they don't want me to throw a rock at it and literally break it. Likewise, if you say, 'I'm going to run to the store,' I'm not going to assume you are lacing up your running shoes. If we can do this in everyday things, surely we can give others the same understanding in our conversations. The reason we often don't give each other that leeway is that we get hung up on what the other person says, and rather than dying to self and accepting what is said, we become defensive and then attack the *words* of the one who has dared offend us.

"God's kingdom does not operate on such a setting. He invites you to 'produce your cause, ... [and] bring forth your strong reasons,' as it says in Isaiah 41:21. If God is willing to hear, then we must hear others as well—not just the words, but also the meaning.

"The fourth principle to effective communication is to be *solution* oriented."

"What do you mean by that?" Marvin queried. "Isn't that the whole reason for discussing a problem in the first place?"

"You're right, but did you and Sue find any solutions in your discussions?"

"Well, no, just a bunch of hurt feelings and blaming each other."

"You are not alone. Most couples strive for a solution without being *solution oriented* and then are baffled when their attempts fail and they find themselves upset and angry. I found this out through hard experience when I started counseling couples. I would ask the wife what the problem was and she would go on for a while listing grievances, amid her partner's objections. Then I would let the husband give his perspective on the problem. He, too, would have his litany of complaints, and she would have her objections. This could go back and forth for hours, like a game of Ping-Pong. Meanwhile, no one was any closer to a solution."

"Sounds kind of familiar," Sue admitted with a rueful laugh.

"Sue," I said, "I had to learn this same lesson in my own marriage and family. We decided to change the way we were handling conflict in our family, and it has worked so well that we started recommending it to the families we counseled. After seeing the results we have never turned back to the old way."

"Don't keep us in suspense, Jim. What is it?" Marvin demanded.

"It's simple. We spend 5 percent of the time on the problem and then all the rest of the time looking for a solution. In truth, it only requires a few minutes to state a problem from every angle, and then we implement our family rule, which basically states that no one is allowed to talk again unless they are going to present a solution. If you think *you* have problems in this area, let me tell you about another couple who came to one of our seminars out West.

"Gerald and Linda came seeking help for their marriage. Linda was going to get a divorce because she just couldn't stand her husband. 'I've had it with his harshness, his negativity and complaining. I'm done with it and with him,' she explained.

"I looked at him and asked if this was true, and when he began to speak, he was so extremely negative that every word just seemed sour. His attitude was so disparaging, I began to see that there really was a huge problem here. Linda truly hadn't been exaggerating, as most partners tend to do when there is a problem to discuss. 'Is he always this way … so negative?' I asked.

" 'Yes.'

" 'Gerald,' I began as gently as I could, 'your habit of negativity is endangering your marriage. For it to have any hope at all, you must break out of this habit. For the rest of this conversation, in fact for the rest of this camp meeting, you are not allowed to say anything, not a single word, unless it is a compliment, affirming words, or unless you are bringing up a positive solution to the problems you and Linda face together. Now, Gerald, I don't know this for a fact, but I would guess that one of the reasons you're so negative about the people you live with is that Linda probably greets you with all her problems. And then the kids pile on their problems, and you've faced problems all day at work. You are probably sick and tired of problems.'

"I studied his expression, but he still didn't speak, just gloomily nodded as if he was dragging a huge burden. 'If you train your family to just state the problem and then look for a solution, the time spent on problems will be drastically reduced, and your home will become much more pleasant. Becoming solution oriented resolves a whole host of arguments and conflicts in the home. Will you do it?' Gerald just shrugged noncommittally. They left shortly after because as Gerald began to implement what I had said, the conversation ceased.

"The next day I ran into Linda. 'How's it going?' I asked.

" 'He hasn't spoken a word since yesterday.'

"Jim, that man makes Marvin look like an angel!" Sue exclaimed. "When you get a glimpse of what others face, it really makes you count your blessings. Whatever happened to them?"

"Well, Sue, Gerald's wife left him thirty days later. My heart really went out to him because I'm sure he had many fine qualities, but his habit of looking on the negative was so ingrained that it was going to require severe, prayerful effort on his part to overcome it, and he wasn't willing to make that investment. I had shared with Gerald that to be solution oriented sometimes means we have to move out of our comfort zone and maybe even choose to compromise on things that may not be necessarily right or wrong, just our preference. Everyone wants his own way, but to think we'll always get it is unrealistic and selfish in the extreme.

"Sally and I have had multiple conflicts over the years about what she wants to buy and what I don't think we need! One day Sally told me she wanted swing time about this subject. We each came armed with our arguments and stated our cases. We could fight for years about this one because we both felt strongly about the subject and there really wasn't a right or wrong involved. We just had different perspectives that led us to different conclusions.

"We laid the problem out in just a couple of minutes and then we used the same rule I shared with you and Marvin. We didn't allow ourselves to talk unless it was to offer a solution. Finally I told Sally, 'You have a right to to decide how to spend the money too. After all, it's as much yours as it is mine. What if we set aside a certain dollar amount each month for you to purchase whatever you desire? If I question it and you tell me the money came from that amount, then I'll not say another word.'

" 'Really?' Sally said enthusiastically.

" 'Sure. It'll be your own private kitty.'

" 'Yippee! I can get my new bathroom scale!'

"You see, Sally had wanted a new scale for a long time, but in typical male fashion I couldn't see anything wrong with the old one. Now she could have the little things she wanted without trying to convince me, which is, well, close to impossible. If you can catch hold of this simple principle, your home will be so much happier."

"Jim, that solution really didn't cost you that much, and it really made Sally happy. Maybe I can try that one with a couple of long-standing disagreements Sue and I have had. Things can't get any worse," Marvin expounded.

"You know, Marvin, one of the most solution-oriented people in the Bible was Daniel. After Daniel's capture and removal to Babylon, he had a problem in that his religious beliefs, the prohibitions given by God to avoid unclean meats, were not understood or accommodated by his Chaldean captors. The Bible, in Daniel 1:8, says that Daniel 'purposed in his heart that he would not defile himself with the portion of the king's meat, nor with the wine which he drank: therefore he requested of the prince of the eunuchs that he might not defile himself.' But when the prince, for fear of the king, refused his request, Daniel did not restate the problem, nor did he demand his own way. Daniel was solution oriented. He proposed another option and asked to try it for just ten days as an experiment. The man agreed this time, and God so blessed the trial that the prince of the eunuchs was convinced that Daniel's course was better and yielded to his wishes.

"If Daniel had stubbornly insisted on his way, the king would have gladly removed his head and our story would be over. Ironically, that is what most of us are doing. We are stubbornly insisting on our way as the only way, and most of us are losing our heads in the heat of argument."

"I never thought of Daniel's story in that way before. It's gives you a whole new perspective on an old story," Sue commented.

"I agree, Sue, and I think you're going to find the fifth principle just as helpful. It's what I refer to as 'time-out.' When I was playing football and things were going poorly, if the other team had us off balance or we were confused as to which play we should run, we could call a time-out and have a minute to recover our equilibrium. If you find a conversation is starting to deteriorate, if passions are rising, if emotions are stirred and threatening a loss of self-control, then either partner must be able to call for a time-out and the issue must be put off for another time, without argument. This principle is a lot harder than it looks and will require a choice based on principles, because after your passions are stirred the last thing you want to do is deny them expression. You will have to restrain your need to give vent to your feelings, and most of us *are not* used to that. I guarantee it will not be a pleasant thing to do the first few times, but the result of this exercise in self-control will sell you on its value. Just not having to face the result of words spoken in anger is worth every discomfort to self when the brakes are applied and the discussion is stopped for another time. Agreeing to allow time-out not only prevents a conversation from collapsing into hurtful accusations, it makes each partner more willing to listen to some hard things from the one they love because they know they can cut off the discussion if it gets to be too much for them.

"I once had a friend who asked me to tell him honestly about his faults, obviously not something I am keen to do, but this man had realized that something about the way he was acting was alienating other people. He honestly didn't know what it was. He asked me to share with him because as he put it, 'I know you will tell me the truth.'

"So I told him and had only listed two or three areas when he said, 'Enough, enough. I get the picture, Jim! I have enough here to work with.' And of course, I stopped. He had all he could handle, and he wanted a time-out. We need to do the same with those we love. The item we want to discuss may be a brand-new thought for them, and it is only fair that they be given time to consider it, just as we had time to consider it before we brought it up with them. Psalm 60:3 states, 'Thou hast shewed thy people hard things: thou hast made us to drink the wine of astonishment.' If you open up communication, real open communication, you may drink the wine of astonishment when you find out just what others are thinking. You may need some time to grapple with these new thoughts.

"When we demand that others give us an immediate response without time to consider, if they are pushed to respond in the heat of the moment, they will likely choose to follow the normal human in-clination to justify and defend themselves. Yet that same person, given time to prayerfully consider the matter, may humbly admit to being in the wrong and repent. Our attitude toward them, and the consider-ation we demonstrate in our conversation, has a lot to do with their willingness to respond and what their response will be."

"Good point, Jim. Sounds like I might get a more favorable an-swer from Sue if I was more willing to wait for it," Marvin said with a sigh.

"I know I have hit you with a lot of information, Marvin, but I want to share one last principle for developing effective communication. It's so basic to the Christian life, you'll probably wonder why I mention it, but it's something we all tend to do—harboring past wrongs. When we are confronted with a problem area in our life, it is the tendency in all of us to bring up the other person's past failings instead of dealing with the issue at hand. But if Sally is troubled by my temper, is it going to help the situation for me to discuss her lack of promptness? This doesn't mean you can't deal with past issues, but there is a time and a place for everything, and when she wants to talk about my temper, it is probably not the time to bring up her lack of promptness. If there are issues that haven't been properly dealt with in the past, those same character flaws are bound to resurface and cause present issues. That is the time to deal with them. In marriage, it is very easy to forget that our husband or wife is different today and to try and hold them in the mold of the past, without appreciating the growth and changes they have made, even if they are only small ones.

"I've shared a lot with you two. Do you think you can stand one more story?"

"Jim, you've given us renewed hope," Marvin admitted. "Go right ahead."

I didn't get a response from Sue, but I knew she was there because I could hear her pulling tissues from a box and then gentle rustling as she dealt with some tears. You see, she hadn't intended to drive Marvin away. She was still in love with him, but she just hadn't had the communication tools to deal properly with the situations in which she found herself once they started talking again.

"All right, Sue and Marvin, here it goes! We met Victor and Janis several years ago when I went to Victor for treatment. I had been injured and needed a specialist, and Victor was good. Even though he wasn't local to us, he had been recommended as the best person for my problem, and we started getting acquainted during the office visits.

"I found out Victor was a Christian, and his wife, Janis, who worked as his office manager, soon joined in our conversations. Before many months had gone by, we had visited in each other's homes and formed the beginning of a real friendship. So when we were scheduled to speak one weekend at a location relatively close to their office, we invited them to come to the meetings.

"We didn't know it, but these two dear people had never really talked in ten years. They lived in the same house, owned and worked in the same business, and were together in one way or another almost every day. They were raising two teenage children together and yet communication was essentially cut off, and they had erected enormous barriers between them. They came that first evening I was speaking, and they arrived from the office in two separate vehicles. Can you believe it? They took separate vehicles from the same office to the same speaking engagement, which shows you just how far they had pulled away from each other and the depth of the gulf that had grown between them.

"I had pre-planned my message that night, but as the time to speak drew nearer and nearer, I just couldn't get comfortable with presenting the message I had planned. The Lord seemed to be impressing me very strongly to change my message that night to one I had previously written called 'Wounding Their Spirits.' So persistent was this impression and so disquieting the idea of preaching the pre-planned sermon that I at last yielded and altered my message for the evening. When something like this happens, and it doesn't happen all that often, I know the Lord wants a different message shared. I don't know whose heart the Lord wants to touch; I just cooperate and let Him lead. This night was to be one of those rare nights when I was able to see exactly what the Spirit had in mind when He impressed me to change my sermon. I watched throughout the sermon as God's Holy Spirit strove with a human heart.

"That night as I looked out at that crowd it seemed that the only person I could see was Victor. 'Wounding Their Spirits' is a message about hurting the very ones we love with our words and actions, and I could see that this message was hitting home with him. He squirmed in his chair and fidgeted. At times he looked like a nervous horse getting ready to bolt. I wanted to go over and put my arm around him and say, 'It's OK. Let the Spirit do His work in your life. You won't regret it.' But of course, that was impossible without embarrassing the poor man, who was already upset enough. I did close by suggesting, as I usually do in that message, that if anyone felt the need to correct a past wrong, if they realized they had been wounding someone's spirit, that they should make it right that very night, either right there in the church or in the car on the way home, and not put it off. The very night when God is pleading with them is the very best time to take action and correct it, for never will His voice be louder nor will they ever find themselves more motivated than that very evening. If they let days go by, the inclination to make things right will fade, and whatever the Lord is bringing to their mind is too important to take that chance!

"I knew Victor had been convicted, so as I left the pulpit I headed toward him. I was afraid he would put off the impression, and I desperately wanted to encourage him to act, if it was at all possible. What happened next put my fears to rest. We stood there in the church aisle, and after looking me straight in the eye, he said, 'Janis, I've been hurting you for years and right here, in front of Jim and Sally, I want to apologize.'

"He kept his eyes riveted on me, as if fearful he might lose his courage if he looked at his wife. I glanced at her and noted the absolute shock on her face. I also knew that when a couple has had a breakthrough like this, you don't just stop it because of trivial things like bedtimes. So while I was sleepy, we encouraged them to continue their exchange, and for the next hour we talked. With another meeting coming in the morning, I finally had to say goodnight and drive to my lodging almost an hour away. Before I left, I said, 'You two really need to come to the meetings tomorrow. We will be covering a lot of things that will be very useful to you as you start over. You can come, can't you?' I asked, noticing the strange expression that now clouded Victor's countenance.

" 'No, Jim, I have previous plans.'

" 'What do you have that could be more important than what you are trying to do in your marriage?' I pressed him.

" 'Jim, you just don't understand. Tomorrow is the opening day of hunting season. My buddies and I always go together,' Victor explained.

"I could feel Sally stiffen beside me, indignant at his sense of values, and one glance at his wife revealed her bitter conclusion about her importance in comparison with his buddies. I tried a couple of times to get him to see the situation more clearly, but I saw his mind was made up, so I felt impressed to try a different approach. 'How would it be if Sally and I came over after our meetings Sunday? Then we can continue talking.'

"Victor agreed to that, and the following Sunday afternoon we found ourselves walking up the beautifully landscaped pathway from the drive to the front door of their impressive home. Set on a knoll, it was exactly what someone would expect of a 'doctor's home,' and through the ornate glass door, I caught a glimpse of Victor in his recliner—sound asleep. Janis let us in, told us they had sent their two teenage girls to a friend's home for the night, and in a hurried whisper admitted, 'We haven't spoken a word since Friday night!'

"I was wondering what I would find, and now I knew. I found myself very thankful we had offered to come and help them. You know, there are a lot of couples like Janis and Victor, who in spite of the breakthrough and Victor's confession only two nights before, just can't seem to be able to cross the void of noncommunication that has grown up between them. These situations grow to such insurmountable proportions and it seems so awkward, so impossible to overcome them that the couples just give up and accept what they have as if it were all they longed for. It is impossible for a couple whose marriage has fallen into such a condition to change, short of divine intervention and often the need for human intervention in the form of a mediator. This is never an easy step, for the one mediating must not only understand and be surrendered to God, but have cultivated the interpersonal skills in conflict management so they can steer the couple away from many harmful avenues of expression. We each need to understand that Satan loves it when he has married men and women in a position of noncommunication, for then they can never enjoy the fulfillment God designed they should find in each other, and that makes both partners vulnerable. He designs that once broken, these bonds shall not be re-established, and he encourages destructive communication that pushes the pair further apart. We can say things that are *true* but they are still hot-button issues specifically planned to rile the one we married. When we do this, Satan has caught us up in his plot, and we become pawns for his use to prevent a real solution.

"Victor and Janis had a new work to begin. They both longed for the possibility they saw before them but how to obtain it, they knew not. It seemed so far out of reach, but it really was not if they would be realistic in their aims. The first step was their desire to change. The very wish for something better is the strongest evidence that God has been working on the heart and has prepared the way for change in the life. They were not going to be transformed overnight, but that was OK if, and only *if,* they recognized it and cherished, indeed, celebrated the small steps in the right direction.

"We helped them follow the guidance of God's Spirit, and they went through the process of correcting the communication problems that had gone on for years. They decided on swing time twice a week, on Sundays and Wednesday nights. Furthermore, they each wanted a night in which they were allowed to lead out in the discussion, so they decided to take turns.

"They were hardly aware of it, but as I watched they began to speak more and more to each other and less and less to us. We had dinner together, and as we did the after-meal cleanup, the sink clogged up. 'I'll fix it,' Janis offered cheerfully, heading for the plunger.

" 'No, I'll do it,' Victor inserted.

" 'We'll both do it!' they cried in unison, laughing, sharing the first laugh I felt they had genuinely shared in a very long time.

"Well, they got the plunger in the sink, and crowding close to each other they plunged that sink with four hands as best they could amid their giggles.

" *'Burp!'* went the sink. *'Glug,'* went the drain as the water followed in a vigorous whirlpool. I wish you could have seen those two as they dropped that plunger and grasped hands in victory. He spun her around the kitchen in triumph. They looked like newlyweds again.

" 'Wow! Just look at you two!' I exclaimed. 'If you can do that with a sick sink, together you can handle anything that comes your way. We're going to go now,' I told the smiling couple as they gazed at each other, firmly locked in a tender embrace. 'I think you two can handle it from here!' And you know what? They could do it, and so can you!"

Let me close with the words of a young lady, whose parents have taken this principle of communication and used it to bring joy to their home, as well.

Learning to communicate in a new and different way,
Leaving arguments behind, having swing time every day.
It will truly change your marriage as you reason with each other
Opening your hearts to love and grace, one unto another.
　　　　　　　　　　　　　　　　　　　　—Janice Van Petten

Activities for Week 7

Sunday

Prayer time: Come close to God today. Commune with Him about whatever is the burden of your heart. Enjoy this special time with the Lord. It seems I've sent you to God frequently in this book, to obtain an open mind, and, yes, again that is what is most needed to gain a perspective of what might be, so you can begin to make the vision a reality.

Activity: Read "Swing Time."

Reflection: How did you relate to the week's chapter? Were you able to imagine you and your partner communicating in this manner? If not, why, and what could you do to remedy the situation? Remember that not every successful marriage uses swing time, but all provide for the need of communication in some manner.

Monday

Prayer time: Ask God to give you wisdom in setting up an experimental swing time with your spouse.

Activity: Plan your first swing time sessions as if you were a general and this project was your most vital battle. No matter how many issues you may have with your partner, keep in mind that this is a long-term investment in your mutual happiness, an investment from which you will never benefit if you chase your partner away by making the time miserable. Taking a day to plan will increase your odds of staying on track and creating a successful transition into a new activity.

Reflection: Do you have an approach that will work with your partner? Can it work, apart from the grace of God, on your heart and your partner's?

Tuesday

Prayer time: Ask God to help you cooperate with Him so that the one you love and want to visit with will see swing time as a positive development and in turn will be willing to cooperate with you in trying it.

Activity: Set up your swing time appointment. There is no perfect technique for doing this, other than asking God to lead and keeping a positive outlook toward your spouse, even if he or she seems reluctant. It might be best to set it up for Friday. You'll have more time to prepare, and often everyone is more relaxed at the end of the week.

Reflection: Was there some resistance? Compliance? Curiosity? Could it be because of the way you've dealt with problems in the past?

Wednesday

Prayer time: Now that your plans have concrete form, ask God what you can do to help the process along, if there is anything in your heart that needs to be taken care of ahead of time.

Activity: Whatever you felt impressed with in your prayer time should be dealt with. There are a number of environmental factors that can hinder effective communication. If the house is messy; if the children are running wild; if the meal flops; if you have allowed yourselves to worry over money; if you have allowed yourself to fall into fighting or bickering over whatever has ruffled your feathers, it is safe to assume that your first attempt at swing time may be less than productive. See what steps you can take to prevent some of the pitfalls I've mentioned.

Reflection: Did you find yourself having some nervous anticipation? Was it almost like a first date?

Thursday

Prayer time: In your quiet time with God, ask Him to help you review the principles of effective communication we learned last week. Remember they are tools given you by God to improve your relationships, but it is only as you use them under God's guidance that they will be as effective for you as He desires them to be.

Activity: Today's activity is to simply remind your partner of your scheduled meeting. Sounds simple, but to many women a man's reminder seems insulting to their intelligence, and for too many men, a woman reminding them seems an awful lot like nagging. So what do we do? You can do anything; use any method as long as you convey how much you are looking forward to the time with them. Act as if you have no worry about them forgetting. Stress its importance to you, and resist, no matter how hard, implying that they might forget to show up. They won't forget, and if you give them the chance to share in a nonthreatening manner, they'll soon be looking forward to swing time.

Reflection: Did it seem like a little too much work just to talk to your spouse? Remember everything worth having requires hard work.

Friday

Prayer time: Surrender to God and ask Him to make you ultra-sensitive to His impressions today.

Activity: If you set up your swing time for the end of the week, today will be your first one. The agenda is yours. If you have done your work well, it will become a regular feature in your life. Not every swing time will require such preparation, but it is important that in this first attempt nothing should be left to chance. Be sure to set up your next swing time now. If possible, schedule them regularly.

Reflection: Was it worth the work? I hope you have had an exciting glimpse of what it may be like in the future. Don't despair if it was a bit awkward; it will become more relaxed in the future.

Saturday

Reflection: Consider how important communication time is to a marriage. What have you learned that you can apply to your relationship with God?

CHAPTER 8

Removing the Thorns

"Because they have no changes, therefore they fear not God"
(Psalm 55:19).

CHAPTER GOAL

Each of us harbors characteristics and behaviors that irritate the one we love like a thorn in their flesh. Removing these is a vital part of our Christian walk. Seeing practical progress in our lives is essential both for our own encouragement and for the enlightenment of others.

I love cutting wood; there is just something about the task that satisfies me in a deep and personal way. Now, before you think I've been up in the wilderness too long, let me explain. I know it's hard work, and that is partly why I like it, but not totally. There is something else, something deeper, more intrinsic and harder to put into words, but nonetheless tangible and real.

For me, my wood represents freedom and independence. There is a tremendous sense of self-sufficiency to know we can heat our house, cook our food, and take long hot showers all for the price of our labor. Beyond the practical considerations of economics, there is something almost magical about a fire. Out of ordinary-looking pieces of wood pour light and heat in a fascinating, ever-changing display of flickering colors and crackling voice. A fire just lends itself to intimacy, banishing pretense and opening the spirits of all who gather around it. Even when you are alone in the wilderness a fire makes an utterly fine companion to spend the evening with, never tiring of your company while at the same time illuminating and sharing your innermost secrets.

With this attitude in their father my boys quickly learned to enjoy cutting wood, and by the time they were ten and twelve, there was almost nothing they liked so well as helping with the wood. And why not? I think the urge to wrest a living from the land, to make our way in the wilderness is as inbred and American as apple pie. In fact, all over the world people relate to my wilderness stories, perhaps because some long-dormant primal instinct recognizes familiar threads of life, long lost to us in that happy Eden home to which we all trace our roots. I truly believe that every man has, to some degree, the desire to live up to the rugged ideal of being a "real man," and my boys, as young as they were, liked cutting wood precisely because it was the "manly" thing to do.

Unfortunately their age, size, and still-developing judgment precluded them from using the chain saw and made it impossible for them to split the wood. They were tremendously helpful in loading, unloading, and stacking the wood I had cut and split. I loved their company, and I'm sure they knew it.

It was on one of these wood-gathering expeditions that Andrew let a chunk of split wood slide through his hands, and as it brushed by his hand on the way to the ground, it left a large, and I mean *large,* splinter embedded in his flesh. It really hurt. I knew it had to. I felt so sorry for the kid because I could just see this huge splinter sticking out of his flesh, and my first impulse was to remove it. Andrew would have nothing to do with this idea, so I suggested that he let his mother do it. After all, she's a registered nurse and she, I was sure, would be very gentle. But the very thought of removal was out of the question. This splinter, this thorn in his flesh, was painful, but the idea of taking it out was even more painful. Every parent can relate to his or her child having a splinter, and many a mom and dad have held a child down and with a maximum of misapplied strength removed the splinter from the child's flesh. But Sally and I decided that at ten, Andrew was old enough to learn an important lesson in life, so if he didn't want to remove it, we would wait until he did. We knew what would happen, and we explained to Andrew that swelling and infection were likely to set in as his body tried to rid itself of the foreign object. This would make his hand increasingly painful, and unless his body was able to expel the splinter, the infection could reach the point were amputation of the hand was necessary.

Now Sally and I had no intention of letting things go that far. We were confident that the pain in the hand would bring him around to the idea of removal long before he entered the danger zone, and that's exactly what happened. It took just a few days of pain and infection before Andrew approached his mother rather sheepishly and laid out his injured hand for her sympathetic care and the removal of the splinter.

The thought of removal was still scary. Big tears glistened in his eyes, but he was trying to be brave. In an incredibly short and painful time the splinter was out. True removal cost Andrew some pain and suffering. Removing the splinter might have even cost him some tears, but I won't confirm that because to me he was a hero. He had learned from his experience and had chosen a little hurt that he might obtain the greater pleasure of a life free of the pain and irritation the splinter was causing. In so doing, he vividly demonstrated the problem that exists in many, if not most marriages. Unlike Andrew, we have not learned to remove the splinters, and we continue to suffer needlessly.

What are the splinters or thorns in your partner that irritate or hurt you daily? I bet that even as you read this, one or two came to mind. If so, you have some thorns to be removed in your marriage. Generally what happens is that we look at these thorns and every time we've touched them they are so painful that we simply try and avoid the thorn in the future. As the years pass by, we find more and more thorns and they become increasingly painful, until at last not knowing how to remove them or because we are too afraid to try, we choose amputation and divorce our partner. Then we look for a new partner, whom we naively believe will have no thorns. Of course, we are living in a fantasy world when we think that. Our new partner may have a different set of baggage than our first, but we will start the same process all over again. How much better to fix what we have, and I don't believe that means lowering your sights and learning to be happy in a less-than-ideal situation.

No matter how hopeless your marriage seems, you can change it for the better. The exercises included in this chapter are not designed to transform your marriage in a week. Rather, they are specifically formulated to put you on the road of change and restore hope that maybe, just maybe, things can be different between you and your spouse. Before we get started, let's look at how the process has worked in the lives of others. So, join me at the front line as I find myself battling to save a marriage in the Midwest.

* * * * *

As Karl approached me during a weekend series, I knew something was amiss. He wore the worried, hunted look of one for whom the bells of fate are chiming. His face told me that he was only one step ahead of whatever unhappy fate awaited him. "Jim, can my wife and I talk with you after the meeting tomorrow? We need some counsel."

"Well, yes … we have some time in our schedule," I replied, but I could tell from the expression on his face that there was something more. "Is your wife interested in counseling too?"

"No, Jim, she isn't," he said, reluctantly opening up. "She's willing to come, but she's already made up her mind. She's going to file for divorce first thing Monday morning."

Now I understood why he looked so worried. "Tell your wife I need just fifteen minutes of her time. If she sees no hope after fifteen minutes, she is free to go her own way."

Karl looked extremely doubtful, as if hesitant to risk everything on a fifteen-minute gamble, but as he had nothing better to offer, he nodded glumly and shuffled away. His reaction was fairly typical, and even though I knew little about Karl or his wife and the problems they faced, I could almost guarantee you that those problems had been discussed, rehashed, and argued about for hours, days, weeks, maybe even years with no resolution. It's no wonder he was doubtful about my fifteen-minute solution. Are you? Is there a better way? I think so.

Unfortunately most of us grow up never learning how to solve problems—practically. Our parents, teachers, and friends all had their own individual "coping mechanisms," which often involved things like the silent treatment, sweeping it under the carpet, or arguing about it for hours. If we're honest, we know that none of them really worked, and we also know that it really only takes a few moments to state the problem, right? And if we were to allow ourselves the few moments it really takes to state the problem, doesn't it seem that we would have a lot more time to talk about solutions? Let's see what happens with Karl and Mary.

Mary was waiting with Karl at the close of the next day's meetings, and her attitude stunk. I don't know how else to describe it. We hadn't even spoken a word, but her demeanor plainly stated that nothing I could say or do was going to change her mind. She had in essence already decided to amputate. Mary had only come out of a sense of obligation. It was almost as if she was saying, "I don't want everyone to view me as the bad guy, so I'll go, but in fifteen minutes I'm out of here!"

My heart sank. From a human standpoint, the whole situation looked bleak, and I could think of a hundred places I'd rather be. I had no assurance that everything would work out just fine. There are many that claim to be Christians and perform so-called "Christian counseling," but do not provide godly counsel. Even the minority that does cannot read the future of every case they handle. No, to provide godly counsel is to persevere when all seems hopeless, not because we know the outcome, but because we know God and the love He has for the troubled individuals with whom He brings us in contact. And gathering courage from this thought, I faced Mary.

"Mary, I'm not going to beat around the bush. I want to ask you three questions. Will you answer them honestly?" I could tell from her expression that my approach had surprised her. She had come expecting me to lecture her, and she had steeled herself to endure for fifteen minutes. But now things had shifted. They weren't following her preconceived ideas, and she showed just a hint of interest.

"Go ahead and ask," she replied coolly, unwilling to commit to answering.

"What is it about Karl that really bothers you?" I queried and pressed on to clarify this first, but oh so important, question. "What are the two things he does that are like thorns in your flesh—constantly annoying and irritating you?"

Mary thought for just a moment, and usually that's all it takes when you ask such a question. The spouse can almost always tell you exactly what the problem with their partner is, and Mary was no exception.

"I'll tell you what really irks me about this fellow," she said, gesturing angrily at her husband. "He goes to church and puts on the big show—pretending that he is religious and spiritual. Everyone listens to his discourses, and they all think he's a wonderful spiritual man. Ha! I wish they could see him at home! Do you know what he does every night at home?"

I just looked at her questioningly, waiting for her to continue. Her manner was hardly Christlike, but I understood the underlying frustration that was causing it. She continued, "He sits at home and watches that disgusting wrestling every night. What about me? What about our children? Why doesn't he have as much interest in us as in those vile programs? It's like he's in love with them."

"And have you talked with him, confronted him about it?" I asked.

"Yes, I have! And you know what his response is when I don't do what he wants? He threatens to divorce me! He is always blowing off his big mouth! That's all he ever does—talk big. Well, I've had it. He's always threatening me with divorce ... so I'm filing and good riddance!"

I paused for a moment, seeking God's guidance before I asked my second question. "Mary, if he were to change—if Karl would agree to put away his wrestling programs for the next thirty days and concentrate on you and the children, would you agree to hold off filing for divorce until thirty days are up?"

Mary sat quietly as she digested what I had said and then turned her gaze from me to her husband. I wish you could have seen the look on her face and the scrutiny and contempt with which she searched his soul. I felt kind of sorry for him there on the hot seat, even though I knew he shared blame for the crisis they now faced. Then she turned back to me and said, "Him? Impossible!"

So I faced Karl and asked, "Do you understand the seriousness of what we are talking about here? Do you hear what Mary is saying? And she is right, you know. It is impossible for you to do what I'm asking of you, no matter how much you may desire it. Karl, you must realize here and now that batteries are not included." I explained his powerless condition and provided a quick overview of the solution. "Are you willing to take the next thirty days and focus on your family, living for the first time as a man led of God and not of yourself?" I entreated him earnestly.

His response was sincere and thoughtful. "Anything, Jim. I'm at rock bottom, and I don't want to lose my wife and family. I really want to be a Christian, but I just never knew how. No one ever explained it in a practical way that made sense before. Yes, I'm willing to do whatever it takes."

Mary sat impassively, taking it all in. I know she saw Karl's sincerity, yet she was still skeptical. "And what about his threats to divorce me?" she demanded.

I amended my earlier statement, and Karl again agreed that for the next thirty days there would be no wrestling and no threats, just a prayerfully dedicated commitment to his wife and family.

"Well, Mary, the ball is in your court. You've heard what Karl has agreed to. Now are you willing to give him the thirty days to begin the process of healing in your marriage?" Silence greeted my question, and as the moments became minutes, the tension grew and grew until I thought the room would burst. The normal human response is to try and say something to ease the tension. Thankfully, the Lord has taught me that this is the very time to keep quiet and let His Spirit do the work unhindered. Alone in that uncomfortable silence, Mary struggled for five long minutes, while I prayed. I'm sure Karl prayed too. Whatever she chose, we knew it would be final. After what seemed an eternity, she looked up and quietly answered, "Yes."

Karl and I didn't leap to our feet and shout, "Praise God," but I know I sure wanted to. Karl looked as if someone had taken a ton of lead off his shoulders. He knew he wasn't out of the woods yet, but there had been a reprieve and he still had a chance to salvage his situation.

"Mary," I said, "I'm delighted to hear your decision. I know it wasn't easy, nor will the next thirty days be either, because change is always hard. So far, Mary, we have been talking about Karl's part—the work he must do, but marriages are always made up of two. Karl has been willing to remove the two thorns that most annoy you. Are you willing to do the same for him?" I asked my third question cautiously.

Another long silence filled the room. You see, she thought he was going to do all the changing. This was going to call for self-denial on her part. It took about half as long as the first time, and she finally said, pensively, "Well, what are they?"

Not the most enthusiastic reply I have ever received, but it was enough. I turned to Karl. "What are the two biggest thorns in Mary's life that bother you?"

"Jim, do you know why I stay up watching wrestling every night?"

"No, Karl, I don't. It's such a stupid thing; I can't imagine what the attraction is. You know it is all fake, don't you?"

"Yeah, I know, but Mary takes the kids to bed with her every night ... in our bed."

"Is that true, Mary?" She nodded and then had a case of what I call the "Yes, but's," which was her long list of reasons for doing it her way. I pushed them aside because we were not trying to debate who was right and who was wrong. We were after a solution. "Mary," I said gently, "do you hear what Karl is telling you?" She did. She knew he felt pushed out of his own bed. Then we moved on to Karl's second thorn with Mary, which was her continued breast-feeding of the two-year-old. Now you can debate the subject of how long to breast-feed. Everyone has a different opinion and study to support their pet theory. But the real issue with this couple was that in breast-feeding Mary received positive feelings about herself—feelings her marriage and her husband were not providing her, so of course she was hesitant to give those up. Yet the very thing she was clinging to as a positive was becoming a negative and coming between her and her husband. At length, Mary agreed to wean the two-year-old and start training the children to go to sleep in their own beds.

I was thrilled with her willingness but felt constrained to remind her just as I had with Karl that "batteries were not included." I told her that her success was dependent on learning to make God the central and ruling Power in her life. I shared with her how to listen to and obey God, just as I did in the first chapters of this book. This time when she looked at me, I saw a different Mary. "I've been a Christian all my life," she began, "and no one has ever explained Christianity like this to me. There have been times when Christ was real to me, but they have only been selected moments. Now I see what I have been missing all these years—a continual connection with Jesus. Thank you!" she ended enthusiastically.

Mary's expression had changed. The hostility was gone, and she truly was a different Mary. Both Karl and she had smiles on their faces and were ready to make a new start. "Couldn't you move your ministry here?" Karl asked wistfully.

I smiled understandingly. I knew what he was really saying. They were ready to make a new start, but there was no one nearby who understood and could help them through their problems as they struggled to start over. This is representative of what Sally and I find everywhere we travel. Marriages are in a deplorable condition and the traditional resources for help, be they counselors, ministers, or friends and families, are unable to truly help resolve the problems couples face.

I have always approached counseling from the perspective of what I know has worked in my life and the lives of others. Too few of those who seek counsel take time to examine the lives and marriages of those who would advise them to see if what they are suggesting really works. In many ways, the changes you are asked to make to save your marriage require a leap of faith, and it is perfectly reasonable to ask the same question I would have asked the Wright brothers if they had suggested I fly in their new airplane: "Does it fly?" If you get, "Well, based on the latest studies, it will," or "Dr. So-and-So developed it after years of field testing," or even "scientific analysis indicates this should work," walk away. All you want to know is if it flies! Is it working in their marriage? Has it transformed others? Show me that and I don't need a government study to validate your principles. So with this in mind, let me share one of the thorns Sally and I had to remove from our marriage.

Long after Sally and I had worked out many of the problems we faced as a couple, we developed and cultivated a thorn that irritated both of us, but it took us a while to realize it for what it was and remove its painful influence from our lives. Let me share an example with you. I was in my own little world concentrating intently on a piece of correspondence when Sally startled me out of my thoughts. "Jim, where do you want to go on vacation this year?" she asked.

What is she talking about? Where did this question come from? I thought. *I don't want to be bothered with this right now.* So I tuned her out and went on with what I was doing. Not getting a response, she must have assumed I didn't hear and quit asking. Well, little sins never stay little for long, and I developed the habit of ignoring Sally whenever I was otherwise occupied. So now the scenario went like this: Sally's voice drifted up from the kitchen, "Honey, what would you like for lunch?" Again I didn't answer, even when she asked again ten minutes later. I had gotten so used to tuning her out that I hardly even noticed. Sally was beginning to catch on to my little trick and felt very hurt and offended. No one likes to be ignored, especially when the offending party shows up for lunch and says, "Why did you make *that?*" It is a tribute to Sally's self-control and patience that I didn't end up wearing some of those meals.

I was bothered by Sally's interruptions, and she was deeply troubled about being ignored. When we discussed our feelings and looked for a solution, we discovered that the solution was simplicity itself. Sally agreed to try and keep nonessential questions for a time when I was mentally free, and I agreed that when she asked a question that required an immediate response I would give her the courtesy of making it my priority and give her the information she wanted. Further, I agreed that if Sally interrupted me with a question that didn't need an answer that moment, I would take a second to write it down and assure her I would talk about it as soon as I was free.

Nothing we came up with was an earth-shattering breakthrough in counseling, but let me tell you, the effects in our relationship were marvelous. I no longer felt interrupted because at most, all I had to do was provide a short answer or write down the subject for later discussion, and Sally no longer felt slighted and ignored.

What I am sharing with you has worked in my marriage, and "removing the thorns" continues to work for us. When each person agrees to remove a thorn and is willing to practice it for thirty days, they will have a new habit, and this new habit will transform the character. Now just because we start a new habit does not mean we cannot go back to the old habits. We do that quite naturally. The thirty days only gets you on your feet. It may take another thirty, sixty, or ninety days to eradicate an old manner of reacting and learn a new one, but what a blessing this brings, as peace and harmony take the place of arguing and bickering, and love and contentment replace hurt feelings and bitter spirits.

This is so simple anyone can understand it, although the implementation may be difficult. As one man told me during a counseling session, "Jim, if you and Sally were not here right now, we would be at each other's throats." It was probably true, too. Many couples will need a mediator to help them remove the thorns because these problems are often such long-standing irritants and the old methods of dealing with them so ingrained that no resolution is possible without some outside intervention. So it was with my friends Connie and David.

I was shocked to see Connie and David threading their way through the crowd to speak with me. I had counseled with their family some months before, but that was more than 600 miles from where we were now. I knew something had to be brewing to induce them to make that long wearisome drive. Vivid memories of their family flashed through my mind in little snippets. First it was David—the leader, super achiever, respected and well-liked by everyone, but harsh and critical at home. Then there was Connie— sweet, affable Connie, who could be a little flighty at times. And last but not least, the two teenagers who, like their mother, just couldn't measure up to Dad's drive and determination. The whole family had been shaken pretty badly when it came out that both of their teens had lost their virginity and lost it in the Christian church and school among associates who were supposed to protect them. They had talked and prayed with us and had been determined to change their home for the better. Now six months later, I could see despair written all over their faces.

"It's just not working for us, Jim," Connie blurted out almost accusatorily. After all, I had taught them about practical Christianity and had encouraged them to try and implement the principles. "All we do is constantly fight, constantly squabble. It just doesn't work for us," she finished hopelessly.

I looked at David, but he just nodded in acquiescence. Then he explained, "The kids are in rebellion. They wouldn't even come with us. Things have gone from bad to worse in their dress, their music, and language. We can't even reason with them anymore. They're so different from what we tried to teach them, so worldly. Why, Jim? Why?"

I paused and then asked tentatively, "Well, David, what are they viewing at home?" Connie shot David a knowing look. I ignored it and went on. "Do you two want to save your children or not? It's up to you."

The question seemed to jar them back to their senses, and they both answered me with a resounding, "Yes!"

"Good," I said. "I thought you did, but if that is truly your desire, then you are going to have to do as Christ did in John 17:19, where He says, 'For their sakes I sanctify myself.' For the sake of your children, you are going to have to sanctify yourselves. And that means doing everything different than you've ever done before. In a practical sense, this means that for the past few months the motivation of wanting a peaceful home and a better marriage was insufficient to actuate in you the changes necessary. It is not uncommon and God knows that to save those we love we will often do things that we might not do just for ourselves. If you are to win your teens' hearts back you are going to have to learn to live in your home the religion you profess in public."

"We can't! We haven't, and we've tried, Jim, really tried!"

"I know you have tried, and, yes, I know you can't, and I'm glad you see that you know it, because now you are in the most hopeful condition for God to do a mighty work in your lives. You see, because you realize now that you are powerless to reform your lives, you are finally motivated to place you dependence upon God, and every one of your past failures acutely reminds you that if you find the victory, it is God in you and not of yourselves. It will be only His grace and not your strength and wisdom. Here is how it works." I shared with them as I have earlier in this book the secret to making Christianity work in the real world—in our homes and with our families. "When you two change the way you relate to each other and transform your relationship, you will, without having to say a single word, influence your children to make the same life-changing choices you have faced. Are you both willing to remove those thorns—those stumbling blocks in your relationship so that your children may see God revealed and working in your lives?"

"Yes, Jim, we are desperate," David said. "We hate what is happening to our children, and we are really uncomfortable with each other. Sure we would like to change things, but we have known so much failure it doesn't seem possible that this can reach our children."

"Listen, Dave, I have faith in what I am telling you. It *will* work. At least try it. Ladies first, so let's start with you, Connie. What are the two areas that bother you most about David?"

She thought for just a couple of moments and said, "Well, he is always negative. He is always putting me down, telling me what I'm doing wrong and what my failures are. It gets so discouraging I don't even want to try sometimes."

"Is that true, David?"

"Yes ... well, sometimes," he hedged a bit, and I could see he had something he wanted to add, but I asked him to hold on until Connie was finished.

"Go on, Connie," I encouraged, turning the floor over to her again. "What is the second thorn that's hurting you?"

"I just wish he would be the spiritual leader in our house that everyone else thinks he is in public. He talks a good game, but he doesn't do it at home."

We discussed this for a little bit, and David admitted these things were true and that he needed and wanted to overcome them. So we worked out a solution for him to begin that process. For the next thirty days, he agreed he would say only encouraging words to his wife. And if he couldn't think of anything pleasant to say, he would say nothing rather than offend her as he had in the past. For the second aspect on his road to change, he agreed to take over the role of spiritual leader in the home and lead the family devotional time. And finally, he was going to begin taking the lead in discipline issues rather than passing the buck or, in this case, the child, to the mother. He saw that to have the time to do this, to be involved with his children, he would have to sacrifice the time he normally spent looking at or reading the news. No longer would he be able to stay late at work, and cruising the Internet was going to have to be a thing of the past. It was going to involve a lot of self-sacrifice, but I could tell by the look on his face that David was willing to let go of these areas if he could obtain what he desired. I looked at David for a moment and then I asked, "What is Connie's side in all this? What are the two thorns she has that are bothering you?"

Immediately he replied, "Jim, if she'd only stop undermining me in front of the children. She belittles me and talks about the lousy job I did on this or that. I know I'm not perfect, but she destroys my ability to lead. My second area is when we make a decision and I think we are working together, I find out she doesn't enforce it or starts to but then refuses to carry through. I'm frustrated! She wants me to lead, but I don't get a whole lot of cooperation!"

As we began to discuss the other side of the situation, Connie was vehement. "I have serious concerns and need to be able to voice them." This is a very common problem among families where the wife has been forced by the default of the husband to assume both roles. She wants him to lead, but she is a little low on faith that her husband is going to do everything right, so she wants to help him a little and keep him on track. Women honestly do not view these little suggestions and course corrections as nagging, but unfortunately men do.

We decided that Connie would bring her concerns to David only when they were out of the hearing of the children. Secondly, Connie agreed that when they made a change, she would write it out on a little index card and keep it in her pocket, consulting it often. That way she could improve the follow-through. She realized that she tended to abandon new programs, not because she didn't want to change, but because old habits seemed to take over and often she couldn't remember what she'd agreed to do.

At this point I wish I could show you their faces. Hope had been restored! With smiles wreathing their faces, we shared a beautiful, heartfelt prayer and said goodbye. They called me three weeks later and exuberantly explained, "We just had to tell you what's going on. We want you to know we have a happy home now! In just the three weeks we have been on this program, our children have seen the changes in us and are already changing and starting to do the things we always wanted them to do. We didn't believe you when you said the way to reach our young people was to change ourselves, but it was true, and it is working for us."

Friends, it can work for you as well. Remove the thorns from your relationships, and when you get rid of one, remove another and another. In a year's time you'll find you've taken care of four, six, or even eight thorns, and very few relationships have more than that. It is a simple method but so very rewarding. May God guide you through the exercises as you allow Him to get out His divine tweezers and begin the process of removing the thorns in your life.

Activities for Week 8

Sunday

Prayer time: Ask God to remove the defensiveness that just seems natural with the sinful flesh we all share and give you a sense of objectivity. Ask Him for the wisdom and courage to deal with whatever problem area comes up.

Activity: Read "Removing the Thorns." Do you see yourself, your marriage, or your home displayed? Prayerfully reflect upon the areas in your partner that bother you, and then contemplate what they might dislike in you if given the opportunity to honestly share their feelings.

Monday

Prayer time: You must seek God for a full and complete surrender because today's activity can escalate into a full-blown fight unless approached and carried out with the Spirit's guidance.

Activity: Approach your partner with the concept of removing the thorns. Be positive about what you will be gaining as a couple. This is especially important if your partner has not yet read the chapter. If you make this sound like a trip to the woodshed, your opportunity is probably lost. All you want today is a commitment to try this concept. The specifics will be worked out in the following days.

Tuesday

Prayer time: Seek God's guidance as to the best manner to begin. Ask His Spirit to impress your mind with the correct course to follow. You want to do this differently than you have in the past or you will find yourselves back in the same old pitfalls. Remember there is nothing magical about the techniques. They are simply tools to be used as God directs you.

Activity: Prayerfully contemplate your relationship. Consider how you react to each other under stress and try and determine if an intermediary would be helpful. An intermediary need not be a professional counselor or minister. It can be anyone whose spiritual maturity is evident and whose judgment you trust. Many couples feel more comfortable with another couple. This is fine as long as they are committed to loving and helping you. They need to have a proven track record of keeping confidences. Sometimes the couple you choose may have a thorn or two they wish to deal with, in which case both couples can help and encourage each other. As a basic rule of thumb I have found that if either partner thinks it might be needed, it is needed. If you decide you need an intermediary, did anyone come immediately to mind?

Wednesday

Prayer time: Ask God for special tact and diplomacy today. You are going to be very vulnerable if you are asking someone else for help and even more vulnerable if you two are committed to going this course alone. Be sure to stay surrendered and open to God's leadership.

Activity: Approach the counselor(s) and ask them if they would be willing to help you pursue a conference to implement the process of change as outlined in this chapter. Share the chapter with them and set up a future date to begin the discussion.

Reflection: Did you find it difficult to seek help or even to admit amongst yourselves that you were having problems? Why is this?

Thursday

Prayer time: Draw close to God this morning and seek to lose yourself in Him, that you may go into your day submitted and willing to consider openly and objectively your partner's point of view.

Activity: If the two of you are going to try it alone, set aside some time to go for a walk or some similar activity and prayerfully share your concerns. Remember when sharing difficult things to avoid direct eye contact and confrontational body language. Phrases such as, "you never," "you always," and "can't you ever," are not only untrue but slam the door shut when you're communicating. Spend only five minutes sharing the problem and then share nothing that is not solution-oriented. Remember if you get stuck or in trouble, *do not* continue. Table the conversation until later, and if you still can't talk civilly to one another, then you need a mediator. If you have already planned on using a mediator, use today to plan your discussion and presentation of the problem in such a manner that it will be as nonirritating to your partner as possible.

Reflection: Did you find the very thought of discussing your problems makes your pulse race? Were you uncomfortable? What can you do to make yourself more approachable?

Friday

Prayer time: If you have decided to remove some thorns, ask for divine help in doing so. Remember your job is to remove whatever bothers your partner. It's up to them to remove the thorn that bothers you; concentrate upon your own task. If you are awaiting a mediator, decide right now that you are going forward no matter how painful it may be to your self-will. If you do this, you will be much better prepared when the time comes.

Activity: If you have a predetermined thorn to remove, your hour has come. Go forth in the strength of God and expect great things to happen. Be merciful if you partner is having trouble changing, just as you want them to treat you mercifully should you slip into old habit patterns. If you haven't yet talked about thorns, pick something you believe your partner dislikes and work at eliminating it right now without being told.

Reflection: Did you find it hard to change old ways and attitudes? If you and your spouse are involved in removing the thorns, did you see them putting forth effort to change? If so, encourage them by expressing your appreciation. Remember no one learns to do these things perfectly overnight. Just as a baby experiences setbacks in learning to walk, there are going to be some falls and bruises as you are learning.

Saturday

Reflection: Enjoy the day with God and rejoice that you have begun the process of change. This is the greatest evidence that God is working in your lives!

Part 3

Empowered Family

CHAPTER 9

Independent Atoms

"If a house be divided against itself, that house cannot stand"
(Mark 3:25).

CHAPTER GOAL

May we see in the stories of others an explanation of what has happened to the family and be motivated to correct these problems at any cost to ourselves.

I don't get to go back home very often to the town where I grew up. And when I do, my time is consumed with family obligations, so I rarely see the friends that I grew up with, but once in a while it happens. Our paths cross and we middle-age men stare out at each other through eyes that last saw us in the prime of life. We introduce our families and talk about the intervening decades, lingering at the goodbye, knowing that such a chance meeting will probably never happen again and this fare-well will likely be the final one we are privileged to exchange.

But last year was different. I had a conversation with a friend that transcended the bonds of the superficial. He turned to me and asked, "What's happened to us, Jim? I've lost my kids, and it's not just me, most of us have. And yours—they're still happy and, well, innocent. What happened, Jim?"

I assured my friend that what happened to him was no accident or twist of fate, but rather the logical outcome of a carefully set and cleverly disguised trap. This trap has captured in its jaws parents and youth, and like some vicious beast is tearing the very fabric of our families apart. I shared with him a short version of the same story I now share with you in depth, the story of independent atoms and the plot to accomplish it.

****

The alarm clock's jarring notes awaken thirteen-year-old Katie Miller, and she groggily hits the snooze button, claiming a few more moments of rest. Three snooze-alarms later, at 5:09 A.M., she finally turns on the clock radio and drags herself out of bed to the bathroom. Then she turns her attention to the algebra problems she didn't get to last night. Her pencil scratches away as she sings along with the song. She glances at the poster of the artist on the wall; the singer's bare chest and tight pants add a certain something to his words about love and create strange longings within her. She wonders about her friends, whether they think and feel as she does. With a final glance at the poster, she sighs wistfully and returns to her work.

After a quick shower, in which she is alternately roasted or frozen as everyone in the family tries to use the water at once, she spends a frustrating half-hour trying to decide what to wear from a closet overflowing with things she doesn't like anymore. Moody over her outfit, she joins seven-year-old Caleb at the kitchen table for some cold cereal. Mom is on the phone with the office while loading the dishwasher. Dad's car is gone, and she remembers something about him having an early sales call. There is no sign of Nancy, her older sister, so she must have left already. Sure enough, it's just a few minutes to seven, and Nancy had an early class.

Mom hangs up, looking flustered. "Katie, my meeting's been changed. Can you see Caleb to the bus before you go? If I don't leave now, I'll never make it in the morning traffic."

"OK," Katie mumbles, her mouth full, "but I can't wait with him. My bus leaves ten minutes before his."

"That's all right. If you get him down there, he'll be fine for ten minutes. I've got to go. See you after field hockey."

"Better get your books together," Katie tells her brother a few minutes after Mom leaves. There's no response. "Caleb, we have to get going!" Nothing. She looks up and screams, *"Caleb!"*

He looks up from the television cartoons and yells, *"What?"*

"We have to *go,* that's what!" She stomps over to the TV and turns it off.

Caleb heads for his room to gather his books, looking very sullen and mumbling under his breath. There on top of the stack is the permission slip for his field trip. He forgot it last night because they got home so late. "Oh, no!" he wails, bursting into tears.

"What's your problem now?" Katie demands from the doorway. After he explains, she takes the slip and signs it, *K. Miller.*

"Is that OK?" he asks with a little trepidation.

"Sure it is. Mom and I have the same initials anyway."

Hustling to the bus stop, Katie barely squeezes in before her bus pulls away. She glances back at Caleb's forlorn little frame. He looks sad and lonely as he prepares to wait the long ten minutes until his bus arrives.

School is a whirlwind of activities, and by four-thirty Katie is playing field hockey. After the game, she sees her mom pull into the parking lot. Eagerly she runs to meet her, hoping to share all the news of the day, but Mom is on her cell phone coordinating the evening's activities with Dad. Caleb is already at his after-school program but will be done at five, and Mom is rushing to drop Katie off at the piano teacher's so she can pick him up on time. It's across town, and she would never be able to make it back in rush-hour traffic to pick up Katie, so Dad will get her on his way home, and they will meet Mom and Caleb at the orthodontist's.

Later, with her braces newly tightened, Katie doesn't feel much like eating. She only has ice cream at the fast-food joint and reads a few pages of a novel a friend has lent her while her family eats.

With one last stop to pick up the poster board she needs for a biology project, the family reaches home long after dark. It has been twelve hours since Katie left, and now there's homework to do. She works away in her room, distracted only by her stereo and the frequent calls of friends on the telephone. She takes a short break to watch her favorite television show and sips diet cola. She worries about her weight. It's so hard to stay thin.

By eleven she's done and turns to gossiping on the phone with her best friend. When Mom calls goodnight through the closed door of her room, she doesn't bother to reply. She's too busy telling her friend how she would just die if she met "him" in person, her eyes studying the poster again.

Katie Miller is a pseudonym, yet she represents a whole host of young people today who live with, and yet, apart from their families. Without a conscious choice, they have become victims of the greatest Trojan horse ever given to the human race. In many ways we are just like the ancient Greeks, falling for things that look valuable, right, and edifying. We seem powerless to see that the very things we embrace are those which seek to kill us. It is no accident that life in the twenty-first century is a constant and never-ending chase after things, which for the most part elude us. Why?

Let's turn the pages of history back about six decades to somewhere around 1945 near the end of World War II. Amid a beautiful grove of trees, where the hillside forms a natural amphitheater, a strikingly handsome being is addressing a small group of followers. With a majestic voice and kingly bearing, Satan confides in his chief imps. "Families!" He rants, pacing before them. "I control most of this world, but I can't accomplish half as much as I want because of their lousy families! Well, we shall put an end to this!

"We must lay our plans carefully because ever since that first marriage in Eden, families have endured wars, famines, political and social unrest. Amid all the upheavals in society, the family units continue to function. We have damaged them to be sure, but still they stand, however imperfect, like a scarred yet still mighty citadel protecting their members from a thousand avenues of our influence. We must change this! Families can never be fully eliminated, so we must undermine their protective influences while leaving the shell intact and apparently healthy. We must separate the members of the family into so many different parts that they resemble *independent atoms.* Yes, yes, I can see it all now," he chuckles with diabolical glee. "To accomplish this task will require all our craftiness and the patience to wait decades for the results … but it *will* be worth it.

"First, bring them prosperity! Prosperity has always been our ally, and never has the church done well under its influence. Now let's try it on the family. Use their reasoning strengths against them. Have them place their emphasis on education. While this helps them in the short term, they will never see the jaws of the trap, which we will be setting for the oncoming generations. Remember that those going to college now are mature men, aged beyond their years by war. They know what they believe and are settled in their beliefs. The young people of future generations will not be so fortunate. They will be easy prey to our influence both from their professors and their peers.

"Remember how we nearly destroyed the children of Israel at the borders of the Promised Land? Entertainment opened the way to infidelity, and so it shall again. We shall use their new technology to full advantage and while television may take generations to alter their perceptions fully, we have *never* had such an open invitation into their homes. We won't just use television, but every other medium of communication too. We will work the *sensual* into advertisements, articles, and photographs, just as we did in Sodom. By beholding they will become changed, and best of all, they will never know it. Ha! Ha! Ha! I love it," he laughs, and his evil angels listen in awe. The mood turns serious again as Satan continues, "Most important is their time. We must invent every scheme possible to consume their time. It matters not a wit whether they are doing good things or bad. As long as we keep them too busy, their families will suffer, and the process of separation will begin *automatically.*

"Now with that overview in mind, let me give you the details and a timeline. I have it all planned out," he assures them. "In the first decade, let them succeed and prosper. Let their homes resemble those they grew up in save for the addition of television. Get them to move to bigger and better homes in the suburbs. These new neighborhoods have no roots; there are no grandma and grandpa just down the lane that might notice our subtle intrusion. Women worked during the war in large numbers, and while the majority will stay home, some will still be willing to work, at least part-time, and many others will volunteer outside the home. Every moment stolen from their families is a victory and prepares the way for its repetition. This generation is tired. They have survived the Depression, then fought and won the war, and now they are beat. They have lost their youth, and their attention is turned to the unfinished business of living that they had to postpone. Few will have any interest in social wrongs, such as segregation or women's rights, and this will set the stage perfectly for the next generation to view them as hypocrites for failing to live up to the ideals of the freedom they profess.

"By the second decade, we can become more proactive in our efforts. Now that the rush of rebuilding is over, we will manipulate events in such a manner that excelling will require longer hours and harder work. With transportation advances making it easier to travel, we must make trips away from home a part of the job for as many as possible, especially among the executives. These leaders are essential. If they conform, they will drag their companies with them. Can you see how it's all going to unfold?" he queries his followers.

"In their rush to make up for lost time, this generation will have acquired something their parents shunned, *debt*—and debt, in combination with a tightening economy, will give birth to the modern, two-income family. In the past, privation has always been the motivating factor forcing mothers to work, but those who start back to work now are the vanguard of a new and mighty shift of attitude. This is the first generation that will leave home to maintain a lifestyle, rather than life itself.

"Families must subtly shift to accommodate these changes, and gradually the accepted 'norms' of acceptable behavior will shift as well. The weaker families will start to crumble under the pressure, the first fruits of our plan.

"Then there will be a flood of scientific discoveries opening new avenues for our attack. New and better medicine and techniques, which might benefit the human race if they were following God, will simply result in healthier sinners. Development of drug-based birth control will set the stage in the next decade, where we shall so dramatically alter their moral components, they will *never* recover from the effects, and that's just what we want." Satan laughs and then continues.

"In previous generations, music was a great unifier in the families. Only as the parents played an instrument or sang was music a part of the home. Later, even radio tended to be something listened to together in the family circle. Anything too questionable came in for scrutiny, and the progression of change was slow. Now, at last, is our golden opportunity to change this, and we *shall* not miss it. This decade's young people will have already been, to a large degree, separated from their parents by having school as the primary focus of social and not just educational development. Items of community interest like dances, at one time major family events, have been ceded to the schools. A new decade will see new music, and the 'happy days' of rock n' roll will captivate young people. For the first time music, the great unifying force, will become a wedge of division between the generations, and, if we are careful, can forever remain so.

"And television," hissed the great arch-enemy, "we *will* control television. Oh, it will seem very innocent and appealing at first. We will let it blossom and bloom with fun and sophisticated programs. This time period will be viewed as television's 'golden age,' with many of their best-loved 'family' programs developed and produced during this decade. Like the pied piper, we shall be leading them down the path to destruction. The slow process of corruption will be advanced enough, even by this early stage, that few, if any, will comprehend what they are seeing. Millions will 'love Lucy,' blissfully unaware that her character is a pathological liar, trampling the principles of God's law while they laugh and giggle. The bickering, argumentative home she portrays is humorous because to a greater or lesser degree, the viewers relate to it from their own home experience. The seeds we've planted will be doing just fine," Satan exults.

"By the third decade, we will begin to reap a harvest from our efforts. The young people who have grown up without the stern discipline of privation that their parents suffered and raised in a culture that values religious form over substance, will discard their parents' belief systems and seek meaning in sensuous lifestyles and social activism. United more by disgust with the status quo than a coherent vision for the future, they will embrace almost any concept that is diametrically opposed to the system of 'normal' behavior that they have come to view in their parents' lives as hypocritical. Music and drugs, communes and communism, as well as free love and free spirits will alter the perceptions of a generation and the viewpoint of the world.

"By mid-decade women will flood the workplace. Daycare will proliferate. Children will leave the parents' side earlier than ever before. Hastily performed studies will show the 'beneficial' results of such environments. In addition to human baby sitters many a child will grow up in front of the television, as the average number of hours watched in many households will start to steadily climb toward the time commitment required by a full-time job. As parents spend less and less time with their offspring, they will intuitively know this is wrong, so we must be ready with the concept of 'quality time' to salve their guilty conscience, while allowing the process of separation to continue. Divorce will become rampant, and with the introduction of 'no-fault' proceedings, what was once clearly understood as a shameful failure can now become an acceptable option. We can begin to introduce thousands to the idea of living together. Quite logically, as they view the devastation caused by divorce they will begin to wonder what difference a piece of paper makes.

"Your job is to make sure the tumult of the times is reflected in music, movies, and art, all of which can push our agenda," Satan instructs his demons. "Put forth extreme efforts to ensure nothing remains taboo and off limits. Horrific crime, drug use, immorality, and even homosexuality can now be openly explored in these mediums, desensitizing their minds for future assaults. In the atmosphere of activism encourage every group to rise up and demand their rights. Let the courts allow abortion as a woman's right. Extend the activism to the churches and unsettle long-held beliefs.

"As the crowning act of the decade, tempt the highest leaders in the land to break the law and then lie to cover it up. Bring it before the people in hideous detail so their trust in public officials is shattered and the government is forced out of office. This will create an atmosphere of chaos, and amid the storm of controversy, the people will find the old standards they used to rely on for their bearings have been set aside, leaving them adrift on the tide of cultural change.

"You see, the people will be so degraded and disgusted, they will enter the fourth decade of our plan completely unaware of the depths to which we will take them. The upheaval has unsettled them, and we must move slowly now or they may become too aware of their danger and seek to return to *God,*" and he spits the name out in utter revulsion. "Bring hard times upon them. That will distract them. This not only encourages both parents to work and further stresses the family units, but it is a great smoke screen for the next phase of our attack.

"Now we will use the human form to seduce them into sin and idolatry, just as we did with ancient Israel, but we shall accelerate the program and speed up the process. Every television program, magazine, and billboard will be saturated with images that suggest impure thoughts. It need not be explicit yet, because most mediums will still restrict such viewing, but we can convey our message just as well with *implied* immoral activities. Movies, however, will allow explicit portrayals, and we shall encourage producers to display such things shamelessly. For it is by 'beholding' that the moral fabric of society begins to break down. Once appetites for such things are created, it requires little effort to turn every convenience-store operator or gas-station attendant into a pimp for the lust mongers, selling their magazines of women for silver and gold. Just see what happens then," the chief demon exults.

"Violence and crime will increase, and they will watch the news reports, saturated with such things with the same horrid fascination that they now reserve for movies, filled with the same shameful, destructive crimes.

"While we keep them increasingly stressed and hassled by the burdens of life, turn their focus to the future with vain hopes that when this or that temporary problem is over, they will slow down, and then they will have time. It's all an illusion." Satan's hideous laughter drifts over the gathering, sending shivers through all who hear him. "It will never happen, and to make sure, we must ever stay ahead of them by laying the groundwork for a new worldwide computer system that will eventually speed their lives up even more.

"Under our clever onslaught, it isn't just the weak marriages that will fail, but the apparently strong ones. Remarrying will become so common," he states flippantly, "that blended families will be just one more stress, further weakening their chances of success. Increasingly, parents will feel the economic pressure to earn more and work longer. As good as the education they possess is, they will wish they had more and pressure their kids to be super-achievers. *Their* kids must get into the best colleges, so they won't have to struggle like Mom and Dad do. Increasingly, colleges will look not just at academic excellence but leadership in sports and clubs. Young people will be encouraged to participate in more and more activities outside the home, and the stage will be set for the fifth decade of our plan.

"Look how successful we will be!" he shouts, and his evil angels hang proudly on every word. "It's hardly been half a century in our master plan and we see only overwhelming acquiescence by the majority to their circumstances. They're too hassled and hurried to even object! They will adapt to the stresses and take an almost perverse pride in their ability to be overwhelmed. Now is the time to increase the pace," he chuckles slyly, "and push them even harder. The birth of the Internet society will seem a blessing to these harried individuals, who must now not only respond to those about them, but answer countless letters, phone calls, messages, and now emails. Time is the weapon to use against them. Even catalogs and junk mail serve our purposes well. Give them call waiting, so that when they are interrupted by a phone call, their interruptions can have yet another interruption. Ludicrous, isn't it?" Satan queries, and his imps chuckle knowingly.

"Couples will be so overwhelmed that they will become little more than ships passing in the night. With no time for true intimacy, their unmet needs will tend to push them toward any avenue of fulfillment. Children, provided with food, clothes, and gobs of toys, will feel like little more than orphans in their own homes. Deprived of the loving attention of parents, which should be their birthright, they are left to fend for themselves and spend larger and larger amounts of time with their peers—all because Mom and Dad are just *too* busy.

"By the sixth decade the family, once the bedrock of society, will crumble, and with it the fabric of civilization starts to collapse. Oh, the 'family' still stands, but like a tree rotted from within, its strength is gone and only the shell remains. Now everything becomes acceptable, except for old-fashioned biblical standards, and that's just how we want it." Satan smiles with a satisfied sigh. "The few who cling to such *antiquated* beliefs are viewed as mentally unbalanced fanatics or simpletons, worthy of pity or contempt by the more enlightened members of society.

"The confused young people of the sixties have raised an even more confused generation of cynical and disillusioned children, who, in turn, with the passing of time, will manage to raise young people in an almost disconnected state from their parents. This generation of parents will receive one of the nastiest wake-up calls imaginable. These children will begin to manifest the same hostility toward their parents and each other that is manifested by society toward them. But don't worry; they won't wake up," the mighty rebel leader assures his listeners. "They won't even understand the causes.

"You see, in removing them from their parents at an early age, these children are deprived of the privilege of an innocent childhood. With parents, who care only that their kids are not 'bothering' them, they provide their little ones all the trappings of success, all the toys imaginable for entertainment, but leave them with no one to guide them through their problems. Is it any wonder these children perceive the world as a hostile place?" he sneers. "Is it any surprise that we can easily entice them to watch movies that aren't fit to be shown in hell and play video games designed by our most inventive devils? Furthermore, does not the message of their worthlessness to Mom and Dad come through loud and clear, as their parents' generation will murder millions upon millions of the unborn in a slaughter so great in magnitude that it will make the Nazi death camps look *merciful?*" he says, laughing sarcastically. His demons sit spellbound as the gruesome plot continues to unfold before their eyes.

"The Jews, so brutally hunted during the war years in Europe, will have carried the memory burned into their collective psyche from generation to generation. Yet, we will so delude the modern parent that while they empathize with the fate of the Jews, they will sincerely believe that the murder of six times as many children will somehow not affect the upcoming generations. Then when their children rise up and kill their parents, or their classmates, these same parents who have manifested a brutal disregard for human life will be so deceived, they will be baffled as to why children have no respect for human life.

"You see," Satan explains, "without a moral compass—and we destroyed that long ago—things once shunned become not only tolerated but also mainstreamed. Three decades ago politicians paid dearly for public indiscretions, but not so by this time. Lying and infidelity will be at least tolerated traits in public officials. Society will have come so far that the chief executive of the United States can now engage in the most disgusting of affairs while elevating public lying to an art form. The populace will greet such behavior with little more than a bored shrug of the shoulders. One of our most effective deceptions will be getting them to believe that *everyone does it.* They will have fallen into the trap of believing that character is unimportant. You can achieve success without it. All that matters is style. Substance will have fallen by the wayside, consumed on the altar of self-indulgence. For you see," he snickers, "the real problem in condemning public sins is that many secretly engage in such activities, and many more who haven't been brave enough to actually do so, have contemplated it longingly." He pauses to quiz his followers. "You get the picture?" And they nod vigorously in approval. "Then I shall continue," he majestically informs them.

"Entertainment will reach its zenith with overwhelming choices and options. They will be able to have news twenty-four hours a day through any medium they like: radio, TV, and the Internet. Publications in every format and to suit every taste, even e-books online, will be available at their fingertips. They will be able to get videos of every movie, on any and every subject, with *nothing* off-limits or forbidden. With the advent of the Internet, even a trip to the local video store is not required to obtain scenes of forbidden passion. With the Internet we can, for the first time, even corrupt them at work. Anyone with a computer will be able to download hours of materials with, well, let's say *questionable* content," he utters with a pleased little laugh.

"By the seventh decade society and government, both built upon the foundation of the crumbling family, will be in the process of collapsing. Now there is little we need to do but enjoy the specter and anticipate the harvest. *If* we have done our job well, and I know we will," he glares fiercely at his demons, "the family, their last refuge in troubled times, will have fallen, and we shall exercise total control over the bedlam that remains. So my friends, victory *is* achievable in just seventy years—in just a single human life span." With a flourish of his hand, Satan closes his mighty address and gazes in triumph at his attentive audience.

A timid hand is raised at the back of the crowd. "O mighty leader," a loyal admirer hesitantly begins, "the humans assigned to me won't fall for those traps. I have the *really* religious ones," he mutters scornfully.

"You're worried about *them?*" the mighty leader replies disdainfully. "They're no trouble at all ... just as gullible as the rest, but I have something special in mind for them anyway. We will use their very churches against them," he continues smugly. "While we entice the worldly characters to be too busy in their pursuits, get the church members too busy with *good* works: too busy in evangelism, too busy with pastoral duties, too busy with outreach, too busy with theological controversy and social activism. It doesn't matter at all that these are 'good' activities. Just make sure," he instructs the inquiring demon, "that every moment is jam packed. Make sure they have no time to experience introspection, quiet contemplation, or worst of all, communion with God," he jeers, momentarily agitated. Regaining composure, he continues. "And so, my friends, go forth with your legions to the victory."

With the passing of time, the echoes of this climactic meeting have faded away, leaving us with only the results to analyze. We are living in the sixth decade of the devil's plan; and in my opinion, he has been more successful than he ever dreamed of being. Today's families are but a dim shadow of what they should be. Time spent together as a family is virtually unknown. Even the family supper hour is a thing of the past in most homes, and in those where it exists, it is usually shared with television. Weekend gatherings with the family have fallen by the wayside as families are scattered across the country.

Parental insecurity over employment has moved from legitimate concern for their children's education to the bizarre. Some parents actually hire expert coaches to qualify their children, not for Ivy League colleges, but for prestigious nursery schools! Have we lost our minds? Some parents have gone so far down this track that they think every act of their child's life should be planned with the goal of Harvard or Yale in mind.

Materialism consumes not just the world but even supposedly Christian homes. I have stayed in homes where the closets are so full I can hardly hang a suit. I personally counted twenty-five pairs of sneakers in one teenager's closet and once visited in a home that displayed the most beautiful china I had ever seen, only to be informed, "We don't eat off those. We bought those to match the draperies." These people are so near and dear to my heart, because they remind me of the life I used to lead. You should have seen my home and my possessions years ago.

One beautiful young family stands out in my mind. They were so stressed by burdens of life and completely stymied in their efforts to

8—E. L.

find a way to spend more time with their kids. In response to their plea for help, I started asking questions.

"You work, don't you?" I asked the wife.

"Yes," she replied.

"And you have two cars, right?" They both nodded. "You have a nice large home, correct?"

"That's right," the husband replied.

"And that home is furnished with beautiful furniture, is it not?"

"Yes, we always buy the best," the wife admitted.

"And yet you are telling me you don't have the time to spend raising your children for God."

"That's exactly where we are," the man of the family confided.

"Well, here is what you do. Your wife should immediately resign from her job. Sell the second car and the expensive furniture. Sell your home and use the equity to move out in the country and buy a little home or even just a piece of property and put a mobile home on it."

I had an ulterior motive in moving them to the country. It's easier to hear God's voice in a natural setting; there are simply fewer distractions, but they could find the experience they were after anywhere, *if* they were willing. Country living is far more a state of mind than a location. Many people have moved to the country and found themselves no better off than in the city. Why? Because it is easy to make an outward reform, like making country living into your religion, instead of seeing it as only a tool to help you in the Christian walk. For many, it becomes a substitute for the true religion they seek. No, *not everyone needs to move to the wilderness, but everyone needs a wilderness experience.*

"Do whatever it takes," I encouraged the husband. "Just make sure you're out of debt. Then you can cut back your work to a minimum, and you will have found the time you need to work with your family."

By the time I finished, I could see it all over their faces. I had struck at the very root of their value system. Would they consent to live in a *trailer,* if that is what it took? They left me, still struggling to come to terms with which ideal they wanted more.

Today's families are fragmented because we have allowed them to be. We have believed the devil's lie that we have to do certain things and make a certain amount of money so we can provide for our children the type of lifestyle we feel they deserve. We are fools if we believe that *things* are more important to our children than our *time* is.

What is your home like? Do you rush out the door in the morning and chase loose ends all day? Do you feel like Mom's taxi service ferrying kids from school to sports, to doctors, to school plays, or a friend's home? How often have you struggled through endless home-work assignments, given out in response to the parental outcry for more and better education, and realized they are robbing both you and your child of the joy of fellowship together? Is there any time left to be a family? Do you really know what goes on in your child's heart?

If your answers to the above questions were not what you desire them to be, then you and your family have fallen victim to the devil's plan. He needs to accomplish nothing more than to separate you one from another to achieve his goal. He wants to split your family into independent atoms. Only you can interfere with his plans, and the secret to that is to stop playing his game. Never play another's game, no matter how appealing it looks. When you play their game, they control the rules and you will always lose.

Satan has intentionally manipulated life so that our options seem limited, but this is an illusion rather than a fact. Ask God what He would have you to do. He *always* has a way out. Discover His plans for your family and then take steps to accomplish His plan, no matter how far afield you may find yourself. This is the key to untying God's hands so He can bless you. As you show your willingness to act, insofar as He has made the way clear, you can be certain He will direct your steps in the future.

The dangers even for intact, church-going families can hardly be overstated. My coauthors recently visited a church whose families demonstrated all the classic signs of impending trouble. They told me about it in a few short words.

"Our daughter, Ellen, attended the class for her age group, but her mom went along because they like to be together and we like to keep tabs on what the children are learning. The class of pre-teens had been studying the life of Joseph, and their teacher asked how they would feel about being separated from their parents at a young age like Joseph was. The response was noncommittal, but a few of the more vocal ones made it very clear that they couldn't wait to get away from *their* parents. Ellen was offended, even though we didn't find out until later. She loves her parents and her family. Quite obviously these young people not only disliked their homes but also viewed their parents with contempt. These parents had lost their children's hearts by age twelve, and worse yet, they didn't even know it!"

Why are these young people so disconnected from their parents at such a tender age? Likely it is because they do not see Mother and Father making those hard choices to protect their family, to make the children their first priority, and to spend the time necessary to bind the children's heart to their own. Materially these children have the best that money can buy, but in heaven's sight they are the most pitifully deprived. Sad, isn't it? Yet it is happening in almost every home and in every church I visit. These same parents who blindly ignore the signs of trouble will find themselves facing rebellious teenagers and throw up their hands, saying, "We took them to church. We did everything we could. I guess we'll have to leave it in God's hands," as if God is somehow at fault for their failures.

Well, what of that family I left struggling with their choice? I didn't hear from them for a long time, but sometime later we were in their area of the country, and we paid a surprise visit to their home. It was after dark when we pulled up, and there was the man installing a new screen door. He looked up at us in shock. We were the last people he expected.

I can hardly find words to tell you what I experienced walking into that house. There was a peace in the home and a oneness between husband and wife. The children showed marked improvement in their attitudes since we last saw each other. "What happened?" I managed to ask.

"We've been having family worship, Jim, and just spending time together as a family," and a grin a mile wide spread over his face.

"And the new door?"

"We're getting the house ready to sell."

That family had made the decision. They had decided to put their family first, ahead of every other consideration, and their home clearly reflected the beginnings of a harvest of joy.

Let me tell you about Cindy, because she exemplifies the courage and determination it takes to succeed in this venture.

In August of 1996, four horses and riders picked their way along the trail leading to a wilderness cabin little more than a mile away. Cindy Parolin, age thirty-six, was riding with three of her children to join their father and ten-year-old brother at the cabin for a backcountry vacation. The horses started acting very strangely. Suddenly a cougar leaped for six-year-old Steven. The horse spooked, and the child fell to the ground. Immediately the cougar had him by the head. Cindy screamed, "I'm coming, Steven!" and, breaking a branch from a nearby tree, she rushed to his aid. As she beat the cougar off the boy, it grabbed her arm, but she punched it hard and threw herself on top of the cat, holding it down, while she yelled for the older children to take Steven and run for help. David, age thirteen, and Melissa, age eleven, obeyed. They picked up their severely injured brother and traveled more than a mile back to the camping area where they had parked the family car. At the campground, they solicited the help of Jim Manion, who grabbed a shotgun and raced to the rescue.

Arriving on the scene after a reckless charge down the trail in his pickup truck, he found Mrs. Parolin, severely wounded but still weakly fighting the cougar as it stood triumphantly over her. A full hour had passed since the fight began. Cindy was only five feet five inches, and the cougar, which weighed slightly less than seventy pounds, seemed to have spent the entire hour wearing her down. Still unconcerned for herself, she asked if her children were all right. Informed they were, she relaxed. "I'm dying now," she told her rescuer, drifting into unconsciousness.

Manion managed to fire at, and wound the cougar, which ran off, but Cindy Parolin died of her wounds before she could reach the hospital. She had gladly traded her future, her dreams and goals, her very life for that of her child, earning newspaper headlines as "The Bravest Mom in the World."

Most of us would like to think that as parents facing the same situation, we would respond as bravely as Cindy did, but the evidence is before us that few, very, very, few of us actually would. I say that because we face an identical situation. The Bible says, "Be sober, be vigilant; because your adversary the devil, as a roaring lion, walketh about, seeking whom he may devour" (1 Peter 5:8).

Whom does a predator target? He always seeks the weakest, usually the young. He is after your children. He wants to break up your flock and scatter your children away from your side, where they can more easily fall prey to his deceptions and thus secure his kill. If you think I am exaggerating, just look at the families about you. Are they coherent? Are they unified in love and in sympathy with each other? Or are they families of independent atoms, scattered here and there? Do the children rebel and fret under the parents' authority? Are their teens too busy living their lives to stay at home and be with Mom and Dad? Is your family too busy to be a family anymore? What is God's Spirit saying to you? Are there things you need to change in order to resist the devil's attack? Take action now before he destroys what is most precious to you. Follow the Bible's recommendation in the next verse to "resist steadfast in the faith" (1 Peter 5:9).

Yes, this battle will cost you something. The price is as high as Cindy's was. It will cost your wishes and desires. It means you must resign your ambitions. You can anticipate no fame or fortune in the path of duty and self-denial. To save your children will require you to die, literally die to self, and to live only to secure the future of your little ones.

Have I frightened you off? Is death too fearful a price to pay? If not, are you willing to die for your family as Cindy died for hers? Are you willing to put up the long, hard fight to the death for the salvation of your children? If so, then come with me while we explore ways to transform your home into a fortress so strong and mighty that it need not fear the empty roars of a defeated enemy. May God direct His plans for your family as together we explore time to be a family. This truly is the key to your children's hearts, no matter what their age.

Activities for Week 9

Sunday

Prayer time: Today is a day for honest assessment, and because this subject is so near and dear to our hearts, objectivity is nearly impossible to achieve apart from the grace of God. As you commune with Him this morning, seek His wisdom and ask that He impress you with His wishes for your family.

Activity: Read "Independent Atoms." Consider how the concepts presented apply to you, whether you have a family, have yet to form a family, have lost a family through death or separation, or even if your children are grown. All of us are part of a home, even if it consists of only one person—you. Have you felt the devil's attack?

Reflection: Most would die to save the life of a child or spouse. Would you be willing to let your personal dreams and goals die so they might live as God intended?

Monday

Prayer time: The process of change is gradual, and success usually does not so much attend the swift, who try to make sweeping changes overnight, but those who carefully and prayerfully plan for the future. With this in mind, ask God to show you the first steps to repairing your family as you do today's exercises.

Activities: Track today's activities as a family. Don't cheat and falsely increase the time you normally spend with them. Track both the amount of time and the activity, making a paper record for future reference.

Reflection: Of the time spent together, what did you enjoy most? Least? And why?

Tuesday

Prayer time: Today, seek comfort with God. You may feel somewhat helpless or even hopeless in your situation, but God knows what it is like to have a family that is fractured and separated. He does not view us as hopeless, and in His love and mercy He has been drawing you closer to Him. He will show you just what to do.

Activity: Using your paper record of family time, separate the times spent traveling from the activities and from the time doing household jobs and watching television. Was there any time spent just being together, maybe just talking? Is there a spot in the schedule that would allow more of this time together?

Wednesday

Prayer time: Try going in before your heavenly Father without a preset idea of what you need and have Him guide your thoughts as to what needs changing.

Activity: Taking the inspiration gained in this morning's prayer time, again take out that paper record and look at it from the perspective of what you would like it to be. What might have to be altered or eliminated to achieve your goal?

Reflection: Would you be willing to let those items identified above go? If so, do it today.

Thursday

Prayer time: Bring your family members before God, asking that He would help you plan ways to spend more time that will appeal to each one.

Activity: Try and talk to each family member at some point in the day. Find out what they would like to see in the way of family time. If your children are older, don't be surprised at the noncommittal response. After all, they likely spent years longing for you to be interested. No, they aren't likely to jump at the chance to interact with you unless you really prove your commitment to them. Finding out what they'd like to do is a first step.

Reflection: Were you surprised by anything your family shared today? Did your family talk freely or did they have to be drawn out?

Friday

Prayer time: In your personal time with God, turn your thoughts to the future. We are going to spend the next three weeks fine-tuning our families. I hope some ideas we share will be familiar. Others are likely to be brand new. In the end, you'll accomplish nothing of value apart from your communion with God. Make the commitment now to have Him lead out in this process.

Activity: Take all that you have gleaned from this week's activities and write it out on paper. Write out your goals and everyone's preferences. Tuck away in a safe place your original paper showing how much time you spend as a family. You will have a use for it in the future.

Reflection: Think back on your most treasured memories of family times in your youth. What was it that made those times special?

Saturday

Reflection: This week we have looked at the problems within our own families, and it is easy especially as parents to castigate ourselves for our failures. Starting tomorrow we are going to look to the future. The solutions ahead of us may be hard, but also very rewarding. Plan today to do what the apostle Paul described when he said, "Brethren, I count not myself to have apprehended: but this one thing I do, forgetting those things which are behind, and reaching forth unto those things which are before, I press toward the mark for the prize of the high calling of God in Christ Jesus" (Philippians 3:13, 14).

CHAPTER 10

Time to Be a Family

"And he shall turn the heart of the fathers to the children, and the heart of the children to their fathers, lest I come and smite the earth with a curse" (Malachi 4:6).

CHAPTER GOAL

If you have a family or are even considering having one, you know it is no easy task to succeed, but anyone can if they wish. It will take a committed investment in time to be a family.

This is Mark's story:

"The screen door creaked as it opened, its painful groan of protest ending in a sharp bang as the springs snapped it shut. If I had been old enough for such thoughts, I would have recognized in that old door an apt representation of my family that looked so good and functional to the outside observer and only rarely allowed the world to hear the sounds of the suffering within.

"Too young to fully comprehend all that I had lost in the death of my mother and unable to prevent my father's advances, I had no one in whom to confide the burdens of my young heart. So I would open that old door into the backyard and finding a comfy spot on the lawn, and I would lie in the grass for what seemed like hours and stare up at the clouds. Gradually peace would come. I didn't have any practical knowledge of God or even religion, but there was something comforting out in that soft carpet of green staring up at the clouds. There, Someone lovingly cared for me, speaking to me through quiet impressions in my thoughts. His voice of love was so appealing to me in my unloved condition that I never forgot the sound or the import of His words, the very first ever in my life that showed what a loving Father might be like. I sought out my refuge on the lawn several times, and that comforting Presence was always there for me.

"As I grew older and life became even more chaotic, these quiet periods of contemplation became a part of my past, no longer actively sought, yet not fully forgotten. Rather, the memories lingered not fully dormant, but simply overwhelmed in the struggle for survival, and survival has been the story of my life.

"Born the third of four children, I was my father's first son. With two older sisters, I was understandably pleased when a baby brother arrived for me to play with, but the carefree days of early childhood were eclipsed by my mother's diagnosis with breast cancer. She was to gradually decline until she died at age thirty-six when I was eight. As tragic as my mother's death was, the changes in my father, prompted by her illness, were worse.

"After my mother became sick, my father began molesting me, setting a pattern that would continue for years and, I would come to find out, a pattern that included my other siblings, although at first none of us knew about the others' encounters.

"When Mom died, Dad sent the girls to live with relatives in New Jersey, and my brother and I went to live with friends of the family in Missouri. It should have been a welcome respite, but as hard as it is to believe, a friend of this family picked up the pattern of molestation right where my father left off.

"My brother became ill while we were living in Missouri, and it was soon discovered that he had leukemia. My father came to visit when he heard the news of his illness and shortly thereafter announced that he was remarrying and intended to reunite his family.

"Our new stepmother had four children of her own, and while any family of ten was likely to garner attention from a curious public, ours was doubly interesting for the people watchers because of the obvious health problems of my brothers. My blood brother had by this time undergone treatments for his cancer. He had lost his hair, and his body was always swollen and puffy from the medications he was on. One of my stepbrothers had cerebral palsy, and another had a congenital heart defect that interfered with the oxygenation of his blood, giving his skin a distinct purple pallor. Needless to say, when we were out together, we were a hard family *not* to notice.

"Yet, with all our oddities, my family looked all right to the outside observer. This was due, in part, to my father's income. As an engineer, he headed a department for a major American company, where he made a very good salary. We lived in one of the largest houses in the neighborhood. What no one could see was that behind the doors of that nice house and in that apparently stable family was a home whose occupants lived a hellish existence.

"It is hard for someone who has not grown up in an abusive household to understand, but the physical abuse, even the inappropriate physical intimacy, does not wound the spirit like the mental abuse that so often accompanies it. My father continued to molest me for many years. However, it was the cruelty of his comments that revealed the pathological evil that motivates someone, who could have been respectable and accomplished much good in the world, to degenerate into a heartless man with dark desires. I grew up never hearing the words "I love you" except in the context of engaging in his animalistic activities.

"My younger brother and I were typical kids, and I engaged in a certain amount of kidding around and teasing of my younger brother. When he died, my father hurt me terribly by stating that it was my teasing and horseplay that had contributed to his death. I excelled in sports and longed for approval from someone, but no one cared. No one ever came to my games. I knew the bitter tears of rejection. As I grew older, the direct physical abuse was replaced by a constant and never-ending fear of ultimately being rejected. With every activity that didn't meet parental demands, threats of being thrown out of the house always brewed beneath the surface. My sister was kicked out of the house at an early age, and as soon as I was able, I joined the Marines, and it was there that my life began to take a different turn.

"I loved being a marine. I was physically fit, and academically I stood at the top of my class. I was invited to attend the United States Naval Academy on the basis of my leadership potential and superior academic record, not to mention placing first in every area of basic training. Some people struggle with the demands of military life, but I thrived. Compared to my struggle for survival at home, it was easy! There were clearly understood rules and expectations, as well as clear rewards for achievement, and compared with my father, the officers, while if not kind, were certainly fair. It wasn't long before my training days were over, and I found myself working as an air traffic controller in beautiful Hawaii.

"I felt I had it made—at last! I had a job I enjoyed, money sufficient for my needs, and I dated a number of extremely attractive women, including some models. I enjoyed all of life's pleasures, including substances, which, even though illegal, grew well in that tropical paradise. I knew a number of guys who smoked marijuana, and I decided it was simply a good business deal to sell to them, since I had to get my own supply anyway. I started packaging the sweet, slightly rotten-smelling, resin-coated leaves and was turning a good profit. I wasn't dealing on the street and never really viewed myself as a 'drug dealer.' I was just taking life as it came and for the first time pleasing myself, and doing what I wanted. Just how long this lifestyle might have lasted, I will never know because my friend Dennis asked me to go on a motorcycle ride with him. I had always loved motorcycles, and I jumped at the chance."

Let me interrupt Mark's story for a moment. After hearing his background of abuse, and knowing the odds that he might follow in his father's footsteps and become an abuser, you would be forgiven if you wouldn't want him as your father. I realize that few homes and families are as destructive as Mark's and yet, there are even fewer homes in which the family members are in love with each other and have truly bonded together as a family. As amazing as it sounds, God's solutions for our families are simple and effective. Over the years the devil has managed in a slow, subtle way to steal away our time—the one element most needed if we are to have exceptionally close and affectionate families. The good news is that we don't have to fall victim to our enemy's plan. Come and explore with me, "Time to Be a Family."

Today's families are stressed, pushed, and pressed for time. With everyone on the go constantly and so much emphasis placed on kid-oriented activities, we have come to view everything from trips to the dentist to after-school sports as family activities. The media has played a role in reinforcing this myth by reporting that modern parents spend more hours with their children than former generations. Only rarely do they confess that this increase is often the result of time spent in the car, commuting to other activities. The idea that families might set time aside just for the sheer pleasure of enjoying one another's company seems charmingly archaic and outdated, like those old black-and-white television programs depicting the traditional family unit. Give the cynics among us their due, however, for they are correct when they say that we can't go back to the "good old days." But in striving for a solution that will work in our day we must identify what it is from that era that we are missing, what it is that makes us feel so nostalgic. In essence, even the most active proponents of traditional family structure really don't want to return to those days of emotionally distant husbands and fathers, nor do they want the limited opportunities for women, the segregation of minorities, and all the other social inequities of that time. We long for the cohesive family units and the sense of worth and value that being a member of such a family instilled.

My father was not a large man, but he was a giant in my eyes. His name and his reputation made me a person of worth and value in other people's eyes, and the way in which people perceived him provided me with the respect of my community, long before I was old enough to earn it on my own. I'll never forget my first year in high school. For the first time in my life I had a teacher who just had it in for me. My father was certainly not the type to side with a student against the teacher and yet, as he listened to my tale of woe, he decided that I was in the right, and Henry Hohnberger had a strong sense of justice. He went with me to a meeting of the administrative board and fearlessly defended me in a verbal confrontation with the teacher. Things became so hostile between the two men that I wondered if they were going to pitch right into each other in the administration offices. When the dust settled, it was the teacher who was dismissed. My father was my hero, and my family had closed ranks and protected me when I was unable to protect myself.

What is it that provides a sense of family? Many things contribute, but none so much as the tradition of time. It is not enough to take time to be a family on vacation or when it is convenient. No, it's just like dating. You have to let the people in your family know they are special by making, looking forward to, and keeping a series of scheduled social engagements. This special time set apart allows everyone to bond with the others, not only in the activity planned but also in the anticipation of that special time. If you want to draw the hearts of your family closer, you will have to provide a minimum of one special time each week that is entirely theirs—time you plan, schedule, and defend at all costs against any activities that would steal away from you those special moments.

In our family, we didn't choose just one night a week, we decided on five nights a week. One, however, is the absolute minimum necessary to get results. The more fragmented your family, the more time you need to heal and build bridges. And yet, ironically, you will likely have more opposition from your family members. If your family is really hurting, push for more, not less, time, but be willing to compromise and negotiate a deal that will work for everyone. Most families try to set aside a portion of the evening hours for their family time. But if your home has a nontraditional schedule you can use just about any time the family is together. You can even set aside part of the weekend if work requires someone to travel overnight. The time can be as short as a half-hour or as long as a couple of hours. Just make it a regularly scheduled part of your life, and soon you will establish a habit, a tradition that no one will want to break.

To be sure, doing this will require some sacrifice. You will have to set aside some social activities, and your kids may have to turn down friends who want them to visit, but most of all, that endless "Things To Do" list must be completely ignored. If you are willing to make the investment, it will be worth it.

If your children are older, they may object to just spending time with Mom and Dad, but press on anyway, knowing only your lack of friendship in the past is to blame. Their objections are the strongest evidence that you are losing their hearts, and prompt action is needed.

So you decide you need family time. Now, what do you do? In truth, anything is better than what you have been doing up to this point—nothing! Your activities will vary with the age and temperament of your children. Ideally recreation should be of such a nature that it supports the goals of spiritual growth you have for your family. Games that encourage competition and build up "self" in one child and discourage another should be set aside for more wholesome fare where everyone can play and have fun, whether they are good at it or not.

When our children were small, we would color, make things in the sandbox, and play with modeling clay or finger paints. Let go, have some fun, and be fun. If your little daughter wants to have a tea party—why not go along? What little child doesn't love to have Dad for a horse? The whole family should play. If Mom is out of shape, don't make her feel slow and awkward. Play tag and design it so that when Mom is "it," everyone has to walk except her. Participation is the key. I have watched many a toddler in the arms of Mom or Dad gleefully reach out chubby arms to tag someone in a game we love to play—freeze tag!

What else can you do? *Read.* Let your little ones play blocks on the floor while your older ones draw or help with the reading. Involve everyone in discussing what you read and ask questions. Choose books that are interesting and build character. We've included a whole list of our favorites in the appendix. Be creative. Record a book on tape for long car trips. My coauthors have a grandma who does this for them, and the kids love it because Grandma has books they don't have, but the best part is that it allows Grandma to be part of family fun even though she's many, many miles away.

Another wonderful family fun time can be special projects. Do you have boys or girls who want to build a tree house, create a hiking trail, or complete a woodworking project? Work becomes play when it is something they want to do and you are willing to lend the time and effort to make it possible. This doesn't mean you pick your pet project and decide they are going to help you get it done.

Swimming, canoeing, tubing down the river, hiking, mountain climbing, biking, and caving are available in the summer. In the winter, sledding, cross-country skiing, building snowmen or snow forts and real igloos, downhill skiing or snowboarding, and ice skating are all wonderful outdoor activities that don't have to involve any competition, yet allow time for the family to bond together and talk. Many families toss around a football, or play kickball or baseball without keeping score. Badminton, volleyball, hide-and-seek, duck-duck-goose, kick the can, and I Spy are other options, but the list is as endless as your imagination.

If you have company, don't let that stop you. Involve them in your games. They will love it, too. Once Matthew sold some real estate to a wealthy man, who owned his own bank and a mortgage company. The gentleman was very impressed with Matthew, and asked if he could spend a couple of days with us. He wanted to know what was different about our home that made Matthew what he was. We welcomed him gladly, and as the time approached for us to have family time, Matthew, my up-and-coming real estate tycoon, turned to the banker and said, "You wanna play marbles?" The banker didn't know what to say, but I did.

"Matthew, don't you think you should pick something different tonight?" I queried, desperately trying to convey to Matthew that this might be a little too undignified for our new friend.

"He's a banker," Matthew calmly observed. "He ought to be able to count them."

And so we all got down on the floor and played marbles, and the banker *loved* it. It made him forget all his troubles. It was the best time he had had in years. We went on to play pick-up-sticks and dominoes, too. It's not just the children that benefit from family time. Too many of us have forgotten how to play, how to forget ourselves and really laugh, and it is making us old before our time.

By playing with our children, we bind their hearts to ours with a golden thread of love, but like a single fiber in a rope, one is not enough to make a lasting connection. So we must make sure that every week we are adding fibers to our ropes of love until there are so many we can't count them, and the bond between our children and us is strong, secure, and virtually unbreakable.

How early can we begin this lifelong work of binding our children's heart to ours? Well, Paul and Carolyn started "family time" when their daughter was a year old. What does family time mean to a child so young? It means lots of cuddle time, reading some books, maybe building with blocks—the same types of activity you normally do with a twelve-month-old infant. And yet Paul and Carolyn soon realized that this infant understood family time as well as they did. On nights when they let themselves get too busy to take the time, or if they just let it slide because it didn't seem important, they soon noticed a correlation in the child's attitude, a fussiness and inability to fall asleep at bedtime. Today family time is alive and well in their home, with a four-year-old and two-year-old eagerly joining in. Infant activities have advanced to early childhood activities, but the fun still remains as they play trains, a great favorite, make pretend food for pretend parties, roll and tumble with Daddy on the floor, or hike in the wilderness and have real picnics. Even simple work projects are enjoyed together—washing the car, painting the garage, and collecting firewood. Once a week they even try to join with some other families and have a joint family time. Maybe they'll pick our family again soon.

As your children grow older, you may find that while you still have family time an increasingly large number of nights are given to family "talk time." We all share openly, with everyone having the right to his or her own opinion. It's helped us to work through in a nonthreatening way many issues, concerns, and interests our boys had, without us trying to force our opinions on them. We kind of sat back and just guided the boys in their thoughts and let them draw their conclusions. Because of that, they were interested in what we had to say. I can't tell you how many years we have spent talking about careers, if and when to date, how to choose the right girl, and other similar topics. I wouldn't trade those "family times" for anything.

Time to be a family sometimes involved more than a few hours and became the investment of days, as we planned trips and then took time out to fulfill our boys' dreams. Are you willing to take that big cross-country trip the kids have been pushing for, to spend two weeks canoe camping in the Canadian wilderness, or to learn how to scuba dive, rock climb, or even (gulp) skydive? Your age, health, and inclination may require less strenuous activities, but are you willing to move out of your comfort zone to keep pace with your children? That is the real issue if you are willing to take the time to be a family.

Families that try this program repeatedly say that it works, but many start and then let it fall by the wayside as the cares and problems of life crowd out their efforts. Children intuitively know when they are a priority and when they are not. When they know they are more important to Mom and Dad than anything else, it provides them with tremendous feelings of security and love.

Tim and Julie's son Travis was in a group of children who were asked to name the most special place they had ever been. Children named off vacation destinations and seashore beaches. Then Travis, who was almost eight years old then, was asked the question. "My home," he replied, to the surprise of everyone present. I am not exaggerating when I tell people that all the world's glitter fades into nothingness when we provide our children what they really want—us!

Still not convinced? Well, you have a right to be skeptical. After all, this program of spending time with your children seems just too simple, right? Well, join me on a visit to one of the most loving, close-knit families I know. They live in Wisconsin, and since I go there often to visit my elderly mother, I try when I can to get over to visit them as well because their home has utilized family time in very practical ways, and it shows in the children.

Sally and I arrive just before mealtime and after an exuberant greeting, we barely settle into the guest quarters before the meal is served. When I arrive at the table, I begin to wonder if they were expecting the president instead of Jim Hohnberger. Everything is just lovely, and the family is delighted with my delight. I feel very loved, knowing in my heart that they did it all for me even though I'm not the president. The food is carefully prepared and artfully arranged. Every item seems to have been specially chosen to not only taste good, but to add beautiful balance and color to the table. They even have my favorite—avocados. Someone took the time to create special name cards at each place. I've eaten many a meal in this home, and even though the food might be simple, it is always presented in a most attractive manner, while the little extras that make the meal and the welcome so special are never neglected.

The conversation just flows naturally around the table, with laughter frequently bubbling from an unseen spring. The children seem as eager for our happiness as their parents and merely reflect the love they feel in the home.

As I help clear my plate, I find a little love note tucked away under it just letting me know how special I am to them. I notice I wasn't the only one whose needs and special likes had been considered.

Soon, almost before I know it, evening has come and four eager faces surround me, as they try to decide what to do for family time. Suddenly their father pipes up, "I know. Let's give Uncle Jim a concert." The children all agree and head off to collect their instruments and set up for a grand concert. Meanwhile, I relax and sink deeper into the sofa, while we visit with the father and mother. "Concert night has been a regular occurrence for years, about once a week, I'd guess. It gives the children a chance to show us what they were learning in a fun way, although it was pretty bad when they were first starting. There were a lot of squeaks and squawks," their father says, laughing. "We always tried to encourage them, even when it was rough on our ears."

The results of their father's encouragement show that night as Rachael, age fourteen, Jonathan, age twelve, Rebekah, age ten, and Esther, age eight, give us a glorious concert. Each child plays at least two instruments, and they include the piano, harp, cello, violin, and viola.

Through hard work, thousands of dollars in lessons, and the encouragement of their family, the children now have a music ministry of their own, in which they travel and give concerts all over the country. And all the while, their goal is to point others to Jesus through the music they love to share.

This is like heaven, I think as the music wafts over my soul. *Surely the angels make music like this,* I muse. So naturally that there hardly seems a ripple of disturbance, family time flows into the evening's climax—worship. Music and songs lift our spirits, and their father tells a story that has me on the edge of my chair, as he changes his voice to match each character. But the father doesn't stop there, just content that he has shared a good story. He gently brings it home personally in family discussion, and when at last they are all talked out, they recommit themselves in prayer and it seems that even more peace and contentment reigns in their home. Tired and sleepy, we loiter by the fire, but it's time for bed, and the children drift off.

I can't help but eavesdrop as the children are tucked in. These budding teenagers still hug and kiss their mom and dad. They want Dad to sit on the edge of the bed and talk—really talk. These children revel in their father's love, attention, and encouragement.

When the father at last returns to sit with me by the fire, I mention the tuck-in routine. He laughs and says, "Yeah, sometimes if I take too long with one, the others will remind me that they want their time too, before they fall asleep. I've even had the other children arrive with their pillows and blankets to bed down on the floor, so they can be close to us while we visit."

"How do you develop such closeness with your children?" I have to ask.

"Jim, I learned a long time ago that I didn't know what to do to be close to my children and to help them. I've known you almost two decades, and our friend Tom [Waters] even longer. When you formed your ministry, I knew you didn't have all the answers. I've just been doing what you do and what you tell everyone else to do—sitting at the feet of Jesus. I go and sit at His feet every day and ask Him what He would have me to do, and He *always* gives me direction."

So, are you wondering who this wonderful father is? Would you be amazed if I told you it's none other than the same Mark, who was abused as a child, who grew up without a good father figure to model, who never felt loved and was never encouraged, even though he could excel? "Mark, what turned things around for you? When we left you last, you were selling drugs on the side in Hawaii and had promised to take a motorcycle ride with a friend. What happened next?"

"Well, Jim, my friend Dennis didn't tell me that the motorcycle ride was to go see a minister. Before I knew it I was at this pastor's church staring out his office window, wondering when we would leave. My friend seemed in no hurry and had an endless supply of questions for the minister. An hour slipped by. *It won't be long now,* I thought and still they talked on. After a while I started to listen, and in their conversation about God, I again heard a voice I recognized. I knew it was that still, small voice that so comforted me when I was a boy, the same one that had lain dormant all these years. Now it rang loud and clear. I knew it was my *true* Father. When I was a child I didn't understand that it was God speaking to me, only that I was loved. Now I knew it had been God, and I turned to Him with my whole heart. We left five hours later, but I didn't leave alone. I had my Father with me. For me Christianity has never been a religion. It's always, always been a relationship with the One I love—my Father.

"My life was instantly transformed. I quit drinking, gave up the drugs, and stopped every activity I thought might displease my Father. Not that I didn't do anything wrong or make some funny mistakes. One that comes to mind is when I quit dealing drugs. I still had a supply of marijuana on hand and didn't want to waste it, so I sold it off to another dealer and gave the proceeds as an offering at church. I wouldn't do that now, but my heart was in the right spot, and I'm sure my Father smiled at me the same way a mother smiles at her child when he proudly presents her with a flower from her garden that she would have preferred he left un-picked. I was doing the best I knew, serving Him out of love. Oh, that everyone could taste of my experience with the God of love, who is my Father and who would be such a Father to them if they would allow it."

"You know, Mark, people often ask me about God. They want a simple 1-2-3 step program to find what you have, but it doesn't work that way, does it?"

"No," he replies. "Perhaps the hardest thing for us to understand in our narrow human viewpoint is that God does not use a one-size-fits-all approach to winning our love and devotion. Oh, there are many biblical principles and such to guide us, but what He really wants is for us to sit at His feet and let Him instruct us personally."

I study Mark's face; the firelight reveals a powerfully built man, softened by middle age, but there is something more … an inner peace. This is a man surrendered to God, ready to obey. We sit companionably in the silence, each of us lost in his thoughts.

"Time for bed," he comments regretfully, rising to his feet.

I agree and head to my room, still contemplating how a home like this can be a little foretaste of heaven and how an abusive home can be a living hell. *That's about it,* I conclude in my thoughts. *Stories like Mark's make you hate sin in all its evilness, and a truly Christian home draws the affections toward our heavenly Father. Only He can bring such joy and peace into a home occupied by failing human beings.*

"Goodnight," Mark calls, his voice floating toward me as I walk to the guestroom. I can almost hear his smile in the darkness, but he doesn't wait for an answer as he walks to his room. This family has taken the time necessary to be a family, and it shows. The children know they are loved without the limits of time or convenience. *If every home could be like this,* I think, *the world would be a better place.* A wave of emotion surges within me, and I give vent to the fullness of my heart as I say out loud, even though he can't hear, "God bless you, Mark, for what you've let God do in this home. Goodnight!"

Activities for Week 10

Sunday

Prayer time: Ask God to reveal Himself to you as you read. Try and enter into the experiences presented and see God as the participants perceive Him.

Activity: Read the chapter, "Time to Be a Family."

Reflection: Consider your family experience in childhood. What was good and what was bad about it? In the home you have formed or want to form, do you see yourself reproducing the type of family you grew up in?

Monday

Prayer time: In seeking God today, bring your family before Him seeking wisdom in how best to structure your home after heaven's order. Enjoy your time with Him. Remember you are part of His family.

Activity: Consider every family member in your home, his or her needs and struggles. Next, think about family time and how a time set apart might minister to these areas you have identified.

Reflection: Most of us would like to think that our dreams and goals are uniquely our own. But if you try to bring the needs of your family down to their most basic elements, you may find that all of us need to be loved and need someplace where, no matter what anyone or everyone else thinks, we are special. All of us need encouragement, and all of us need a place to grow as we get to know God, grow to love Him, and experience peace through Him.

Tuesday

Prayer time: Take time to feel God with you today. Strive to make sure that you maintain a real relationship with Him and not just a casual contact.

Activity: If possible, start to experiment with time to be a family. If your current commitments do not permit it, lay definite plans to implement it in the future. Start small and increase the time commitment as your family learns to enjoy family time. If you are unused to getting along and cooperating together, it may take some time to learn these skills, and extended time together could be awkward if you're really estranged, but with time and patience you can learn to enjoy each other once more.

Reflection: What is the biggest hindrance to taking time to be a family in your home? Are you separated, divorced, still single? Remember that even if you are alone, you are a family, for you are part of God's great family. And in setting some time apart for something you enjoy, you are not just getting some refreshing recreation, but also training yourself for the day when you will have a family to care for. This is one habit they will be very happy you developed.

Wednesday

Prayer time: Ask God for courage and wisdom as you begin the process of implementing change.

Activity: Take a few moments to write a note to each family member telling them what makes them so special and why you want to spend more time with them. It may seem awkward, but I think you will find it worth the effort. Remember you have probably not been giving them the type of attention they deserve, and they may be skeptical. It is your job to convince them, as the Lord gives you wisdom and guidance.

Reflection: What was the reaction to your notes? Did they think this is just a phase you are going through, or do they see genuine change? Why did you answer that way?

Thursday

Prayer time: Because today's activity involves another family, ask God whom you should pick. Try to be open to whomever God should bring to your mind, even if they are not close friends.

Activity: Try and schedule a get-together with another like-minded family just for the purpose of having fun together. Arrange it so that it will not fail to be fun and then make sure everyone has a good time. I know of some families that had a great time playing games in a picnic pavilion while rain came down in chilly torrents. Remember time to be a family depends on nothing more than a determination to be a true and loving family, even if it rains on your picnic!

Reflection: How far out of the way are you willing to go to provide for your family the fellowship and the family time they need?

Friday

Prayer time: You have spent a week thinking about time to be a family, and today take a few moments in your prayer time to reflect upon the God you have been coming to know. God planned a special garden for our first parents and then planned a special time each and every day when He would come personally and walk with them in the cool of the evening. God wants to spend time being a family in just so personal a manner with you. How can you assist Him in the process?

Activity: If in your reflection on your family this week you remembered a special something done by a parent, a spouse, or sibling, take the time to express appreciation, even if decades have gone by. For it is only as we express gratitude that we truly possess the gift given. And the gift of time—time to be loved, to appreciate, to be involved with, and time to actually be a family is a precious gift all of us should be privileged to enjoy.

Reflection: How many families do you know who are taking the time to be a family? Any? It is a rare thing to be one of those exceptional families. If you are determined to join their ranks, and I hope and pray you are, then you are going to be out of step with the world, and you must plan to be misunderstood and considered a little odd by others. Are you willing to be different?

Saturday

Reflection: After God created the world He set aside one day, the Sabbath, to enjoy what was made and for His created beings to enjoy Him. If God considers time with Him so important for His created children, what does this teach us about the importance of time with our children?

CHAPTER 11

The Family Firm

"Train up a child in the way he should go: and when he is old, he will not depart from it" (Proverbs 22:6).

CHAPTER GOAL

To dramatically change the way our homes work by an equitable distribution of work between the family members, and to invest the time redeemed from Mom and Dad's schedule in the children.

The rains of spring and the snows of winter were a thing of the past and the forest was garbed in a variety of new green growth not yet tempered by the rainless heat of late Rocky Mountain summer. The call of the out-of-doors on such days is almost audible, but I delayed, finishing my tasks inside, knowing that our guests should be arriving soon, and wanting my time free to spend with them.

Sally was kneading bread, her hands rhythmically pressing and turning the dough and forming loaves that no bakery can equal, when the phone rang. It was our friends, leaving Kalispell and headed toward the North Fork and our house. Hanging up the phone I thought of this family, one of the many God has brought into our lives, and as always I wondered what God had in store for their visit. Would they see something of value, something they wanted for themselves, or would they, like so many others, look at our lifestyle and decide it required just too great a sacrifice?

Bob and Samantha Cutter had a boy and girl about the ages of our teenagers. We had met at one of our meetings, and they had told us excitedly of their planned visit to Glacier Nation Park. Learning where we lived, they had grasped hold of a new possibility. Might they come and visit us while they were there? Amazing to both of us, primarily because our lives are planned anywhere from twelve to eighteen months in advance, the time they planned to visit was free, and now they were on their way.

Inwardly, Samantha mused to herself, *It's a long drive up those fifty miles of gravel road to their home; I hope they like us. The closer I get, the more nervous I feel. Jim and Sally are so nice, I'm sure everything will be all right. I guess I've kind of made them into spiritual supermen in my mind, but they're just people like us. Still, I'm afraid my family won't measure up.* Her reverie was broken as Bob asked her to look up something on the map and the normal car chatter resumed.

One advantage to living in the wilderness is that when you hear a car, you know it's for you. So we were out on the back porch to greet our friends as they drove up. They climbed stiffly out of their car, and Samantha graciously turned down our invitation to come in and sit down. "Thank you, but after the trip here, sitting is something I'm not quite ready for," she said with a laugh.

"Jim, who did the rock work around the foundation of your cabin?" Bob asked.

"We did."

"You did?" Bob exclaimed. "Wow! It really sets off the cabin beautifully. I didn't know you were a stone mason."

"Well ... to tell you the truth, I'm not. We wanted the boys to get a taste of different construction techniques, so we came up with this project to teach the boys masonry skills. It took about two years to complete it all."

"You mean the boys did this?"

"Well, not all of it, of course. We dug the footings and did all the preparatory work together. We did the first wall as a family project with the boys, so we could all learn how, and then the boys and I each did one of the remaining sides by ourselves."

"And these swings?" Bob continued, giving his daughter a playful push as she relaxed in one of them.

"Andrew built them for us. This is what we use for 'swing time.' I'm sure you've heard us mention that in some of our sermons."

He nodded and then queried, "How old was he?"

"I think he was around twelve," I replied. Since we had already begun an impromptu tour of the property, I decided to continue showing them around. I tried to convey that our home when we moved in was just a simple mountain cabin and the land around had been very rough, but of course, that was hard for them to imagine as they gazed at the neat, attractive yard and trim house. Bob had heard me mention the workbenches our sons had made in previous talks, and now he just had to see them! So we stopped at the garage before heading to the garden. The boys had completed this huge project themselves, and now the benches provide plenty of workspace. The largest is almost twenty feet long and three feet wide, with shelves and storage drawers. "The boys put in every board, nail, and bolt," I told Bob. "They really enjoyed it and used most of their spare minutes over a period of many weeks. It really kept them busy and gave them a sense of accomplishment when they were done."

Samantha may have been nervous about visiting here, Bob was thinking, *but I'm astonished. I have to twist my son's arm to get him to mow the lawn, and their boys stick to a time-consuming project like this for weeks! There's something more here than meets the eye. I've got to know more.*

Suddenly Bob noticed a little door. I could tell he was trying not to be nosy, so I grinned and said, "Go ahead, Bob. Open it." He gasped as he stepped inside and discovered Andrew's all-cedar sauna.

"Jim, this is just the ticket for relaxing at the end of a hard day. No sore muscles for you." Bob was still engrossed in his exploration of the sauna as everyone headed for the garden. As the silence settled down around him, he realized he was alone and hurried to catch up.

"We had to truck up all the dirt from an old farm in the valley," I explained. Our soil is just too rocky here. The greenhouse was an early project back in the days when we were just getting started and so very limited on funds that we cut the timber in the woods and milled it with a chain saw mill. Matthew was six then, maybe seven, but even so he pounded about every third nail."

After admiring Sally's thriving crops, we headed down to the creek using the trail that had been another of our special projects. Our home sits up on a forty-foot rise, and the creek is at the bottom of a steep descent. The boys had suggested, and we had agreed, that we build a trail into the hillside providing a gentle grade for easier access to the creek. Many family times in the evening were given to this trail, cutting the trees, building retaining walls of logs, and at last spreading gravel over its whole length.

As we wandered down the winding trail, Samantha found her mind wandering as well. *This project must have required their family to spend hours and hours working together, and yet they never tell stories of frayed nerves and rising tempers in the process. How do they do it? Bob and I can hardly write a letter together without fighting.*

As the guest cabin came into view, I heard Bob ask, "So, when did you and the boys build the guest cabin?"

"Well, this project wasn't our idea. It was the brainstorm of some Lutheran men who run a construction business here in the valley. You see, back when I was selling real estate, clients often asked me to recommend a builder, and I referred a lot of clients to these men. They really appreciated it, especially when they were just getting started. This cabin was their 'Thank-you' present. They even provided all the materials."

"Oh," said Bob, a little disappointed. "I was just sure this was another of your wonderful family projects."

"Bob, I'll tell you what. There is more to the story. If you can wait until lunch, I'll tell you the rest of the story about the cabin.

Right now we better head inside because Matthew and Andrew should have the meal ready.

"Mmmmm, smells like we are in time for lunch," I said, leading the group into the cabin.

"You sure are, Father," Andrew said. "Glad you're here too. I was getting hungrier and hungrier just smelling it all. I just finished the salad, so everything is ready."

Wow, Samantha thought, *the smells in here would give credit to a world-class restaurant. It's clear those smiling boys didn't just warm up food their mother had already prepared; they have actually made the meal. I can tell because Sally is going around peeking into this bowl and that pot to see what they've made. She trusts them to make a meal for company without her supervision or even her insight! Incredible! Something's going on here. I've got to find out how she does it.*

"You mean your boys cook as well as do the more traditional men's work?" Samantha asked.

"Sure, we do," Andrew replied.

"And clean, and can, and iron, and ... " Matthew was on a roll and probably could have kept going for quite some time, not complaining or even boasting, but sharing with the understated pride of mastery. A gentle touch from his mother's hand on his arm stopped him mid-sentence, reminding him of the other young people there, who might feel overwhelmed with too detailed a recitation of activities. And so lunch began.

"You see, Bob and Samantha, our philosophy has always been that if our sons expect to head a household someday, and they do— then they must know how to perform every task and duty of the household in order to be in a position to manage these tasks done by others," I explained. "It's kind of like working your way up from stock boy to president."

"Jim, you promised me a story about the guest house," Bob broke in. "By the way, this lasagna is great!" he added, passing his plate for seconds.

"All right," I said, smiling broadly, "if you think it wouldn't be too distracting." I watched them busily devouring the meal.

"Please, continue," Bob said with a chuckle. "It'll give me a chance to slow down and take a breather."

"When the builders suggested the guest cabin, Sally and I agreed, but only on one condition. We wanted our boys to work with them, so they could learn how to build a structure from the ground up. I knew they were hesitant both to have the boys and to voice the real reason for fear of offending us. They weren't too crazy about the idea, but we persuaded them to give the boys a one-day trial. I told them, 'If they don't work out well or are too much trouble, you won't have to put up with them again.' They reluctantly agreed, steeling themselves to endure for just one day. And they loaded Matthew and Andrew down with 'go-fer' jobs all day, expecting them to tire out or lose interest. Later I found out about their conversation. It went something like this. 'Matthew, do you know how to measure and cut ... accurately?'

" 'Yes, I think I can.'

" 'Well, get one of those two-by-sixes and cut me a five-foot, seven-and-three-eighths-inch length,' one of the builders commanded as he put down his tape measure and went back to work with his companions.

" 'You don't really expect him to get that right, do you?' asked one of his friends doubtfully.

" 'Naw, but I didn't expect them to last this long, either.'

" 'Here is the board you asked for, sir. Anything else?'

" 'Yes, why don't you unload the rest of those two-by-sixes from the truck and stack them near the power saw.'

" 'By George, I think this is cut right. In fact, I couldn't have cut it better myself.'

" 'Beginner's luck,' his friend countered. 'Let's see if the other boy can do it.' He paused momentarily. Then without waiting for an answer, he whipped out his tape and made a quick measurement. 'Hey, Andrew,' he called, 'I need a two-by-six cut to eight-foot, four-and-three-quarter inches. Would you mind cutting it for me?' That's how it all began. When the builders saw they were accurate and diligent, they started giving them more responsibility. Eventually, they hired the boys to help on other building projects, and through these men, Matthew and Andrew have learned every aspect of the building trades."

Makes sense, Samantha thought. *Everything in these boys' lives has been placed there to prepare them for success. You might say it was luck to know the right people at the right time, but if the boys hadn't been taught to work properly and well … it wouldn't have mattered anyway. I sure have a lot to teach my kids.*

"How did you know what to teach your boys?" Bob asked.

"I didn't. I merely tried to involve them in every task I thought they might be remotely capable of doing. We started at a very early age. I also tried to teach them to anticipate my needs as they helped me."

"Anticipate?"

"Yes. For example, when I was changing the oil in our truck I would train the boys to try and think ahead of me so I wouldn't have to say I needed the wrench. They were supposed to think out the sequence of events in changing the oil so that when they saw I was ready for the wrench they were ready and I wouldn't have to ask for it. It took a number of times to train the thinking process, and it was a real trial of my patience, but they soon learned the art of planning ahead. In fact, it became almost a game to keep out in front of me in thinking out the job!"

Bob nodded thoughtfully. "When I tried to involve the children in my work, I just gave up because it was so aggravating. Besides, it was easier to do it myself. Guess I was pretty short-sighted."

"Bob, it's a problem at least as old as parenting. To train children for service requires of us an investment of time and self-denial that tends to really rub parents the wrong way. Recently I read a story of a woman writer who had suggested parents teach their children by working with them. Her article generated various letters, one of which she responded to and I'll paraphrase. 'You asked, "Don't your children bother you when you work with them?" Of course my children bother me, but I never let them know it.'

"That is the crux of the whole matter, Bob. It doesn't matter that it is hard for us to do. It only matters that we do what is best for our children. I suppose the real inspiration for wanting our boys trained differently than most came from running my own business. I vividly remember trying to hire a new secretary for my insurance agency. Let me tell you, it was an uphill battle to find a qualified person. I interviewed thirty-two young women for the job, most of whom were obviously unqualified for the position. They came in dressed unprofessionally, chewing gum, semiliterate, or with horrible inter-personal skills. It was discouraging, until a college graduate applied. She had a degree in elementary education and had just moved to the area with her new husband. Unfortunately, there were no positions in the local school system, which explained her appearance at my of-fice. She could file, take notes, had a pleasant phone personality, and good interpersonal skills. I thought my problems were over until I asked her to demonstrate her ability to handle a cash transaction. I gave her the petty cash box we keep in the office and told her, 'I want you to pretend that I am a customer who wants to pay his premium. My bill is $87.36. Here is a hundred-dollar bill. Please make change.' She looked at me and then the cash box. For the first time, she seemed flustered. 'It's OK,' I encouraged her, 'just take your time and figure it out.' She started and stopped, then blushed all over, because she had no idea how to figure out someone's change. She was embar-rassed and should have been. I was embarrassed for her. How could she teach school if she couldn't even do something that simple?"

"I came home that night and told Sally about my thirty-three ap-plicants. She wasn't surprised at all. You see, she taught in the church youth division and knew all about the young people who were cur-rently growing up and how unprepared they were for the real world.

"I didn't want our kids growing up like that, not fully realizing that at that point, Sally and I had made a decision for which we would be forever grateful. We started to give our children greater and greater responsibilities, far beyond what their peers experienced, but the greater efforts demanded of them did not make them sullen and re-bellious. In fact, the more we pushed and demanded, the sweeter their personalities became and the easier it was to get them to surrender. Day by day, every job crossed their wills and required them to submit to God's will for them, and as they did so, He increased their natural strengths and abilities. We have just continued that way, running our family like a business with Matthew and Andrew as the junior partners."

"So, you started the family firm," Bob said, laughing, and then he turned serious. "Will it work for us? Even though our children are older?"

"Bob," I said, glancing at his kids, "you have good kids, and it's not their fault they haven't been trained. Why don't we pair them up with ours for a day and see how they react?"

"But, Jim," Samantha interjected, "I haven't even taught my daughter to cook yet!"

"It's all right. She has to start sometime, and it might as well be here." And so we did. All day long I saw her daughter chop wood with Andrew while her brother helped plan meals. Those kids worked hard all day, but every time we saw them, they seemed happy. We ate fantastic meals and enjoyed great conversation.

It was a hot evening, and we got out the tubes for a cool, relaxing river trip. The water was so refreshing; I just relaxed and let myself drift downstream. Suddenly my world turned upside down as someone dunked me! *That Matthew,* I thought, *he'll do it to you every time if you don't watch.* I came up sputtering to the surface, only to see him far away, resting lazily on his tube—laughing. Who? Then I saw Bob's daughter. Why, my boys had taught her too well. What a fun time we had together.

Later that night I heard them laughing and retelling my dunking story as they headed toward the guest cabin. I shamelessly eavesdropped, enjoying the sounds of a happy family.

"What did you think of their program?" I heard Samantha ask. And I listened intently for the answer.

"It was great!" their son responded enthusiastically. I heard the voice of her daughter, that rascal, exclaim, "It was the best day ever! Can we follow the Hohnbergers' program at home?"

They had moved beyond my hearing at this point, and I hoped and prayed the answer was "Yes." I remembered all the hard choices we had made along the way, and my eyes misted with unshed tears at the thought of what lay before them if they chose to go forward. *That girl was only mistaken in one thing,* I thought as I turned to enter my own home. *It isn't the Hohnberger program; it's God's.*

When God designed the first family in Eden so very long ago, He never intended the situations that families have allowed themselves to be placed in today through tradition, chance, and social pressure. Today the family is composed of two parents who carry a disproportionate amount of the household responsibilities. This is harmful in many ways to all parties, but it especially robs the children. They do not view themselves as vital, contributing members of the household, and with that lack of responsibility they lose the wonderful sense of self-worth that comes from being needed. They also lose their parents' time and attention because it is consumed in the tasks that might have been done by others. Their parents have less energy for play and grow weary. They tend to become less cheerful, bringing an oppressive atmosphere of gloom into the home. This situation is even more pronounced in single-parent homes where one adult must carry the whole load of household burdens, often in addition to full-time employment. So, how do we rectify such problems?

First and foremost, it will take a schedule. The majority of families we counsel have no schedule. They often think they do, but on examination we find the schedule is something imposed by others, such as schools, employers, etc. Just because you have to be at work or at school by a required time does not mean you are scheduled, any more than driving the speed limit when there is a police officer following you proves you are a law-abiding driver. No, it is what you do when there is no external authority exerting control that proves whether you are scheduled or not.

We have found it helpful to divide the day into three parts. The first part is the early morning hours. That's the time we rise, spend our personal devotional time with God, take care of personal grooming, have family worship, and finally breakfast. The second area is the working hours of the day, where tasks begin. Depending on who you are, it may be outside employment, housework, or schoolwork.

The third area is the evening hours. This is the time set aside for family recreation, and it should be guarded from interruption as rigorously as the work hours are. I usually remind people that the early morning hours begin at the end of the evening hours, because the time we retire in the evening determines our willingness to get up on time the next morning. New schedules should always be adopted and implemented in the evening before the start of a new day. That way any new program can start fresh and doesn't have to begin by dragging the baggage of the previous day's intemperance.

The purpose in scheduling our family life is not just efficiency, but rather that we understand the schedule as a tool used of God to redeem time now wasted, and as a gift for our happiness that He may draw us closer to Himself. We all want to be like Jesus, and a schedule will help achieve that goal.

In helping countless people plan schedules that work practically in the real world, we have adopted this philosophy: Do only those things necessary to your temporal comfort and happiness, then you will find the time to read your Bibles with prayerful interest and raise up a well-ordered, well-disciplined, Christ-centered family.

God is a God of order. This is self-evident from the natural laws visible in nature. Ecclesiastes 3:1-8 says, "To every thing there is a season, and a time to every purpose under the heaven: A time to be born, and a time to die; a time to plant, and a time to pluck up that which is planted; a time to heal; ... break down, ... build up; ... weep, ... laugh, ... mourn, ... cast away ... gather ... embrace ... refrain from embracing; ... rend, ... sew; ... keep silence, ... speak; ... love, ... hate; ... a time of war, and a time of peace." Our schedule should reflect a time for everything that needs to be done in our households.

The best way to make a schedule is to simply launch right into it. Write out your purposed schedule. If you don't know how or where to start, look at the sample schedules in Appendix 2. Keep in mind that you must tailor your schedule to fit your family and you will gain far more cooperation if the various members of your household are involved in the decision-making process. Then try it out for a week. At the end of that time rewrite it, amending it as needed to accommodate any problems that came up. Continue tweaking and adjusting your schedule until you have it in good working order, and then leave it alone and in place.

A working schedule is a tremendous blessing. Children thrive on the consistent expectations of what is required. And as my coauthor Julie, puts it, "When I don't feel well or I'm just not motivated, my schedule is my salvation. I don't have to make any decisions; my family knows what is expected; and the household runs without Mother having to crack the whip or supervise."

After years of experience, I can emphatically state that the people who have the most trouble staying on schedule are the parents, not the children. The children enjoy knowing what to do and when to do it. It is the parents who will make or break the schedule in the home. If you keep the schedule, allowing nothing to interfere, your children will do likewise. If you allow this or that temporary problem to intrude, then soon everyone will view the schedule with contempt.

Every company has rules, principles, and by-laws under which they operate. Our homes need such rules as well. They should be simple and adapted to your children's ages. There is one more very important principle to remember: your household rules must be enforced!

The ideas I've presented in this chapter are not complex theology. In fact, they may seem too obvious to even merit discussion. But we have found there is no substitute for a well-ordered and well-run Christian family. It speaks louder to the community than all the sermons preached. It reaches deep into the hearts of children and binds them to life-long principles that will serve them no matter where they may be called or what they do. Becoming a member of the family firm is the training ground for real life. The future of your family is before you, and the only question left to ask is, "What do I want for my children?" May God be with you as you decide.

What Do I Want for My Children

What do I want for my children?
Do I seek for them worldwide fame?

Do I treasure for them wealth and riches?
Do I want their lives to be like a game?

What do I want for my children?
Is it power and wisdom and might?
Do I want for them untold blessings?
Do I want everything to go just right?

I'll tell you what I want for my children:
A heart full of peace from above,
A life of serving others,
A heart of patience and love.

I want them to know my Saviour,
To be free from the power of sin.
This is what I want for my children.
I want them to walk with Him.
I want them to be like Him.

—Ruth Anderson

Activities for Week 11

Sunday

Prayer time: Ask God to show you weak areas in your family that He would like to have you correct. Remain sensitive to His impression and remember that the area we may feel like tackling the least may be the very area most needing to be addressed.

Activity: Read "The Family Firm." Counsel with your family and arrange to have a family council Tuesday evening.

Reflection: Was there anything in the chapter that crossed your will? Why do you suppose that was so? Consider thoughtfully your own family's schedule. What is good already and what needs improvement?

Monday

Prayer time: As you pray, remember that the reason for organizing your family is to gain a closer walk with God. Therefore, seek His will in this area of your life today.

Activity: As far as possible, write out your family's schedule just as you are living now. If you really don't feel you have a schedule, then note the outside influences such as work and school that require you to run on their schedule.

Reflection: Did you notice that you were busy all day, but on paper it seems like there should have been areas of free time? If so, you are not alone. Life in our day and age is very demanding, and unless we block out time for specific projects or items of interest, countless things will steal away our time moment by moment.

Tuesday

Prayer time: Ask for wisdom today so that you may order your life after heaven's design and not your own. Try as best as possible to approach rescheduling your life with a neutralized will, your spirit willing to submit to whatever God shows you to do.

Activity: Today is the day. Get out a sheet of paper and write up a new schedule. Get out a second piece and make up new job assignments for your whole family. Really work on your presentation just as you might a task at the office. Plan to present it to your whole family tonight. Keep your plan open to suggestions from others. Remember that some tasks such as cooking may not be able to be done until the children have been trained in the skills necessary to accomplish them safely.

Reflection: Think of each member of your household, their strengths and weaknesses, and plan your presentation in such a way that it will appeal to each in their own personality. Remember that a successful schedule begins with a proper bedtime the night before.

Wednesday

Prayer time: Seek patience and wisdom for today's conflicts.

Activity: Start running on your new schedule. Remember that while you may be convinced of the need for change, everyone else is going to have to be sold on its worth by experiencing it. If you get grumpy or short with your family, they are not going to be inclined to want your new program. If they find you have more time to invest in making them happy and you use the time gained for this purpose, you will quickly gain converts to your new schedule.

Reflection: How did it go today? What could be improved?

Thursday

Prayer time: Ask God to help you make correct judgments as you fine-tune the scheduling process.

Activity: Today you may need to tinker a little with specific areas of the schedule that just didn't work well yesterday. Don't be afraid to adjust both the schedule and the household tasks until you have a well-working system in place. It may take some time, but stick to it and enjoy the extra time as a family.

Reflection: After two days, have you seen some benefits? Some shortcomings?

Friday

Prayer time: Seek for God to guide you through this process. You will need His help to stay with it and to iron out the early difficulties.

Activity: Seek to help each child through their new tasks, even if you think they are old enough to do them on their own. Unless you have previously trained them in these household tasks, they may not have learned all the tricks you know that make the jobs go faster and easier. Be an encouragement, not a nag!

Reflection: Have you been devoting more time to your family? Make sure they stay a priority.

Saturday

Reflection: If you get a chance, look back at the story of Creation in the first two chapters of Genesis. God is a God of order and schedule too—take courage!

CHAPTER 12

Family Councils

"Provoke not your children to wrath: but bring them up in the nurture and admonition of the Lord" (Ephesians 6:4).

CHAPTER GOAL

To start implementing family councils in such a manner that they are a constructive tool to alleviate conflict and bring about the type of family government the Lord envisioned, empowering all members to reach their potential.

"Father, can we have a family council sometime soon?"

I turned from my yard work to see Matthew gazing at me with sober eyes. Clearly something was bothering him, but I had no idea what it was. In our family anyone can have a family council if they wish. They just have to come to me and ask for one, and then I schedule it in where it seems appropriate. Sometimes you need a little more information to make sure you plan on a time that will work. For example, if someone has a vacation suggestion we might do that very casually, but if someone is upset or has a serious concern we may need a larger period of uninterrupted time. I decided to probe just a little. "Is something bothering you, son?"

"Yes, and I would appreciate it if we could talk about it this week."

"Well, son, this evening is free. How about seven-thirty?"

"Sounds fine, Father. Thank you!"

After he left I racked my brain to see if I had done something to offend him, but I came up with nothing. The Holy Spirit didn't bring anything to mind in that moment, and so I concluded it must have been Sally who was responsible. She must have asked him to do something that was not his job or pushed too hard in his schoolwork. *Whatever it is, we will be able to deal with it tonight,* I thought, and secretly I relaxed a little knowing that I was not the cause of the problem and wouldn't be on the hot seat, so to speak.

That evening as the family gathered, I reminded everyone of the purpose of family councils. It's not to condemn or condone, but to find a solution. I also reviewed the ground rules. The first one is that the person requesting the council has the right to speak without interruption until they feel they have stated the problem sufficiently. Then no one else is allowed to speak unless they have an idea for a solution, a suggestion, or need clarification on a point. That being said, we prayed that God would lead us. We asked that self be surrendered and controlled, no matter what the issue. Then we turned the time over to Matthew, eager to hear his complaint.

"Father, you used my brand-new chain saw today and didn't ask my permission," Matthew stated indignantly.

I sat there in stunned silence. I had been so sure that I wasn't the cause of his problem, and now this! I struggled just a moment to pull my relaxed mind back into gear. Yes, I had borrowed his saw. There were some small limbs behind the greenhouse that I wanted to clear out. When I went to the workbench to get my saw, Matthew's brand-new lightweight model was right there, and it seemed the perfect tool for the job, so I borrowed it. He was now thirteen, and it was the first real power tool he had ever owned. Of course, he had paid for it himself, but as it sat there temptingly in its shiny red paint, I never even thought to ask *permission.*

I had always been strict about requiring the boys to ask before they used *my* tools. That way if something was missing or broken, I knew who to check in with, and the very act of asking cultivated respect for others' property and responsibility when an item was borrowed.

As I sat there on the hot seat, I suddenly saw the situation through Matthew's eyes and could imagine how he felt when he heard a chain saw running and looked out to find me using his brand-new saw that he hadn't even used yet. He was offended that I hadn't extended the same courtesy of asking first, and rightly so. I was beginning to feel very small in my seat.

The big picture loomed before me, and I began to wonder what would have happened if we didn't have a mechanism like family councils for dealing with such conflicts. Imagine, if you will, Matthew feeling hurt and angry and blowing up at me. Or if he had come to me to speak privately, I might have been tempted to say, "Listen, I make the rules around here. That's just the way it is. When you get your own home and pay the bills, you can make the rules." In my heart, I knew that responses like that just embitter the children against the parents.

With every eye in the room riveted on me, I knew I had to respond, and every word I said mattered. "Matthew, I can't think of a biblical principle for this problem, but I've always believed that 'What is good for the goose is good for the gander.'"

"Huh? What does that mean?" he asked, perplexed.

"It means I'm sorry I used your saw without permission. If it's good for you to ask first, it's good for me too. I promise I will do so in the future," I concluded. His face relaxed and melted into a smile. I knew it was all over, dealt with justly and fairly, and peace flooded my soul too. Harmony was restored.

Family councils can be used as a tool to work miracles when dealing with conflict, but it doesn't stop there. We've had family councils gathered around the table, planning for vacations or around a fire deep in the wilderness with only the cry of loons to accompany our words. We've even had them in the car as we travel. Yet many families are reluctant to try them. The underlying sentiment seems to be "That's fine for your family and the Waters family, but it won't work in our home or with our kids."

Would you be willing to at least give it a try? Join me, as we visit one struggling family who did just that and came to see the value of the family council. Nancy, a successful doctor, together with her husband, Don, was trying to keep her own surgical practice going and raising three boys. While Don had a small business of his own, it was Nancy's practice that provided the majority of the family support, and it was Don who was home with the boys. The only problem was that Don is what I'd call a softy, a gentle, kindly man who had allowed some bad habits to develop in his sons that were causing tremendous conflict and tension in the home. The boys had learned to overstep the bounds of Don's kindness and wanted to debate any instruction that crossed their will. They had become indolent in their work, stalling and delaying until simple tasks like washing the dishes could drag out for as much as an hour. This indolence, coupled with the debates, made tasks seem to last forever and prevented the family from completing household jobs in a timely manner. You can imagine what life was like in their house. All day long the father reminded and badgered the children, who ignored and antagonized his efforts. It was a losing battle that frustrated everyone involved. Worse still, instead of the home being a refuge from the cares of the world, it became a place of conflict and strife. The children felt they could never succeed, the father felt impotent, and the mother was sorely tempted to become impatient with both the children and her husband because her expectations of what they should be accomplishing were continually being disappointed.

When I suggested that we might be able to resolve most of these problems in a family council, they were incredulous. Even though they were desperate for a solution, they drew back from what they felt would just be another long, contentious battle ending in futility.

I asked my son, Andrew, who was twenty-one then, to take their boys out on their property and set up a grizzly run. Where we live, grizzly bears roam freely, and they are renowned for their unpleasant personalities and short tempers; so when we set up disciplines for our boys, we planned some long runs referred to as "grizzly runs." These were supposed to be tough enough to take the "grizzlies," or the *fight,* out of them. It works like this: If we crossed the will of our child and they became upset or refused to do their work properly because of stubbornness, we would send them for a grizzly run instead of trying to deal with them when they were all worked up. The rules are that they had to run it at their best speed, and if they didn't come back winded and sweating, we knew they had tried to pull a fast one, and off we sent them again!

This is not designed to be punitive, but rather a way to neutralize those energies that are poised to do wrong and divert them into a harmless outlet like running—hard. We trained the boys that the time spent running was not to be used for self-pity, but to give them time to gain self-surrender. So, when I assigned Andrew to set up a grizzly run, he knew just what to do. Their new grizzly run ran across a field and up a hill along the crest and then down a long slope to the house. He had beautifully used the hundred-plus acres they called home, and the run was still less than a mile. The boys helped Andrew with the design, and then we timed them as Andrew led them at top speed in the initial run. Timing is very important if you are to know your child's best speed. When we started grizzly runs, we used to run with our boys until they got used to the idea. Nancy and Don's boys were huffing and puffing when they got back with Andrew, and their view of the "grizzly run" was suddenly a lot more serious.

Nancy and Don asked me to lead out that evening in moderating their first family council, to kind of walk them through it. The first thing I did was lay out the ground rules we follow and introduced the parents' concern about their poor job performance. I asked the boys if the parents were correct in their judgment or if their parents were exaggerating. The boys hung their heads, and I knew the description was accurate. In many ways they were good kids who really desired to do right, but did not understand how to submit to God and surrender their wills in order that He might change their feelings and desires and enable them to do what deep down they knew they should. It was in this context that I shared the grizzly run concept as a tool to help them clear their minds so they could respond to the Holy Spirit and find happiness in obedience, instead of continuing in misbehavior. Then I asked the boys to decide how and when they should be supervised.

I guided their thoughts a little, but soon they had compiled a list of "problem" activities, like the dishes, that even they admitted would benefit from a new and different approach. I emphasized that it was at the parents' sole discretion to use the grizzly run tool, and its purpose was to change their attitudes and make them willing to listen and be reasoned with.

We had to make sure they understood that the battles they faced in the home were being won or lost in their thoughts. When any activity crosses our wills, the natural tendency is for feelings and attitudes to rise up and encourage us in the wrong path. It is the manner in which we deal with those "natural" feelings, either by surrendering them to God or by indulging them, that determines our success or failure in the Christian life. This is why our children need training far more than "punishment." Consequences are only good when they lead or motivate a child to do right instead of wrong. The inherited tendency we obtained from our parents and passed on to our young ones is a self-will that wants its own way, right now! You don't have to teach your child to be selfish, to throw a fit or be demanding; they know how to do it naturally. It is only through the grace of God that any of us can overcome these natural tendencies. Nancy and Don hadn't been able to get the behavior they desired because they had never addressed the root cause.

The grizzly run designed to provide motivation for change was already working. Because the boys had already run a trial one with Andrew, they were beginning to think that grizzly runs weren't as much fun as they thought and that maybe cooperating with Mom and Dad wasn't such a bad idea after all. Nevertheless, they enthusiastically began assigning grizzly runs to what they felt were likely misbehaviors.

Children have a strong sense of justice and tend to be harsher on disobedience than adults if given the opportunity, so I was happy to hear the youngest boy protest when his brothers promptly assigned a grizzly run for some rather minor violations. "No," he objected, "that's only worth half a grizzly run." And everyone agreed.

Without even realizing it, the family council had the boys working together toward the family goal of reform. The parents looked stunned and later shared, "We thought that a family council meant you told the children what was expected and that was that, but you almost turned it over to them!"

"That's right," I agreed. "Children are much more likely to support a government in which they have had some input." These parents were just beginning to learn that everyone, not just the children, want to be part of the decision-making process or at least have their feelings taken into consideration. Family councils are a natural extension of the Family Firm that we talked about in chapter 11. It is by giving those junior partners the ability to participate in the family government that they learn self-government. It's not just a symbolic representation either, but a real, meaningful voice in the family. Children appreciate and respond to that consideration.

Nancy and Don had begun the process of sharing family government, and now they must willingly and consistently continue the program. I have found that in any household, it's not the children who have a problem with change, but the parents. We parents are most guilty when it comes to lack of follow-through. The results achieved always depend on how motivated we are. God often uses desperate circumstances to motivate us as adults to try forms of change that we might normally dismiss as distasteful. I remember one family who was so desperate that they had piled everyone in the car, including the grandparents, and driven most of the day in order to counsel with us.

It all began with an unexpected phone call from Kalispell. It was a family that lived many miles from us. We had met them at a weekend series of meetings. They were having a family crisis and unable to come to any resolution, so they wanted us to help solve it.

Now this is hardly the type of unexpected guest we want to have dropping in on us, but our hearts went out to them in their despair.

We understood their frantic emotions and extreme exasperation. Fortunately, we had a fairly free afternoon in which to accommodate them. Not everyone who wants to drop in for a visit is so lucky. One of the hardest things I have had to face since forming the ministry of Restoration International is saying No gracefully to the many requests that people make that simply cannot be accommodated.

I gave this family the specific times we would be available to them, along with the directions to find our home. It was a pretty motley crew that stepped out of their car some hours later. We shared the normal pleasantries, but there was a certain something, an undercurrent of discontent that went far beyond any surface issues. The parents, Robert and Claire, looked ill at ease, and the children's expressions spoke volumes. Seventeen-year-old Barbara looked heartsick and weary, while Susan, her fifteen-year-old sister, seemed more disgusted than angry. It was their nine-year-old brother whose face told it all. His attitude seemed to be "Go ahead, do your worst. You can't touch me." He was becoming hardened, shutting people out to keep from being hurt any longer. The grandparents, who had accompanied them, looked like nice people who were worried to death about their daughter's family. We chatted for a few minutes, then settled into our living room and began to talk seriously. I organized the discussion on the basis of a family council and made everyone aware of the rules of conduct. Further, I stressed that in this setting the family members should be free to speak honestly about their problems without fear of retaliation later.

Deciding to start with the youngest, I asked Todd what he felt the problem was. He looked at me as if I should already know. After all, he knew, and he was a lot younger than I was, but at last he consented to tell me anyway. The disgust he felt for the situation couldn't be missed. "Mommy and Daddy just fight all the time," he said dejectedly. Clearly he was ready to discard his parents as hopeless cases. I waited a moment, but nothing more was forthcoming, so I turned to Susan with the same question.

"Mom always talks so harsh to us. She has these Bible verses to tell us what we should do and shouldn't do, and she wants us to live up to them, but she treats us so harshly, I can hardly stand it anymore," she confided hesitantly.

I glanced at Claire; she was in tears, but I felt impressed to continue, so I asked Barbara her opinion. This poised young woman was an adult for all intents and purposes. Her words demonstrated both the longing she had for a happy home and the bitter fact that she felt it was pretty near impossible to obtain. "If only Mom and Dad would quit fighting," she commented flatly. Her anger seemed spent, replaced by regret over what might have been. "Then when they fight," she continued, "they take all those upset feelings out on us and treat us badly."

"Is one parent more responsible than the other?" I probed.

"Yes, it's Mother. She is always picking at Dad."

Her mother was crying harder now, and I felt for her. Here she was sitting there with her parents listening as her family recounted her failings. "How is your dad at home?" I asked the children.

"Oh, Daddy is OK. We can usually talk to him, but he's never around." The other children nodded in agreement.

A picture of their home life was slowly emerging, but to be fair I needed to hear the parents' perspective as well. "Claire, your take on the situation is a little different, I'm sure. Why don't you share it with us now?"

It was as if a dam had broken, and Claire poured forth her tale of woe, telling how she had tried to uphold biblical standards, but her husband didn't help her and the children wouldn't cooperate. She felt she had to yell to get a bare minimum of compliance. Obviously, the children weren't the only ones who were miserable at home.

Finally I turned to her husband, Robert, and asked, "Are these things true?"

He shrugged and said, "Yeah, Claire kind of puts up with us as long as she can and then loses it and lets us all have it." He admitted that he was a softy, who tried not to rock the boat. He wanted to keep everyone happy, but wasn't really that involved in the family.

The last piece of the puzzle was falling into place. Clearly the father wasn't the spiritual leader he needed to be, and the mother, sensing the lack, had picked up the burden, but while she had a zeal for the things of God, she had gone about it the wrong way. It was, as the Bible says, "not according to knowledge." The children were just a reflection of the home environment.

Their family was on the verge of collapse. Failure to act in a positive, upward course at this point would likely lead to the disintegration of the family unit, with all of them in rebellion to the God in whose name such injustice and mercy had been wrought.

I glanced at the grandparents. "How long have you been with them?" I asked.

"Two weeks."

"Is there anything you'd like to add?" I queried.

"No, the way things have been described is pretty much the way it is," Claire's father observed sadly. An even deeper gloom settled over the room as the grandfather made his pronouncement.

Somehow I had to present them a picture of hope, and it had to begin with the parents. *Lord, give me the right words,* I prayed silently. "Robert," I began, "surely you can see that you must take over the spiritual leadership in the home if your family is to survive." He nodded his acquiescence, so I went on. "Claire has been carrying that burden for some time, but she's not suited to the task. You must begin leading out in family worship, in discipline, and most importantly in setting the overall tone of the family. Further, the problem of you two fighting must be dealt with by creating a time when you can *talk,* not *fight* about your concerns and needs and eliminate this constant battling." It took about forty-five minutes to help them set up swing time and understand the rules for effective communication. Then I turned to Claire.

"The mother is more responsible than any other single person for the attitude of the home. If she is cheerful and happy, the home will be the same. Claire, you have an extra burden because you have cultivated a negative, judgmental spirit. It will take concerted effort to choose to be happy and break that habit. The children benefit most from your happiness, and they are hurt most when it's absent. From talking with your children, I can tell that each one longs for you to be happy. What I'm going to suggest now might be viewed by some as a dangerous step, but I think it is appropriate at this point in your family life. If the children see you slipping back into old habits, they can say *respectfully* to you, 'Happy face,' and smile themselves. This is not to be done to upset you, but to encourage and remind you that the whole family is behind your efforts to change and praying that you will gain a victory."

I looked at the children, and they nodded. All they wanted was for their parents and their home to be happy. "You young people have an obligation as well," I said, addressing three pairs of questioning eyes. "If your parents are going to try and change the atmosphere of the home, you can make that task much easier by cooperating with their efforts. You know just those actions that tempt your mom to lose control, don't you?" They nodded shamefacedly. "All of you can choose to use your proper behavior to help your mother in her battle to be cheerful. Will you do that?" Again they nodded.

"Now, Claire," I said, turning my attention back to her, "you face a problem in that, even with your desire to change and all this help and encouragement, you can't do it. You don't have the power to alter what you have been doing. That's right," I explained, noticing the shocked expressions on their faces. I think they expected something more encouraging, but I paused to let the full import of my words sink in. "Not one of you can do what I'm telling you to do, not of yourselves and not even with God's help! *Only* as you let God do it in you, will you be able to succeed." I then shared with them the same material I've shared with you in "Batteries Not Included," "Crossing Over," and "Attached and Receiving." They were a family that looked good to the casual observer, and it was going to be hard for them to accept that all the good things they did and all the reforms they practiced were not of any true value compared with a life led under the control of God.

"But it's such a drastic change ..." Claire began and then trailed off.

"Yeah," Susan chimed in. "We're so used to being angry and upset, I'm not sure what's it's like to be nice," she said with all the honesty of childhood.

"I have an idea for you," Sally exclaimed, jumping into the conversation. "I have talked with a number of families, and from their experience, as well as my own, I can tell you that your reaction is normal. We can get so focused on being negative that to even contemplate doing something nice or giving a compliment seems almost fake and awkward. Most stores carry those cute little sticky notes these days. I recommend that each of you get some and make sure you pick a color or design that makes you feel good and positive. Then every day, you can, in fact you should, write something nice, positive, or encouraging to each member of your family. Then stick it up where they will be sure to find it. You can make it a fun surprise, and then it won't seem so awkward! You know how a muscle will get weak and atrophied if it's not used?" Everyone nodded. "Well, the muscle of kindness does too, and it may complain a bit about the exercise at first, but in time it becomes easier and easier."

We prayed there together, each one committing themselves to the task before them. When we rose to say goodbye, it was a different family than the one that had arrived three hours earlier. They had hope for a peaceful home that would make life worth living and a plan as to how to achieve it. The hugs those children gave me when they left about knocked me over. I could just sense their relief. They were so happy! I hoped that someday soon they would be hugging their parents the same way.

As we waved goodbye, we wondered what would happen. Would they go through with the changes or fall back into the old ways? Two weeks later, the first Thank-you cards arrived in the mail. The children were ecstatic! It was working! They were using the sticky notes as Sally had suggested, and it had eased them over to verbal communication. What a marked contrast their notes presented to the sad faces that had greeted us two weeks earlier. This family had learned and was learning that the transformation is available even to those who have made a mess of their lives. And it is available to you as well!

In closing, I want to tell to you about a young woman named Sarah. Sarah's parents divorced, tearing her world apart, and she experienced all the pain anyone would when the two people she loves and depends on for security fail her. "I wish that parents could understand what divorce does to their children," she told me. Sarah understands why God says, "he hateth putting away [divorce]" (Malachi 2:16).

Unsettled, she faced a bewildering array of choices. Her father's place had the world and all its allurements, and at home was a conservative Christian lifestyle.

Back and forth the battle raged as she felt a stranger in both worlds. Rebellious under restraint, she liked the perceived freedom of her father's home, but she had tasted too much of the truer joys, the more meaningful and sober pleasure of life in her mother's house, to ever come away from a period of self-indulgence at her father's place feeling satisfied. Instead, it seemed the more she tried to find happiness, the more it eluded her.

As is usually the case, the bad situation just got worse, until she felt she had to separate from her mother and live exclusively with her father. Mother was a constant reminder of things that hindered her living a self-directed life, and that life still seemed to hold out the hope of happiness for this young woman who felt so unloved. At last in a family meeting she informed her mother of her decision. Unexpectedly her mother replied, "You're not leaving!"

And this brings us to the final, but most important point in family councils. No matter how much a child may want their own way and no matter how much we may desire or even feel obligated to grant them their wish, it takes leadership to run a household, and this young woman's mother had it. She did not have any legal right to force her daughter to stay, and the father had joint custody, but the mother, although terribly tried in this difficult conflict, had something far more compelling—the faith that God would not have her give up her daughter without a fight.

Sarah was at first taken aback, even angered, but she soon came to see that in that very action of not allowing her own way, her mother was proving, in a way that nothing else could, that she loved her more than anyone else and was concerned for her happiness. Sarah still had a long road to travel before she found the peace with God that she longed for, but the turning point was a parent's love that would not, could not let her go.

Friend, it is the same today in your home and in your marriage and in your life. Jesus stands before you as you try to find fulfillment in this world's false pleasures and so-called freedoms, saying, "I love you! I cannot let you go!" Will you respond to His plea today and take those first hard steps to bring about a resolution to the conflicts that Satan has been using to ruin your happiness at home?

Activities for Week 12

Sunday

Prayer time: Ask God what He has for you in this chapter; then seek a willingness to follow through. Chances are that God's methods will cross your will and will require you to go deeper in your surrender to Him if you are to succeed.

Activity: Read "Family Councils."

Reflection: Can you recall a recent situation in your home that might have been easier to resolve if you and your family had established a specific method whereby conflicts could be addressed and a forum where suggestions might be considered?

Monday

Prayer time: Ask God to bless your efforts today by giving you clarity in both memory and reasoning.

Activity: Go back in your mind's eye to your own childhood. Think about the ways in which your family dealt with conflict and how you felt about it.

Reflection: How do you feel about conflict resolution in your home now? Have you carried into your home the same patterns of conflict resolution? If so how do think your children feel?

Tuesday

Prayer time: Reflect with God about how He runs His government, which is also His household. Are there clearly understood rules? If so, why?

Activity: Review your household government today. Is there participation from all parties as their ages allow, or do you run a benevolent or even a not-so-benevolent dictatorship?

Reflection: If you could choose to be a member of your home, would you? Would you if you were a child, even the youngest child?

Wednesday

Prayer time: Ask God for guidance as you seek to correct any wrong ways of dealing with things He has shown you.

Activity: Plan today to try family councils. Read Friday's activity today and start laying out your plans.

Thursday

Prayer time: If you and your spouse haven't yet talked about family councils, today is the day. Seek God's wisdom and timing.

Activity: Make some notes to speak from when you share with your family about family councils. Consider using your first family council to set up your family's ground rules for using the family council effectively.

Reflection: Who in your family is likely to be the least cooperative with implementation of the new program? How can you win them over?

Friday

Prayer time: Ask the Lord to help you present family councils to your family as a winning idea, as something special for them!

Activity: Plan to present the idea today or tonight depending on when your family is together. If the morning meal is the best time, make it special, like a Sunday brunch. If the evening is best, make it as special as if company was coming. Your preparations are an important signal not only that the "times, they are a-changing," but in letting your family know they are special, and no matter how poorly you have done it in the past, you are determined to make sure they know it now. Schedule the next council before you leave this one.

Reflection: How did it go? Build on what worked for your situation. There is no specific plan, no one-size-fits-all approach with God. He knows and loves your family. Every member is special to Him. If you are willing to receive it, He will give you the wisdom to reach them.

Saturday

Reflection: Think about expectations. All of us expect certain things from our families, and when we don't get them we are displeased. By clearly laying out the family council as the expected way family problems should be dealt with, the expectation has been created that both you and your family will use that method for resolving them. Are you willing to stick with it, even when it is inconvenient? Are you willing to persevere when it's not easy and let self die when your will is crossed? If so, you will find your family government markedly improved, and you'll be able to instill in your children a model of what a home should be like. May God attend your efforts.

CHAPTER 13

Failure Is Not an Option

"With men it is impossible, but not with God: for with God all things are possible" (Mark 10:27).

CHAPTER GOAL

We must learn to choose the attitude of victory, even in the face of defeat. The task of reforming and restructuring our lives, marriages, and families can seem a daunting job, but it is not the problems we face but our attitude that determines the outcome as we set our hands to a seemingly impossible outcome.

It was July 20, 1969 and NASA had just landed the first man on the moon. Do you remember the circumstances? My memories of it are so vivid that I can recall exactly where I was. I was returning home from a date with my girlfriend, Sally, in Milwaukee, Wisconsin. As I drove my convertible toward home and listened to the news reports over the radio, I would glance up toward the bright sphere of the moon and think, *What an awesome event!* The whole world was looking on as the first man walked on the moon. It was an accomplishment of historic proportions equal perhaps to Columbus discovering the New World.

But on April 11, 1970 another spacecraft was launched toward the moon, and I doubt that any of you remember its launch. Space flight had become a routine—so much so, that none of the TV networks provided live coverage of the launch as they had in the past. Newspapers buried the story many pages away from the headlines. The media was, after all, reflecting the attitude of the public, which as a whole had little interest in the mission of what were to be the fifth and sixth men to walk on the moon.

No one outside of the space program cared or took much notice of the flight until a short, poignant radio message crackled down, slightly delayed because of its passage through 205,000 miles of space: "Houston, we have a problem!"

Stranded more than 200,000 miles into their mission, astronauts Fred Hayes, Jack Swaggert, and mission commander Jim Lovell found themselves in the Apollo XIII command module facing a situation no one believed could ever occur. The Apollo command module was considered almost indestructible, yet something had gone desperately wrong in their fuel cells, and they were losing electrical power. If their power went out, they would lose their oxygen supply as well. Now, facing almost certain death, the crew joined with mission control in a desperate struggle to save their lives and bring their crippled ship back home. News of the disaster was broadcast, and television commentators estimated their odds for survival at no better than one in ten. Even NASA, whose news releases were always known to be optimistic, conceded that the astronauts' lives were threatened.

Today we face a similar situation as the God of the universe is in a desperate battle to bring us home from this planet. We too must repair our crippled lives, marriages, and families, and I'm not speaking of the world's lives, marriages, and families, but those who are already within the Christian churches. Christians are supposed to have the power to bring the gospel to the world, but today we have lost our fuel cells and we are powerless to do the job. Just like the Apollo XIII mission so long ago, our families are broken and we have fractured lives. Like mission control then, God needs your cooperation now. He desperately needs your cooperation!

As the crew and ground control of Apollo XIII examined the data streaming back from their sensors, the first impulse was to try and discount it. It was so bad that they thought it must be an instrumentation problem—no way things could have gone *that* wrong. But gradually those brilliant men, whose expertise was the ability to send spacecraft more than a quarter million miles to the moon and back, drew the conclusion that the command module was dying, and when it died it would take the three fragile creatures inside with it. Worse still were thoughts that transcended a dead crew, as horrible as it was, and affected the future of space flight itself. The ship, as Jim Lovell put it, "would never go away. It would be there forever, a shining, mocking monument to the technology of the twentieth century." It would enter "a permanent egg-shaped orbit 24,000 miles around the Earth in a hideous, endless circuit that could easily outlast the very species that had launched it." With such a specter before them, it was little wonder that rumors flew fast and furious that this might be NASA's greatest disaster, and people around the world were horrified at the idea of astronauts dying in space.

Once mission control drew the right conclusions about what they were seeing and properly understood the gravity of the situation, hard decisions had to be made. What about you, my friend? You have spent twelve chapters with me. Have you been facing any hard decisions? It is hard. I know it's hard because almost two decades ago I had to make those same hard decisions about the saving of my crew. Are you willing to do whatever it takes, or will you stubbornly cling to your dreams at the cost of your family?

The crew of Apollo XIII faced hard decisions. The plan to land on the moon had to be scrapped. These men had trained much of their lives to obtain the goal of walking on the moon, but it had to be set aside just to try and bring the crew home alive. You may have to give up your career, you may have to give up your fortunes, you may have to give up your occupations, and you may not be able to continue living where you do. It may require you to give up your toys too. In fact, it may take everything you have if you are to save your family, your children, and yourself from perishing in this world.

There was only one hope for the crew, and mission control quickly implemented it. The lunar excursion module would have to be used as a sort of lifeboat, if you will, to sustain the crew's life until they could return to earth. They had less than two hours to power up the ship and transfer the data before the command module died. Once the transfer was complete, mission control and the crew breathed a short sigh of relief, but everyone knew that they couldn't sustain the drain they were putting on the batteries and the life support system. They had merely moved from a ship in which they were sure to die in the next couple of hours to one in which they could not survive more than a couple of days. Emergency meetings were called, and experts grappled with the challenge. Oxygen was the least of their worries; the ship had more than enough, but it wouldn't matter because the lithium hydroxide filters used to remove CO_2 would run out before two days were up. No matter how much oxygen there was, the crew would suffocate. If that problem could be solved, the power supply became the real obstacle. No matter how many ways they looked at it, there just wasn't enough power to make it home. Examining the figures, a NASA engineer gave voice to his conclusion. "We've got to figure out a different way to run this ship." Up in the spacecraft, Jim Lovell was also doing some figuring and drawing exactly the same conclusions. Turning to his crew, he said, "We got to figure out some other way to run this ship."

Have you drawn the same conclusion? Too many of us have moved our families out of the world, out of certain death, into the church where there seems to be apparent safety, only to realize with the passage of time that all we have done for our families was to delay destruction—not prevent it. In the NASA structure, the senior flight controller was in charge of all flight decisions, and no one could overrule him. Gene Kranz was that powerful man. He pulled his control team off the monitors and assembled them in a vacant conference room. Basically he told them that he hadn't lost a spacecraft yet, and he wasn't planning to start now. He wanted options to bring these men home, and lots of them. Then he left the fifteen men he expected to save the astronauts' lives to their task, confident that failure was not an option.

What is your attitude? Have you accepted a crippled marriage? Have you decided that stale and humdrum is just the way it's going to be? It doesn't have to be that way, friend! What about your children? Have you accepted worldliness and disrespect in your children? Have they come to believe that sin is just part of their lives, something they can't overcome? Is your life fractured and broken? Is your Christian experience just like that of all the other powerless Christians about you in the churches? Do you believe that failure is not an option? God believes it. He says in Mark 10:27, "With men it is impossible, but not with God: for with God all things are possible." God holds that attitude because it's true. Isaiah 42:4 describes God by saying, "He shall not fail nor be discouraged."

The first crisis to be conquered is our attitude. Before God called His people to go into the Promised Land, He told Moses to send out twelve spies and have them report back to the people. Two of the spies came back with the attitude God wanted them to have: "Failure is not an option." But the majority of both the spies and the people decided it was impossible. What is your attitude? Are you with the majority who feels failure is likely and victory too difficult to obtain?

Time is critical, my friend. The longer mission control struggled to decide what to do, the less power would be available to them in working out a solution. How long is it going to take for you to decide to make your family, your marriage, and your own personal walk with God a priority and make everything else subordinate? Will it take thirteen chapters or thirteen books? If you put this book down and fail to decide to go forward, you have decided. When we fail to decide, we in essence have decided, even though we haven't outwardly rejected God.

There are four simple steps to take when rescuing our crew. The first step is to say, "Houston, we have a problem." We must admit that we are broken and realize we are in need of help. You can't fix something when you won't admit you have a problem with it. Two decades ago, Sally and I decided we had a problem. We didn't decide the church had a problem; we decided that we had a problem, and it wasn't going to be fixed unless we took some drastic action. We had been in the church and considered ourselves Christians, but we didn't know how to walk or talk with God. I was the head elder, but if I could have given everyone in my community my religious experience, they would have still been yelling at their wives and getting irritated at their children. It wasn't until I admitted to myself and then to God that I had a problem that there was a chance any healing could take place.

I had come into the church and the church had told me I was converted and I was spiritual, but in truth I was doing everything in the power of Jim Hohnberger and not in the power of God. I was self-directed, and the vast majority of those in the churches are exactly the same as I was—self-directed. They are getting along in the power of their knowledge, and the power of their reforms, but they are not empowered by a living connection with Jesus. That's why it is so easy for us to pick on the faults of others but so hard to look inward at our lives. We don't like admitting even to ourselves the idea that something might be deeply and fundamentally flawed in the religion we practice. Yet, as I looked at myself, I had to draw the conclusion that I was an unconverted man. I came to see that without dramatic changes I was a lost man in spite of my church offices, reputation, and theology. We are crippled Christians, and yet we think we are OK.

It was not until I realized just how crippled and lost we were that my entire focus became the saving of my crew, just as the entire focus of the Apollo XIII crew was survival. We determined to go back to God at all costs. We set our sights high and set out to achieve the impossible, and do you know who did their best to discourage us? It was our fellow church members. "It's impossible! Your sights are too high; it can't be done! You're becoming fanatical."

But we weren't fanatics. No, true Christianity is something so rarely seen that when it is glimpsed by the worldly majority, it seems so extreme and so difficult compared with the compromise commonly practiced, that the desire of the carnal heart is to dismiss it as fanatical, freeing the observer from any obligation to practice it. But if you, like me, see that you or your family is endangered, then I advise you to take whatever steps are necessary for its survival. When you are confident that God is guiding, dismiss your critics, for no one ever enters the pathway to life without feeling to one degree or another the animosity of those who have a form of religion but never truly enter it. They are described in the Bible as those who will neither enter in at the straight gate nor allow others to enter in.

Step number two is communication. What is your communication like with your Commander-in-Chief in heaven's mission control? Is it continual or is it broken? Do you talk occasionally? Never? Do the day's activities sever your communion? In my travels through the United States and thirteen other countries, it has shocked me to see how few who claim to be Christ's followers actually communicate with Him on an ongoing basis. This is serious because God says, "I will instruct thee and teach thee in the way that thou shalt go: I will guide thee with mine eye" (Psalm 32:8). How can we be led if none of us are listening? If the crew of Apollo XIII hadn't maintained contact with mission control, they would have been lost. Apollo XIII waited eagerly for every instruction from mission control. They asked repeatedly for more instruction, often looking for information that mission control had not yet prepared. Why were they so insistent? Because life itself depended upon the data they received. Do you wait that eagerly for God to tell you what to do?

While you and I may not realize the value of open communication, our enemy realizes it, and he is doing everything possible to jam heaven's signals. Why do you suppose there is music in every store, in every waiting room, and even on the telephone when you are placed on hold? We are being jammed, friend. I have met people who have gotten so used to the jamming noise that they get antsy without it, and I can't help but wonder if the real reason they are so eager for constant background noise is so they can silence the voice of conscience. Others are used by the devil himself as mobile jamming stations. I've had kids pull up next to me at stoplights whose music was so loud my car actually vibrated because of what was going on in their car. If you are having trouble hearing God, eliminate as much as possible these distractions and see if His quiet voice is not easier to hear. I know from my own experience that as I took steps to shut the noise out and tune God in, I learned to hear Him better and better. And so can you!

People come to me and say, "I don't hear God's voice." Jesus Himself says, "Everyone that is of the truth heareth my voice." Do you hear God's voice speaking to you? If you don't hear God speaking, you are in charge of your life, and God isn't.

The third step we must follow is carrying out the instructions we receive. The crew of Apollo XIII had to put into effect the changes ground control asked for, and they were extremely difficult. But the crew was willing to allow mission control complete management of their destiny. Many of you have given God some management in your life, and your lives are a mess because God can't do a whole lot without complete control. Power had to be drastically shut down. In the lunar excursion module, all nonessential items were eliminated and then many items normally thought of as essential had to go. Heat was turned off, wastes could no longer be vented, and water was in tight enough supply that the crew had to think carefully before taking even a sip. Their food froze. Their bodies shivered, and the lack of water caused kidney infection and fever, but all could be endured if that was the price of saving life and returning home. What God asks of you may not be comfortable, but it is for your survival. You are in a life-and-death situation, and everything is at stake in your compliance to mission control.

Step number four is courage. It takes courage in the face of discouraging odds to take the attitude that "failure is not an option." If courageous, daring men had not been part and parcel of the NASA team, that crew would have been lost. The crew of Apollo XIII demonstrated a positive response to a difficult situation and a resolve to carry out their task to the end, when the odds seemed totally stacked against them. We must have that same boldness if we are to succeed, and succeed we must!

On April 17, 1970 Apollo XIII splashed down in the Pacific Ocean. Their mission to the moon was not even considered in the celebrations that followed. The mission was a success. The crew was saved. Praise God! I hope some day to complete the mission God has given me—that of saving my crew.

Someday, not that long from now, I shall see a city whose gates are set with pearls and whose streets are paved with gold. Meandering through its avenues are the banks of the river of life flowing from the very throne of God. Outside the gates, the wide-spreading plains will swell into hills of beauty with majestic mountains rearing their lofty summits. With my wife and children beside me, I want to explore those peaceful hills and living springs. I want to walk with my sons through heaven's gate and see them receive a crown of life from Christ's own hand, and as I gather my family together in a giant hug, I want to respond to my crew, as Jim Lovell did to his after splashdown, "Fellows, we're home!"

A Closing Note to Readers

We hope the presentation you have just finished is helpful to you. We strive to make the principles of God's Word as practical as possible. When we say that we desire more than anything else to uplift Christ and draw you to Him, we believe we are speaking for everyone who graciously allowed us to share his or her story in this book. If you desire to contact any of the individuals identified in the acknowledgments, please write in care of:

Empowered Living Ministries
157 Turtle Mountain Road
Kalispell, MT 59901

For more information or an email address please visit our Web page at http://www.empoweredlivingministries.org. The authors may be reached either at the above address or in care of the publisher.

May God's richest blessing be yours as you seek to know Him better.

Yours in Christ,
Jim, Tim, and Julie
Polebridge, Montana
Henryville, Pennsylvania

Appendix 1

Recommended Book List

This list is not intended to be exhaustive, but rather a compilation of the best of the best that we have experienced in our families.

Title	Author	Publisher
Bruchko	Bruce Olson	Creation House
Endurance	Alfred Lansing	Tyndale House
Evangelist in Chains	E. Wagler	Rod and Staff Publishers
For His Honor	Terry Johnson/ Kay Rizzo	Pacific Press
From Wealth to Faith	Mollie Zook	Christian Light Publications
History of the Waldenses	J. A. Wylie	Cassell and Company
I Will Die Free	Noble Alexander	Pacific Press
In His Steps	Charles Sheldon	Honor Books
My Bible Friends (5 vols.)	Etta B. Degering	Pacific Press
My Escape From the Auto De Fé	Don Fernando	Shiloh Publications

Of Whom the World Was Not Worthy

	M. Chapian	Bethany House Publishers
Paula: The Waldensian	Eva Lecomte	Loizeaux Brothers, Inc.
Singer on the Sand	Norma Youngberg	Pacific Press
Sunshine Country	Cristina Roy	Rod and Staff Publishers
The Bible Story (10 vols.)	Arthur Maxwell	Pacific Press/
		Review and Herald
The Pilgrim's Progress	John Bunyan	multiple sources
The Secret of the Cave	Arthur Maxwell	Pacific Press
The Seventh Escape	Jan Doward	Pacific Press
Thrilling Escapes by Night		
	Albert Lee	Rod and Staff Publishers
Tip Lewis and His Lamp		
	Pansy	Rod and Staff Publishers
Uncle Arthur's Bedtime Stories (5 vols.)		
	Arthur Maxwell	Pacific Press
War-Torn Valley	Joyce Miller	Rod and Staff Publishers
Whom Shall I Fear?	Kendra Burkholder	Rod and Staff Publishers

Appendix 2

Time Management

"To every thing there is a season, and a time *to every purpose under the heaven: A time to be born, and a time to die; a time to plant, and a time to pluck up that which is planted; A time to ... heal; ... break down, ... build up; ... weep, ... mourn, ... laugh; ... dance; ... cast away ... gather ... embrace, ... refrain from embracing; ... rend, ... sew; ... keep silence, ... speak; ... love, ...hate; ... a time of war, and a time of peace" (Ecclesiastes 3:1-8, emphasis supplied).*

The schedules enclosed are intended to provide you guidance in preparing your own. There is no magical formula for you to follow that will make everything work out just fine. You will have to create a basic schedule and then fine-tune it to your family and your circumstances. The following quotes helped the Hohnberger family as they started to see and develop the principles of becoming scheduled.

• *"In order for children and youth to have health, cheerfulness, vivacity, and well-developed muscles and brains, they should be much in the open air and have well-regulated employment and amusement." [Direct all their work time and free time.]*

• *"The monotony of continuous study [book learning/mind work] wearies the mind, ... any effort that exalts intellectual culture above moral training [the exercise of the will to choose to do right over wrong] is misdirected." [Teaching practical household duties, quick, thorough workmanship, self-control, and self-denial is a vital and all-too-often neglected education.]*

• *"The education of most youth is a failure. They overstudy, while they neglect that which pertains to practical business life.... The constant application to study, as the schools are now conducted, is unfitting youth for practical life.... In order to preserve the balance of the mind, labor and study should be united in the schools [homes also] ... a portion of the time each day should have been devoted to labor, that the physical and mental powers might be equally exercised."*

• *"Each member of the family should understand just the part he is expected to act in union with the others. All, from the child six years old and upward, should understand that it is required of them to bear their share of life's burdens." [Even the two- to six-year-old can have a daily chore list that is their responsibility and beginning training. Teach them early.]*

Plan to be misunderstood in your attempts to be organized, but that is all right; you will be in good company. John Wesley taught such practical principles, causing him and his followers to be called Methodists by their critics because of their methodical practices. They were organized and had a method to their work. May God bless your efforts.

Hohnbergers' Home Schedule
(Boys ages 12-17)

5:30 A.M.   Out of bed, shower, personal care, water, govern yourself

	Prayer time (30 min.), personal Bible study (1 1/2 hrs. +)
7:30	Meal preparation—prepare dish and place in oven before family worship
	Matthew (Tues. and Fri.), Andrew (Sun. and Wed.), Mother (Mon. and Thur.), All (Sabbath)
7:45	Feed and watch deer, feed birds, practice self-government
8:00	Family worship—have all books out and ready, start early or on time
8:30	Finish meal preparation—set and prepare table
	Son #1—sweep all floors, 2 porches, shake rugs, make bed, vacuum
	Son #2—stack firewood in house, fill carrier with wood, burn trash, make bed, make parents' bed, help brother on meal preparation
	(These chores are done daily for 1 month, then boys switch chore list.)
	Mother—clean bathroom, start laundry, ironing, oversee all
9:00	Breakfast—we will eat on time
9:30	Son #1—washes, rinses, dries, and puts away dishes
	Son #2—clears and cleans table, puts away all food appropriately, neatly, cleans up the floor as needed (son #1 washes A.M. dishes; son #2 washes P.M. dishes; switch weekly)
	Fold and put away laundry that is ready, ironing
10:00-2:30 P.M.	Begin day's work, schoolwork, writing a book, ministry work, etc.
	All work/school to be done neatly, orderly, thoroughly, and timely
	Bedrooms, garage, and all home to be kept clean and orderly at all times
	Consult Mother's chore list for the day for extra

	things to be done
	Examples: cleaning/cooking/organizing/errands/office work
	ministry work/fill orders/duplicate tapes/photocopy articles and booklets/computer work/bookkeeping/any other help
	Consult Father's chore list, change oil in car, chop wood, errands
	organize/clean garage
12:00-12:30 P.M.	Personal break (up to you), 15 min. alone with God
2:30	Meal preparation and associated chores
3:00	Supper—eat on time
3:30	Dishes, clean up, vacuum, firewood
4:00-6:00	Personal projects, e.g., building workbench, make a trail, rock work, letters, typing, etc.
6:00-7:00	Family time—walk, talk, work together on project, freeze tag, etc.
7:00-8:00	Quiet personal activities—tub bath, reading
8:00	Family worship
8:30	Bedtime—lights out by 9:00 P.M., if not before

Winter Schedule

(When Matthew and Andrew were ages 9 and 7)

6:00 - 8:00 A.M.	Rise, personal prayer time (15 min.)
	Shower, brush teeth, drink water (3 glasses), proper dress (15 min.)
	Personal study (1 1/4 hour), Bible study
	Review learning with Father or Mother (5-10 min.)
	Ready for worship before 8:00
8:00 - 8:30	Family worship
8:30 - 9:00	Individual chores—done daily, changed monthly
	Son #1: Sweep floor, shake rugs, vacuum, make his bed

	Son #2: Empty waste baskets and burn trash, fill wood bin and carrier, make his bed, make parents' bed
	Mother: Clean bathroom, start laundry, do ironing
9:00	Breakfast
9:30 -10:00	Son #1—wash, rinse, dry, put away dishes
	Son #2—clear table, put away food, vacuum, fold and put away clothes
10:00-2:00	School
12:00 P.M.	15-minute break with God—alone, quiet
2:00	Outside work, if school and chores are all done
	If work is done—cross-country skiing, walk, personal project
2:30	Help Mother prepare supper
3:00	Supper
3:30-4:00	Son #2—wash, rinse, dry, put away dishes
	Son #1—clear table, put away food, vacuum
	Consult Mother's chore list for today's needs
4:30-6:00	Personal time—build birdhouses, walk with a parent, play marbles, pick up sticks, play trucks in the snow, other innocent activity
6:00-7:00	School with Father, nature lessons
7:00-8:00	Quiet activities—draw, color, read stories, art or gift project
8:00	Family worship
8:30	Bedtime—lights out

Typical outside work, beginning at this age and as they got older also:

Shovel snow around buildings/shovel snow off greenhouse roof/ shovel high snowbanks down/attach plow to truck with Father/ organize and clean garage, attic, or specific areas.

When 12 and older: snowplowing around buildings/pack ski trails with snowmobile/drive the car and attach trailer/wash car weekly and put into garage/drive car to attach and plow the half-mile driveway/ministry work such as duplicating tapes/ photocopying articles/writing messages/filling orders/computer work.

Spring: prepare greenhouse for planting/plan food and seed needs to order, then plant them/clean upstairs attics/go through everything we own, discard, sell, give away unnecessary items/scrub all logs and walls and spring cleaning/any painting that needs to be done.

Summer Schedule

(When Matthew and Andrew were ages 10 and 8)

6:00 A.M.	Rise, personal prayer (20 min.)
	Shower, brush teeth, drink water, proper dress (15 min.)
	Personal study (1 1/4 hr.), Bible study
	Review time with Father (5-10 min.)
	No talking—ready for worship before 8:00
8:00-8:30	Family worship
8:30-9:00	Individual chores (previously listed), emphasize thoroughness
9:00	Breakfast
9:30-10:00	Clean-up chores (previously listed)
10:00-12:00	(April) start greenhouse, apply plastic, till, plant, water
	(May) rake and clean up lawn as soon as snow melts, put up swing
	(May/June) clean up all 6 flower beds, half-mile driveway rut repair
	Mow lawn, trim grass
	Till garden, plant, weed, and water gardens and greenhouse
	Harvest fruits and vegetables, bulk canning (600+ quarts), drying
12:00-12:15 P.M.	Time with God, prayer, read, recommitment, review day

12:15-1:00	Personal time
1:00-2:30	Summer projects such as: help carpenters build the guest cabin, collect, cut down trees for building jungle gym, build swings
	A directed activity—to teach practicals
2:30	Help Mother in meal preparation—son #1
3:00	Supper
3:30-4:00	Clean-up chores (previously listed)
4:00-4:30	Consult Mother's chore list
4:30-6:00	Personal time if all is completed properly—sand box, saw boards, pound nails in boards, build bird houses, etc.
6:00-7:00	Bible drills, memory work, family reading
7:00-8:00	Personal time—family walks, talks, games, art project
8:00	Family worship
8:30	Bedtime

Typical summer projects: beginning at this age, projects progress as they get older:

Remodel their own room/build walls/closets/shelves and doors/ wire new lights for bedroom/help carpenters build our guest cabin/ plumbing experience/help put in gravity-feed water line from a spring 1,600 feet away/collect firewood as a family/clearing woods and burning/build jungle gym out of trees/(age 12) cut firewood with chain saw/work for neighbors in yard/garden care/build a 12-foot workbench/build 9-foot chain saw workbench/build 8-foot-tall storage cupboards/masonry experience: rock work on flower beds/rock work with foundation around back porch/work with neighbor hand-pouring basement foundation/rebuild the front porch/rock work around front porch.

Home School Schedule
(When Matthew and Andrew were ages 12 and 10)

5:30 A.M.	Rise, shower, personal care
5:45	Personal prayer time
6:00-7:00	Bible study **School subject #1**
7:00-7:15	Review with Father
7:15-7:30	Spelling **School subject #2**
7:30-8:00	*Son #1 on meal preparation
	Son #2 begins math drill exercises
8:00-8:30	Family worship (church history, etc.) **Extra-curricular subject**
8:30-9:00	*Chore lists to be completed, see other schedule for details
	*Son #1 on meal prep. and does his chores
9:00-9:30	Breakfast—on time
9:30-10:00	*Clean-up chores, see other schedule for details
10:00-11:30	English **School subject #3**
	Read, study, discuss and do exercises
11:30-1:00 P.M.	Complete any unfinished school subjects
	*One hour of practical outside work (shovel snow, car care, etc.)
	15 min. personal time with God
	Remaining time is free time
1:00-2:00	Math **School subject #4**
	Mother does oral drill with son
2:00-3:00	*Meal preparation by Son #2
	Son #1 does extra math drill as needed
3:00-3:30	Supper—on time
3:30-4:00	*Clean-up chores, see other schedule for details
4:00-6:00	Personal time, if all else is completed
	Mother completes any lesson corrections not done
6:00-6:30	English review, grammar **School subject #5**
6:30-7:30	*Personal family time and activity—walk, talk, play tag, family projects
7:30-8:00	Quiet-time activities—personal, family reading, art
	School Subject #6

8:00-8:30	Family worship **Extracurricular subject**
8:30	To bed—quiet reading time optional
9:00	Lights out, if not before

* Denotes **Practical education**—becoming efficient in daily life duties.

Pictorial Schedules

Many families have used pictorial schedules when their children were too young to read. These are effective tools, and they work like this: All morning activities like making the bed and brushing teeth to doing the dishes and family worship are marked on poster board with pictures and a clock illustrating the time. Children can learn schedules before they learn to read or tell time.

Canutesons' Daily Schedule

Ellen, age 12, and Travis, age 8

4:30 A.M.	Parents rise, personal time with God
5:30	Ellen rises, personal time with God
6:00	Travis rises, family cuddle time in the big bed
6:10	Travis and Ellen make beds and get dressed; parents in shower
6:30	Ellen starts breakfast preparation
7:00	Travis's worship with Mom
7:30	Family worship
8:00	Breakfast
8:30	Morning jobs for all the family
9:00	Home school begins, Ellen—piano
12:00	Midday worship and story
12:30	Playtime
1:00	School
2:00	Lunch preparation
3:00	Lunch
3:30	Afternoon jobs

4:30	Free time for jobs or play as needed, finish extra schoolwork
5:45	Unload dishwasher
6:00	Family time
7:45	Bath time
8:00	Bedtime for children
9:00	Bedtime for Mom and Dad

Read these Pacific Press Bestsellers

Escape to God

By Jim Hohnberger with Tim and Julie Canuteson

Jim and Sally Hohnberger were young, educated owners of a successful business, a beautiful home, and expensive vehicles, and they had a great reputation in their church. But under the veneer of success, Jim's life was too busy, pushed, and stressed. His marriage was stale, his Christian experience superficial, and he didn't even know his children.

Convinced that the pursuit of the "American Dream" was robbing them of an authentic walk with God the Hohnbergers sold everything and set off for the Montana wilderness in search of an "Enoch" experience. What this family found forever changed their lives, and yours could be next!

0-8163-1805-0. Paperback.
US$13.99, Can$22.49

It's About People

By Jim Hohnberger with Tim and Julie Canuteson

Desiring a deeper understanding of Christ's sacrifice for man, the author is challenged to the depth of his being as God reveals to him the *true* meaning of the cross. Using real-life illustrations the author shares what we as Christians all too often fail to understand amid the theological jargon, doctrinal intellectualism, and the liberal, moderate, or conservative biases prevailing in the church today—namely, that the gospel is about people.

Prepare to be challenged to learn to love others as God does—without an if. Without question *It's About People* is one of the most important books on practical Christianity you will ever read!

0-8163-1964-2. Paperback.
US$10.99, Can$17.99

Empowered Living Ministries

Empowered Living Ministries has become acclaimed by those tired of Christianity's failure to realistically provide its adherents with the ability to live a life hid in Christ Jesus. The "Practical Gospel" has been the hallmark of this unique and vibrant ministry. If you would like to learn more about the services of Empowered Living Ministries, contact:

Empowered Living Ministries
157 Turtle Mountain Road
Kalispell MT 55901
http://www.empoweredlivingministries.org
Toll free: (877) 755-8300

Order books from your ABC by calling toll-free **1-800-765-6955**, or get online and shop our virtual store at http://www.adventistbookcenter.com so that you can

• read a chapter online
• order online
• sign up for email notices on new products.
Prices are subject to change without notice.